"The power of an idea can often be m
settings and geographies. With this n
have demonstrated a reach that goes t.
riculum. Giving Voice to Values has truly become a methodology, .e
development of ethical leaders … anywhere they might be! A truly valuable compendium of reports and insights."

Leonard A. Schlesinger, *Baker Foundation Professor,*
Harvard Business School, President Emeritus—Babson College

"In business ethics teaching we often remain stuck in analyzing what is wrong out there. You want to equip students and professionals with a hands-on action framework? Use the Giving Voice to Values framework. This book will further spur Giving Voice to Values' success as the leading action framework for business ethics."

Markus Scholz, *Chair and Endowed Professor of Corporate*
Governance & Business Ethics, Head of the Institute for Business
Ethics and Sustainable Strategy (IBES), University of
Applied Science Vienna

"The Giving Voice to Values approach to ethical leadership has already empowered countless individuals worldwide. This has been a great benefit to all who seek to develop responsible leaders and this volume provides timely lessons learned and important insights in pursuit of that goal."

Scott Beardsley, *Dean, University of Virginia*
Darden School of Business

"Companies need to get beyond the debate about why people don't speak up in challenging situations and instead focus on helping their people become more skilled at speaking up effectively. GVV is an innovative, evidence-based approach to building those skills, and in the challenging times we are facing, we need them more than ever. This book helps us to understand why integrating GVV into your curriculum for employees at every level, from recent college graduates to the members of your C-suite, will undoubtedly have a positive impact on the ethical culture of your company for years to come."

Victoria Sweeney, *Principal – Ethics & Compliance*
Group, KPMG LLP

"The broad appeal of Giving Voice To Values' innovative approach to values-driven leadership development is rooted in its practicality – an orientation toward *acting* on one's values, effectively and with conviction. Goodstein and Gentile's new book chronicles how this methodology has expanded well beyond its original roots in business education – to cross regions and cultures, professions and sectors – and it offers an exciting glimpse into its potential future applications and impacts."

Judy Samuelson, *Executive Director, Aspen Institute Business & Society Program and author, The Six New Rules of Business: Creating Real Value in a Changing World*

"This publication provides convincing evidence of how GVV developed into an effective and sustainable approach to values-driven action for individuals faced with everyday ethical dilemmas, teachers wanting to develop the moral competence of their students, and leaders building ethical organizational cultures. While being fully at home in the conventional arena of face-to-face engagements for over a decade, its digital homecoming is no longer a distant reality – it is happening already."

Arnold Smit, *Associate Professor of Business in Society, University of Stellenbosch Business School, South Africa*

"Values can be tricky in the realm of innovation where we often ask to hold back judgement. Leave it to Jerry, Mary and all the amazing contributors to thread a very small eye of the needle. Obviously this book has never been more relevant and teaches us how not to kill innovation while respecting people's values."

Fred Dust, Author of *Making Conversation: Seven Essential Elements of Meaningful Communication*

"FASPE believes in the importance of professional ethics: ethical behavior and ethical leadership of professionals. Mary Gentile brings life and energy to the requirement of ethical behavior through her unrelenting and creative attention to practical and effective strategies. Mary converts ethics from philosophy to action."

David Goldman, *Chairman, FASPE (Fellowships at Auschwitz for the Study of Professional Ethics), www.faspe-ethics.org*

GIVING VOICE TO VALUES

Giving Voice to Values, under the leadership of Mary C. Gentile, has fundamentally changed the way business ethics and values-driven leadership is taught and discussed in academic and corporate settings worldwide.

This book shifts attention to the future of Giving Voice to Values (GVV) and provides thought pieces from practitioners and leading experts in business ethics and the professions on the possibilities for sustaining its growth and success. These include the creation of new teaching materials, reaching different audiences, and expanding the ways in which GVV is making a difference in classrooms and the workplace and acting as a catalyst for organizational and societal change. The book closes with a reflective chapter by Mary C. Gentile, looking back at where GVV has been and looking ahead to where GVV might go.

Jerry Goodstein is Professor Emeritus of Management at the Carson College of Business, Washington State University Vancouver. He has taught graduate and undergraduate courses in the areas of business ethics, managing innovation and change, and leadership in organizations. Dr. Goodstein has published widely in high quality business ethics and management journals and has contributed a number of cases for the GVV curriculum. He served for many years as Associate Editor at *Business Ethics Quarterly* and has served on the editorial boards of *Administrative Science Quarterly*, *Academy of Management Journal*, and *Journal of Management*.

Mary C. Gentile is Creator/Director of Giving Voice to Values, Professor of Practice at the University of Virginia Darden School of Business, Senior Advisor at The Aspen Institute Business & Society Program, and consultant on management education and leadership development. Among numerous other awards, Mary was named as one of the 2015 "100 Most Influential in Business Ethics" by *Ethisphere* and one of the "Top Thought Leaders in Trust: 2015 Lifetime Achievement Award Winners" by Trust Across America-Trust Around the World, January 2015. She was also named one of the "Top Minds 2017" in ethics leadership by *Compliance Week*.

Giving Voice to Values

Series Editor: Mary C. Gentile

The *Giving Voice to Values* series is a collection of books on Business Ethics and Corporate Social Responsibility that brings a practical, solutions-oriented, skill-building approach to the salient questions of values-driven leadership.

Giving Voice to Values (GVV: www.GivingVoiceToValues.org) – the curriculum, the pedagogy and the research upon which it is based – was designed to transform the foundational assumptions upon which the teaching of business ethics is based, and importantly, to equip future business leaders to know not only what is right – but how to make it happen.

Engaging the Heart in Business
Alice Alessandri and Alberto Aleo

Shaping the Future of Work: A Handbook for Building a New Social Contract
Thomas A. Kochan and Lee Dyer

Professionalism and Values in Law Practice
Robert Feldman

Giving Voice to Values in the Boardroom
Cynthia E. Clark

Giving Voice to Values: An Innovation and Impact Agenda
Edited by Jerry Goodstein and Mary C. Gentile

For more information about this series, please visit: www.routledge.com/ Giving-Voice-to-Values/book-series/GVV

GIVING VOICE TO VALUES

An Innovation and Impact Agenda

*Edited by Jerry Goodstein and
Mary C. Gentile*

Routledge
Taylor & Francis Group

LONDON AND NEW YORK

First published 2021
by Routledge
2 Park Square, Milton Park, Abingdon, Oxon OX14 4RN

and by Routledge
605 Third Avenue, New York, NY 10158

Routledge is an imprint of the Taylor & Francis Group, an informa business

British Library Cataloguing-in-Publication Data
A catalogue record for this book is available from the British Library

Library of Congress Cataloging-in-Publication Data
Names: Goodstein, Jerry, editor. | Gentile, Mary C., editor.
Title: Giving voice to values : an innovation and impact agenda / edited by Jerry Goodstein and Mary C. Gentile.
Description: Milton Park, Abingdon, Oxon ; New York, NY : Routledge, 2021. | Series: Giving voice to values | Includes bibliographical references and index.
Identifiers: LCCN 2020056342 (print) | LCCN 2020056343 (ebook) | ISBN 9780367768331 (hardback) | ISBN 9780367768362 (paperback) | ISBN 9781003168744 (ebook)
Subjects: LCSH: Business ethics. | Social responsibility of business.
Classification: LCC HF5387 .G558 2021 (print) | LCC HF5387 (ebook) | DDC 174/.4—dc23
LC record available at https://lccn.loc.gov/2020056342
LC ebook record available at https://lccn.loc.gov/2020056343

ISBN: 978-0-367-76833-1 (hbk)
ISBN: 978-0-367-76836-2 (pbk)
ISBN: 978-1-003-16874-4 (ebk)

Typeset in Bembo
by Apex CoVantage, LLC

CONTENTS

CONTRIBUTING AUTHORS

Christopher Adkins is an associate teaching professor in the Management and Organization Department at the University of Notre Dame and serves as the Rex & Alice Martin Executive Director of the Notre Dame Deloitte Center for Ethical Leadership. Empathy is the core theme of his research, providing a diverse set of strategies for the contexts of: ethical leadership, innovation and design thinking, leading change, diversity and inclusion, effective communication, conflict management, sustainability, and social entrepreneurship. In June 2015, he was awarded "Master Teacher of Business Ethics" by the Wheatley Institution at Brigham Young University.

Prior to joining the faculty at Notre Dame, Chris served as Executive Director and Associate Dean of the Undergraduate and One Year Master Programs at the College of William & Mary, Mason School of Business. In this role, he led the Giving Voice to Values programs with both undergraduates and MBA students, and developed new programs in sustainability and diversity and inclusion.

In addition to his teaching and research, Chris creates innovative, engaging training programs for business professionals that translate insights from neuroscience, social psychology, and behavioral economics into practical strategies for everyday leadership.

Partners and clients have included: Prudential, LPL Financial, World Bank, Deloitte, GlobalFoundries, IBM, Agilent Technology, The Aspen Institute, Novelis, Huntington Ingalls, The Conference Board, *Compliance Week*, TXU Energy, Express Scripts, and Kaiser Permanente.

Daniel Arce is the Ashbel Smith Professor of Economics at the University of Texas at Dallas and a UT System Regents' Outstanding Teacher. He holds a PhD in Economics from the University of Illinois. Professor Arce is a game theorist who has published extensively on business ethics, collective action, counterterrorism, conflict resolution, and cybersecurity.

Rebecca Awuah is a mathematics lecturer at Ashesi University. She holds a Bachelor of Science degree from The Evergreen State College and a Master in Teaching degree from Seattle University, USA. She has taught mathematics at different levels for more than 20 years. Since joining the faculty of Ashesi University in 2008, she has worked to develop mathematics curricula that emphasize conceptual understanding, problem solving, application, and the use of technology. She led a collaborative effort to adapt the Giving Voice to Values curriculum to the Ghanaian undergraduate context and has spearheaded faculty training and efforts to increase writing and critical thinking across the curriculum. Research areas include a longitudinal household survey of Berekuso assessing changes in Ashesi University's host community over time, the impact of student community service on students' leadership competencies, and statistics education. She is Board Chair of the Odeefoo Oteng Korankye II Education Fund and is currently pursuing a PhD in comparative education at the University of Minnesota, USA.

Ira Bedzow, PhD, is an associate professor of medicine, UNESCO Chair in Bioethics, and Director of the Biomedical Ethics & Humanities Program at New York Medical College (NYMC). He is also Senior Scholar of the Aspen Center for Social Values, a contributor at the MirYam Institute, and a regular contributor in Forbes for their Leadership, Diversity and Inclusion section.

Jane Cote, Emeritus Professor of Accounting at Washington State University Vancouver, conducts research examining how the quality of inter-organizational relationships affects profitability; identifying the mechanisms to support professionals facing ethical issues; and the effectiveness of corporate social responsibility reporting.

R. Edward Freeman is University Professor, Olsson Professor, and Academic Director of the Institute for Business in Society at the University of Virginia Darden School of Business. He is best known for his award-winning book, *Strategic Management: A Stakeholder Approach* (Pitman, 1984; and reprinted by Cambridge University Press in 2010). His latest book is *The Power of And: Responsible Business Without Trade-offs*, with Bidhan Parmar and Kirsten Martin (Columbia University Press, 2020). He has received six honorary doctorates (Doctor Honoris Causa) from: Radboud University in the Netherlands; Universidad Pontificia Comillas in Spain; the Hanken School of Economics, and Tampere University in Finland; Sherbrooke University in Canada; and Leuphana University in Germany, for his work on stakeholder theory and business ethics. He is the host of The Stakeholder Podcast, sponsored by Stakeholder Media, LLC.

Mary C. Gentile is Creator/Director of Giving Voice to Values, Professor of Practice at the University of Virginia Darden School of Business, Senior Advisor at The Aspen Institute Business & Society Program, and consultant on management education and leadership development. Among numerous other awards, Mary was named as one of the 2015 "100 Most Influential in Business Ethics" by Ethisphere and one of the "Top Thought Leaders in Trust: 2015 Lifetime Achievement Award Winners" by Trust Across America-Trust Around the World, January 2015. She was also named one of the "Top Minds 2017" in ethics leadership by *Compliance Week*.

Jerry Goodstein is Professor Emeritus of Management at the Carson College of Business, Washington State University Vancouver. He has taught graduate and undergraduate courses in the areas of business ethics, managing innovation and change, and leadership in organizations. Dr. Goodstein has published widely in high quality business ethics and management journals and has contributed a number of cases for the Giving Voice to Values curriculum. He served for many years as Associate Editor at *Business Ethics Quarterly* and has served on the editorial boards of

Administrative Science Quarterly, Academy of Management Journal, and *Journal of Management.*

Claire Kamm Latham, PhD, CPA, CFE, is an associate professor for the Washington State University Vancouver's Carson College of Business. Latham conducts empirical and behavioral research involving ethics with a concentration on efforts to enhance ethics training of students and professional accountants. Latham has been honored with several Outstanding Faculty Teaching Awards and the Woman of Distinction Award.

Brian T. Moriarty is Assistant Professor at the University of Virginia Darden School of Business, where he serves as course head in the residential MBA program's communication area. He teaches courses in leadership communication, strategic communication, and corporate communication. Previously he served as Director of the Institute for Business and Society and of the Business Roundtable Institute for Corporate Ethics. He has been selected as one of the "Top 100 Thought Leaders in Trustworthy Business" by Trust Across America four times.

Debra Newcomer leads Nomadic Learning's Content and Instructional Design where she works with an incredible team of entrepreneurs, teachers, writers, and filmmakers to push the boundaries of what's possible with online learning. She has 20 years of professional experience on four continents focused on getting the necessary stakeholders to the table to better solve complex problems through innovative and inspiring approaches to education.

Carolyn Plump graduated from Duke University and Boston University Law School. Before joining La Salle, she worked as a partner and associate at several law firms, as an Assistant Chief Counsel for the United State Senate, and as a Deputy District Attorney. She authored two books: *Giving Voice to Values in the Legal Profession: Effective Advocacy with Integrity* and *A Student's Guide to Business Law.*

Rachel Schaming is a University of Florida graduate. Rachel's career has included executive and senior human resource positions at NASA, The Texas Medical Center, two New York City law firms, a technology company, and higher education institutions. She is a professional certified coach specializing in coaching leaders facing cringe moment decisions and conversations.

Dr. Heidi Waldron is Director of Clinical Teaching and an educator in the Communication and Clinical Practice Domain at School of Medicine Fremantle, the University of Notre Dame Australia. She manages the communication skills course and recently received an Australian Award for University Teaching for producing a comprehensive video library.

Jessica McManus Warnell teaches business ethics, sustainability, inclusive leadership, and business in Japan at Notre Dame's Mendoza College of Business. Her recognitions include a teaching award from the North America chapter of the UN Principles for Responsible Management Education (UN PRME), and publications include her book *Engaging Millennials for Ethical Leadership: What Works for Young Professionals and Their Managers* (2015), part of the Giving Voice to Values collection.

Liang Yu is passionate about business education, leadership development, and entrepreneurship. Liang works in Duke Kunshan University overseeing its executive education department. He collaborates with the leading companies to grow their leadership and organizational capability and enjoys the process of designing transformational learning journeys for leaders from around the world.

INTRODUCTION

Giving Voice to Values: an innovation and impact agenda

Jerry Goodstein and Mary C. Gentile

Giving Voice to Values: An Innovation and Impact Agenda is dedicated to exploring the future of Giving Voice to Values (GVV). Over the past few decades GVV, under the leadership of Dr. Mary C. Gentile, has fundamentally changed the way business ethics is taught, discussed, and practiced in over 1,200 academic, corporate, and non-profit settings around the world.

While GVV continues to have tremendous impact and momentum with its existing initiatives, in this book we not only share lessons from current experience but also look beyond where GVV has been and where it is now, to explore future directions for GVV. We invited a wide range of contributors to offer their thoughts on possibilities for sustaining the growth and impact of GVV in the classroom, in the workplace, and more broadly in the community and society. These contributions come from GVV's diverse and committed global network of academics and practitioners, including authors from multiple disciplines (e.g., business ethics, economics, and healthcare) and contexts (e.g., academia, corporations, and professions). They represent pioneers, among the first to adopt

GVV in their classrooms or workplaces, as well as innovators, who have extended the reach and impact of GVV through their efforts to introduce GVV into new contexts. Collectively these authors offer their ideas and insights – based on their experiences to date – on potential opportunities for enhancing what is taught within GVV, to whom GVV is taught, how GVV is taught and delivered, and where GVV is taught.

Over the course of GVV's evolution there have been a variety of books that have described the genesis of GVV (Gentile, 2010) as well as texts describing the application of GVV in a variety of geographical regions (e.g., MENA); across functions (e.g., accounting, marketing, communications); across professions (e.g., medicine, law, corporate governance); to different issues (e.g., sustainability, racial justice, young adult development) and on and on.[1] We saw an opportunity at this particular point in GVV's history for a book that would take stock of GVV's extraordinary growth and how this growth might be sustained over time. We wanted to reach out to GVV's network of "ambassadors" from around the world who have been at the forefront of putting GVV into action, and who we felt could offer a rich, diverse, and grounded discussion of innovative ways GVV has developed over time, its impact within and outside academia, and its possibilities for GVV's future growth and development. The following chapters reflect their experience and insights working with GVV in the classroom, in the workplace, in the community, and across the virtual network.

Giving Voice to Values: An Innovation and Impact Agenda is divided into two major sections. Part I, "Strengthening the Impact of GVV Within Higher Education," is devoted to exploring innovations in the development and delivery of GVV and their potential impact within higher education settings and programs. The opening chapters of this section consider novel ways that GVV can draw on important moral traditions including virtue ethics (Ira Bedzow) and pragmatist ethics (Brian Moriarty and Ed Freeman), to reinforce and expand GVV's contributions to the teaching and practice of business ethics.

In a series of subsequent chapters authors focus on how GVV can extend its scope and impact within business school contexts and in other domains of higher education. Jerry Goodstein considers new possibilities for GVV teaching and practice by shifting the traditional GVV perspective from those who are voicing their values, to those who are in the role of listeners. Daniel Arce elaborates a variety of strategies for integrating GVV across a range of business disciplines within traditional business school settings. Chris Adkins and Jessica McManus Warnell share their experience with institutionalizing GVV within the University of Notre Dame, as well as highlighting opportunities for developing "allies" and extending GVV's influence across the university. Ira Bedzow and Heidi Waldron consider as well how GVV can reach beyond business school classrooms, specifically by introducing GVV into other academic programs and professions such as training healthcare professionals. Finally, we close this section of the book learning more about how GVV is expanding around the world and future challenges and opportunities for its global growth. Rebecca Awuah discusses the integration and institutionalization of GVV into Ashesi University in Ghana, and a series of programs and initiatives to introduce GVV throughout other countries in Africa.

In Part II, "Strengthening the Impact of GVV Beyond Higher Education," contributing authors highlight how GVV is being implemented outside the classroom and university and the opportunities for further innovation whether in the workplace, within local communities, or throughout virtual communities. Carolyn Plump shares a series of mini-cases that illuminate the potential role GVV can play in helping lawyers meet important professional and ethical challenges within their law firms, and in their interactions with clients. Jerry Goodstein interviews leaders from four organizations in diverse industries and presents their insights and guidance regarding implementing GVV in workplaces around the world. Liang Yu extends this theme, focusing on China and highlighting, through the use of an in-depth case study, how GVV might be implemented in workplaces in China. He considers as well the broader question of what the future of GVV might be within China. Rachel Schaming shares her experience from a unique perspective as a professional executive coach and presents a series of examples of where she has utilized GVV to help her coaching clients confront challenging values conflicts in diverse workplace contexts.

The final two chapters of Part II highlight how GVV might be communicated in novel ways to audiences within local and virtual communities. Jane Cote and Claire Kamm Lathan reflect on their experience taking GVV out of the classroom and offering community-based GVV workshops to CPA professionals, women working in various roles, and social service agency professionals. Debra Newcomer offers a fascinating, forward-looking discussion of how GVV has expanded over time through the use of digital technology, and the potential role emerging and new digital tools and technologies could play in significantly increasing GVV's future global reach and impact.

We conclude *Giving Voice to Values: An Innovation and Impact Agenda* with the voice of GVV's founder and guiding spirit – Mary C. Gentile. In this personal reflection, Mary shares an "untold" story about the founding and early development of GVV and identifies some of the challenges she has confronted in guiding GVV's growth over time. She ends her chapter and the book offering her vision and hopes for the future development of GVV.

We thank these authors for their contributions to this book and most of all for their contributions to GVV. Our hope is that *Giving Voice to Values: An Innovation and Impact Agenda* inspires readers to join with these authors, as well as many other GVV "ambassadors," and move GVV ahead in ever more imaginative and impactful ways.

Note

1 Gentile, M. C. (2010). *Giving voice to values*. New Haven, CT: Yale University Press. Retrieved from www.routledge.com/Giving-Voice-to-Values/book-series/GVV

Part I

STRENGTHENING THE IMPACT OF GVV WITHIN HIGHER EDUCATION

1

GIVING VOICE TO VALUES AS A WAY TO TEACH VIRTUE ETHICS

Ira Bedzow

The focus of this chapter will be to explore how two major premises of the Giving Voice to Values (GVV) methodology parallel those of the philosophical school of virtue ethics and how, therefore, GVV can serve as a programmatic and practical means to implement the process of moral growth that virtue ethics describes. Virtue ethics has been a moral philosophical framework since Plato and Aristotle, yet it has made a significant resurgence in moral philosophy since the 1980s. The uniqueness of virtue ethics over other moral frameworks is that it conceives of ethics as a form of personal character development rather than simply as a means to determine how to act in individual situations. It also explicitly recognizes the relationship between improving one's process of making decisions and acting on them, and it conceives of moral excellence in terms of personal capabilities rather than adherence to universal or communal norms. GVV shares these conceptions of ethics. The importance, therefore, of showing how GVV can be grounded in virtue ethics is that virtue ethics as a moral philosophy gains a practical method of instruction and GVV gains a theoretical foundation, which bolsters its legitimacy as a philosophically grounded moral pedagogical framework.

Exploring two key premises for GVV and virtue ethics

While there are many intersections between GVV and descriptions of how to inculcate moral growth in the virtue ethics literature, two premises that this chapter will discuss are as follows: First, moral action should not be understood as an automatic consequence of moral deliberation. Ethical decision-making and moral action consist of different skills and face different challenges. For example, even when a person knows "what to do" in terms of what the moral decision might be, he or she may still not know "how to do it" in terms of what particular steps are required to act on that decision. Moreover, there is a moral gap between decision-making and acting that is closed (or narrowed) through the development of moral habits in conjunction with the development of practical reasoning. In other words, even if the person might know "what to do" and "how to do it," knowledge does not always compel a person to be motivated to act on that knowledge. Only through creating a habit of acting a certain way does it become second nature to continue to act in that way.

Second, moral rules are not abstract universal codes of conduct that individuals should utilize to guide their moral actions. They are community-wide standards that apply to general situations and are embedded within a community ethos through its laws (or organizational policies, depending on to which community one refers). As such, one must understand moral norms to be approximate; they will cover the majority of typical cases, but they will not perfectly match the particularities of actual cases. There will be many times when simply following a rule will not be the best way to respond to a situation or when a rule will not state specifically how it should be enacted. Rather, in these cases, successful moral action will demand the use of practical wisdom, or the ability to think pragmatically to ensure that one can successfully implement his or her values-driven decision. Practical wisdom is developed through personal experience yet is grounded in the values which community standards attempt to impart on the community. Because of this shared foundation, there is a strong relationship between personal decision-making and recognizing community norms, both when considering what one should do as well as in determining how one can persuade others to act in kind.

The point here is not that through GVV people will find ways to rationalize action based on community norms; rather, a person must consider how to act on their own values in light of community norms. Those norms may either be levers of persuasion or potential obstacles if not confronted strategically. In either case, the person tries to answer the question of how he or she can act successfully on his or her personal values, given the community or organizational context in which he or she must act.

In summary, virtue ethics and the GVV methodology both offer a more complete understanding of how individuals can learn to give voice to what they believe in ways that they can achieve personal growth and even social or organizational change for two particular reasons. They both recognize that there is a difference between ethical decision-making and moral action, and they both appreciate that there is a relationship between an individual's behavior and the ethos of his or her social or organizational community.

Outline for chapter

After introducing how virtue ethics conceives of moral development, the chapter will examine two premises that virtue ethics and GVV share. It will first discuss how virtue ethics conceives of how one can develop skills of moral action and how GVV provides educational opportunities for students to develop those skills on their own terms, and how the development of those skills gives rise to the virtue of practical wisdom. The chapter will then describe how virtue ethics explains the ways in which community norms serve to inculcate virtue and the skills of practical reasoning so that a person's use of practical wisdom entails consideration for a community's code of moral conduct. Building on this description, the chapter will also explain how GVV instruction provides ways for students to practice these skills of ethical deliberation and moral action in a community or organizational setting. By showing how GVV provides moral education, the chapter will show how GVV, like virtue ethics, is a practical education where students consider both their own choices as well as the environment in which they choose to act.

The chapter will contribute to the primary themes of the book in two ways. First, it will provide an overview of how moral philosophy and the GVV methodology complement each other. This recognition would allow moral philosophers to expand their ethical discourse to include suggesting ways to confront many of the practical and professional challenges that people face. It would also allow business and professional ethics educators to understand the benefit of the GVV methodology *as ethics training*. Second, once one appreciates the similarities between virtue ethics and the GVV methodology, educators and professionals who are already utilizing the GVV methodology can appreciate some of the philosophical social assumptions that it presupposes, making their ethical inquiry that much richer and deeper.

Short introduction to moral development in virtue ethics

Virtue ethics is a theory of moral growth and character development. With proper instruction, people can improve their ability to act on, and identify with, the moral values that they and the community in which they belong hold. Virtue ethics is different from other contemporary moral philosophies in that it does not possess a moral maxim, such as Kant's categorical imperative, or a utilitarian formula through which moral questions are processed in order to reach a conclusion. Rather, one's skills of moral deliberation and habit formation develop through a recursive process of continual decision-making and action, where previous experiences lend insight to future experiences, and current challenges compel one to reevaluate previous choices so that the moral actor learns how to incorporate effectively nuance and various factors into his or her decision. In this sense, virtue ethics appreciates that wisdom develops through experience rather than simply application of a universal moral law, and it seeks to explain how people's choices and habits improve through mindful reflection and building one's "moral muscles."

The philosophy also recognizes that previous action facilitates both readiness and competence to be successful in acting on one's moral values in the future. As such, virtue ethics is the ethics education equivalent to continuous quality improvement. Moreover, because, for the virtue ethicist, moral improvement occurs over time and incorporates both a person's actions and how he or she identifies with the values those actions embody, the question of primary importance for the virtue ethicist is how one can improve his or her response to a moral challenge. This consideration includes the response's efficacy, the individual's disposition and personal capabilities, and the person's identification with the values that the response embodies. This is in contradistinction to deontological and consequentialist ethical frameworks, which focus moral inquiry on the right or best choice for a given situation in the abstract, without considering the personal characteristics of the person making or enacting that choice.

In a virtue ethics framework, a person starts his or her ethics education under the assumption that he or she has the potential and the aspiration to act in ways that best exemplify the values that he or she has. Personal moral development stems from a combination of influences. For example, people initially learn what is right or good from community norms. They then learn how to apply general community norms and values to everyday decisions and habits. As they develop a moral sense, they learn how to interpret and respond to their personal experiences so that they can choose to act on values in ways that are effective in more challenging situations. Through practice in acting on values in more difficult situations, people not only improve in figuring out how to act more effectively, they also come to identify more closely with their moral purpose based on their own moral values. The culmination of moral development is when the person achieves moral integrity, which is defined as having consistency within one's set of principles or commitments and having coherence between one's principles, actions, and the motivations behind them.[1]

Ethical decision and moral action

When confronted with moral challenges, the virtuous individual will not only be able to make the appropriate decision, but he or she will be able and motivated to carry out that decision so that it achieves the desired result. The virtuous person is able to do this through the exercise of practical wisdom. According to Aristotle, practical wisdom is a combination of practical reason, i.e., the intellectual skill of knowing what one wants to achieve in a given situation as well as knowing the means through which one can achieve it, and the possession of moral virtues, i.e., as one's identification with certain values through their embodiment as regular habits.[2] To make a proper moral choice, therefore, necessitates that a person has the knowledge required to make that choice; he or she must choose the desired option voluntarily, and the choice must reflect the person's moral values.[3] Values are the priorities that a community imparts on its members and that members hold as personally significant.

Choices must reflect values ∧ virtues

Virtues are the capabilities that adherents develop so that the person who acquires virtues is motivated and able to express the corresponding values in his or her behavior. However, practical wisdom and choosing the best course of moral action is not simply a matter of knowledge and desire. One gains practical wisdom through experience, which implies that one hones both the skills of practical reasoning and the reinforcement of one's identification with certain values over time and practice.[4]

Aristotle thus calls the moral choice that a virtuous person makes a "deliberate desire,"[5] meaning that it is both intellectual, as it results from deliberation, and affective, since the person desires to act on that choice.[6] This does not mean that moral choice consists of two separate and distinct components, i.e., the goal one wants to achieve through acting and the means through which that goal can be achieved.[7] Rather, the two parts are connected in the same way as the concave side of a lens is connected to the convex side. They are two sides of the same lens.[8] For this reason, even if a person identifies with certain values and has cultivated a desire to act in a way that promotes those values, it is possible for the person nevertheless to fail to choose the proper way to carry out the decision. Furthermore, even if a person knows intellectually the proper response to a particular situation, he or she may still not be motivated to act upon that decision because of other personal or situational factors.

Given these dispositional and situational factors, it becomes readily understandable that not only do the intellectual and affective components of a person's decision allow a person to want to make the moral choice, both components will also allow the person to make the proper moral choice for the person himself or herself. In other words, through the exercise of practical wisdom, the virtuous person will choose a particular moral response and choose to perform it in a particular way, both in terms of what the particularities of the situation demand for that choice to be effectuated and in terms of the choice taking into account the person's abilities and disposition. Practical wisdom can thus be described as the combination of a ready disposition to respond to situations in a certain way and an intellectual ability to discern the best way to respond *for that person*.[9]

Factors that influence how a virtuous person responds to a situation of moral difficulty include not only what one would want to do generally, but also the various stakeholders and what would be most persuasive to them in a given situation, what consequences the virtuous person foresees

for himself or herself as well as the other stakeholders, the systemic or
organizational limitations or opportunities the virtuous person might
encounter when implementing his or her decision, and whether the interpersonal ethos in which the virtuous person acts seems to support or
disallow the desired ethical choice. While important in many social and
interpersonal contexts, the utilization of practical wisdom is even more
important in giving voice to one's values in a hierarchical or professional
environment, which demands that one persuade other stakeholders who
might have different goals or varying weights of authority and/or power
to support or reject one's desired choice. Therefore, knowledge and ability to be persuasive and to recognize the needs and goals of other stakeholders are critical. In other words, practical wisdom will provide more
than simply general notions of what is right; it will give a person the skills
to create scenario-specific plans for how to act in practice.

Virtue ethics, GVV, and personal values

Virtue ethicists, starting with Aristotle, ground their theory of moral development in the assumption that those who seek moral education already
have a good idea as to the values with which they aspire to identify and
the types of behaviors that will put those values into action.[10] Similarly,
the GVV methodology starts with the assumption that a person should not
consider the moral response to a situation abstractly or generally conceived.
Rather, he or she should look at how one can act on one's own values in
response to a situation of moral tension. Therefore, for both approaches,
moral pedagogy begins with the premise that each person must choose
a path of action that fits with his or her own sense of self and his or her
personally held values. At the same time, the person should recognize that
moral challenges require people to grasp the nuances of the social environment in which a person must act, which includes appreciating social
conventions that might help or hinder the success of one's actions.

Thus, the primary purpose of moral pedagogy for those who appreciate the philosophical foundation of virtue ethics when incorporating the
GVV methodology is that education must include the opportunity for
students to refine their understanding and ability to act on their held values, so that their learned moral behavior becomes second nature. It is not
enough to evaluate case studies for what should be the "right decision."

Evaluation of case studies should include what would be the "right and best decision for each student" and how that decision reflects each student's and the community's values for the case at hand, in relation to overarching goals and in relation to other decisions that have been made in the past and will be made in the future. As a primarily post-decision-making method, which emphasizes the presumption that students know which values they want to incorporate into the ethical decision, GVV cases do not simply ask, "What would you do in this situation?" Rather, they ask students to consider the following "Thought Experiment" – "What if you wanted to enact your values? What might you say or do?" In thinking about past cases, it asks, "Do you think that you would have been more confident and more effective in voicing your concerns if you had rehearsed ahead of time?" These questions demand that students conceive of moral education as a *training activity*, where they can develop tools and skills to express values efficaciously.

The programmatic frame shift for case-study evaluation exemplifies the manner in which students learn how successful enactment of their moral choices becomes what Aristotle called a "deliberate desire." Moreover, the education is similar to other types of practical training, such as in business, law, and medicine, where students are explicitly taught how to carry out decisions in practical and particular detail. For example, in order to test the worth of a given business idea, business students learn different strategies to carry out and different means to evaluate whether the given idea can be successful. Similarly, law students learn not only whether a lawsuit is warranted but also how to file one properly and argue one's position persuasively to win one's case. Medical students learn not only whether a certain medical intervention is indicated or not, but they also learn how to provide that treatment, given the goals of care and the wishes of the patient. In the same way, through the GVV methodology, ethics education can provide students with the tools to evaluate whether their choice of action fits with their values and how they can carry out their choices successfully. GVV case studies demand that students develop scripts, which incorporate decision-tree types of strategies, where students account for various rationalizations to be prepared for multiple possibilities. Furthermore, by accounting for various ways in which they can respond, all of which are in line with the person's habits and nature, moral action strategies strengthen both the person's practical reasoning as well as reinforce his or her current moral habits and virtues.

In thinking through and constructing practical action strategies and communication scripts for the moral questions that a GVV curriculum asks students to consider, students develop skills of effective moral action for particular cases at hand. They learn both how to come to a decision that gives voice to their own values, which is informed by ethical reasoning and critical thinking, and how they can act on their decisions, given the complexity of the environment in which they must act. By having students repeatedly engage in creating practical and effective strategies for action, in rehearsing how they would communicate with various stakeholders in the respective cases, and in participating in reflective peer discussion and coaching on how to improve, students develop "moral muscle memory" to respond to the challenges they will face in the future. This is not only an important component of the GVV methodology, but it is also an explication of the relationship of practical reasoning and habituation in virtue ethics. It also reinforces the premise that both virtue ethics and the GVV methodology holds, namely, that ethical thinking and moral action are two sides to the same ethical lens and that students must continually look through both to be successful.

Virtue ethics, GVV, and practical wisdom

When virtue ethics began its resurgence in the modern era, many moral philosophers perceived it in contradistinction to rule-based or maxim-based ethical frameworks. For example, G.E.M. Anscombe argued that one cannot reconcile the contradiction of conceiving of ethics through a rule-based framework and as a matter of acquiring and acting on virtues.[11] Anscombe is correct that, for Aristotle, moral action based on the exercise of virtues does not correspond with acting in fulfillment of a moral law, as in Kantian deontology, or according to a moral code, as many professional codes seem to presume.

Yet, the difference between rule- or code-based ethics and virtue ethics is not simply that virtue ethics focuses on the development of character traits while rule- or code-based ethics focuses on particular actions. Rather, as stated earlier, virtue ethics recognizes the limitations of applying general moral maxims to particular situations. It also recognizes that there is a difference between understanding the prescriptive nature of a moral code and willingly acting in the spirit of it. This last point, however, is shared with Kantian deontologists. Nevertheless, compliance with codes of conduct does serve a moral purpose in terms of delineating generally what the moral choice should be and in creating opportunities to develop moral virtues. This is because many moral and professional codes are attempts to put values into prescriptive activities. Therefore, by learning the rules of the code and abiding by them, one can learn and create habits that engender moral and professional values.

Similarly, for Aristotle, law orders society according to "objective" practical reason. By "objective" practical reason, he means that the rationality of the law is based on the consensus of the community and is not the product of any one individual.[12] However, as stated earlier, even if the law is created through the utilization of objective practical reason, its insufficiency stems from its inability to take into account the particularities of moral life. Of course, because laws and many professional codes are derived from political compromise, one should not simply rationalize actions based on a rule's existence. There may even be times when a rule may be found to be unethical when applied in practice, and strategies and tactics for working through such situations require extreme care and thought.

The difference between Kant's moral law and Aristotle's view of the moral foundation of law is that for Aristotle ethics begins at the level of society, and it is society's conception of the good that shapes individuals' characters and moral growth. For Kant, on the other hand, ethics begins at the level of the individual, and it is an abstract, rational conception of the good that ultimately should guide a person's moral actions. Therefore, for Aristotle, the law is not set against ethics; rather, it is both a cause,[13] albeit indirect, and a consequence of it. It is a cause by virtue of its effect on its adherents, and it is a consequence of ethics in that legislation and judicial decisions are made, and improved, by those ethical legislators and judges who have been shaped by the community's laws but use their own practical wisdom to improve upon those laws.

Study of the law alone, however, would not enable a person to develop practical wisdom, even if intellectual study of how the law applies to cases would enable a person to learn how one should act in a given situation. For virtue to develop, intellectual study would still not provide for the person a means to acquire the moral motivation and facility to act morally, since those skills are only acquired through practice and habituation.

Motivation and habituation, or as the GVV literature states, "the building of moral muscle memory," occurs through personal engagement in real-life moral situations. For professional and business training in ethics, these situations are part of everyday professional and organization interactions. For ethics instruction, the relevance is that it is insufficient to learn ethics concepts and laws or codes of professional ethics. It is also insufficient to discuss those concepts and interpret those laws or codes for the sake of understanding their underlying values. The development of virtues and practical wisdom stems from incorporating discussion of ethics concepts and interpretation of laws or codes into practical implementation exercises where students must create moral action strategies and scripts – in other words, the GVV format of ethics training.

The goals that an individual aspires to achieve, and the values that he or she holds dear, are realized through the person's choices and actions. By living according to his or her choices, made within a communal or organizational setting, a person will engender a disposition that allows him or her to recognize the values embedded within them and will aspire to become the type of person who identifies with those values. Edmund Pellegrino and David Thomasma explain the integration of moral action and communal principles through a virtue ethics framework as follows:

> Moral acts are inextricably tied to the who, what, where, how, and why of our lives. We are saved from the errors of situationist, emotivist, and egoist ethics by principles. But, by themselves, the principles can depersonalize and dehumanize. Virtue-based ethics link principles and obligations as abstract entities to the circumstances of our personal lives through the virtue of prudence [i.e., practical reason, inclusion by author].[14]

The person's moral growth is thus based on how he or she internalizes those values and learns to act on them through practical wisdom. Internalization of values so that one develops corresponding virtues arrives through seeing how one engages his or her community or organization and its ethos as a matter of choice. When faced with a situation that challenges either a personal or social value, the person has a choice as to whether he or she wants to uphold that value or not. Seeing values as entailing choices allows the person to take control over his or her decision rather than seeing value-based norms as being imposed upon him or her. When one conceives of values as choices-turned-virtues, acting on those values gives a person a sense of empowerment in transforming them into virtues.

According to the GVV methodology, when faced with the question of how to respond successfully to a moral challenge, a person must consider organizational policies and/or various laws that are relevant to their desired choice of action. In doing so, students do not simply see the law or organizational policies as exclusionary reasons, i.e., reasons for acting *as well as* reasons why one cannot act in any other way. Rather, they consider why the law and/or policy was created, which values are intended to be instilled in those who comply with it, and how or whether compliance gives voice to that value in the given situation. This deliberative practice and the strategy students create through it will not only help in persuading other stakeholders either to comply with the law or policy or to revise or change it, depending on the case; reflection will also facilitate internalization and identification of the values and norms of the community or organization when appropriate. From a pedagogical perspective, the process of learning how to accept, internalize, and identify with laws and guidelines can be taught by asking students what their current conception of the law or guideline is, what assumptions they made that led to that conception, and how they can adopt a more positive understanding of the policy if they disagree with it. Reinforcement of proper attitudes to laws and guidelines in developing good practices and habits occurs through practice and case studies that ask students to create action strategies that must consider how one can act, given legal or policy constraints.

By having students confront the practicalities of cases and understand how systems-based policies and laws may support or hinder fulfilling their desired choice of action, students learn how personal and communal values relate to each other. They are also given the opportunity to identify with the community (whether it be a civil, organizational, or professional community) of which they are a part.

Conclusion

The GVV methodology demands that each student considers not what an abstract person should do in an instance of moral challenge but rather what he or she could do, as an individual with particular values and personal capabilities, to respond successfully to that challenge. The emphasis on personal development of one's "moral muscle" – in terms of being able and motivated to create and act upon practical strategies that respond to the realities of a given situation – reflects the description of moral growth and character development in the philosophical school of virtue ethics. This chapter outlined how GVV and virtue ethics share two major premises, which would also allow business and professional ethics educators to understand the benefit of the GVV methodology *as ethics training*. It also gives teachers using GVV a lens through which to see it within a broader philosophical school. Whether one is engaged in examination of ethical theory or increasing ethical integrity in practice, the GVV methodology can serve as a means to convey many of the themes that virtue ethicists have been teaching for centuries to a new generation of moral leaders.

Notes

1 For similar definitions of (moral) integrity, see the following: Taylor, G., & Gaita, R. (1981). Integrity. *Proceedings of the Aristotelian Society*, Supplementary Volumes, *55*, 148. McFall, L. (1987, October). Integrity. *Ethics*, *98*(1), 5–20.

2 Aristotle. Nicomachn Ethics. Trans. Martin Ostwald. Addison Wesley Longman; Package Ed edition (November 1, 2000). *NE* 1138b18–30, trans. Ostwald; Ibid. 1106b21–24.

3 Ibid. 1105a30–1105b1.

4 Ibid. 1142a12–16.

5 Ibid. 1139a24.

6 Ibid. 1144a7–9.

7 Arist. *EE* 1227b36–7, trans. Ogle.

8 Arist. *NE* 1102a31, trans. Ostwald.

9 Ibid. 1144b30–3.

10 Ibid. 1194b28–1095a5.

11 Anscombe, G. E. M. (1958). Modern moral philosophy. *Philosophy*, *33*(124), 1–19.

12 Arist. *NE* 1287a.32, trans. Ostwald.

13 With respect to how prescriptive codes can engender moral action, according to Aristotle, abiding by the law of the state is a necessary precondition to moral development, but only an indirect cause for it. This is so, because humans do not voluntarily choose to obey the law to become

virtuous. Moreover, the law in essence becomes irrelevant as practical wisdom develops, since through practical wisdom a person will be able to determine the proper mode of conduct for each situation. Aristotle does admit, however, that because people may falter in their practical reasoning at times in their life, the laws of the state will in effect always be necessary as a backdrop to ensure proper conduct (Ibid. 1179b32–1180a5). The moral relevance of obedience to the law is because the law forms a continuing part of character education that is begun at home, where the political community plays the role, albeit at the level of the state, played by parents at the level of the household.

14 Pellegrino, E., & Thomasma, D. (1993). *The virtues in medical practice* (pp. 23–24). Oxford: Oxford University Press.

2

VIEWING GIVING VOICE TO VALUES THROUGH A PRAGMATIC LENS

Brian T. Moriarty and R. Edward Freeman

The body of work and tools that constitute Giving Voice to Values (GVV) is aimed at ameliorating a specific type of challenging situation that most people will face during their professional lives. In the workplace, sometimes people are asked to take actions that conflict with their values. Social pressure to act in a way that contradicts deeply held norms can lead to moral anxiety and moral confusion. The experience is usually emotionally upsetting and can be extremely difficult to navigate – especially when a situation is particularly complex and involves several stakeholders who view key factors differently.

At the center of GVV's origin story is the fact that many people facing this type of moral dilemma in the workplace fail to act on their values. The tendency of people to go along with actions that conflict with their values in the face of organizational pressure is often unconscious and not wholly attributable to purposeful deliberation. Mary C. Gentile's self-described "crisis of faith" emerged from her recognition that while a person's acquiring knowledge of ethical frameworks is crucial for developing moral awareness and maturity, this is often not sufficient for enabling a person to enact their values effectively.

And yet, it is critical to note, some people do find effective ways to enact their values within their organization. The aim of GVV is three-fold – to encourage the belief that action is possible, to guide people who have decided to act, and to promote practices such as pre-scripting and rehearsal that build "moral muscle memory."

This chapter argues that one way in which the three objectives of GVV can bear further fruit is through a dialogical conversation with pragmatic philosophy – particularly with that of John Dewey. As we make evident, the relationship of GVV to pragmatic philosophy is one that is mutually reinforcing, much like the water dynamics operative in a thriving rain forest. As a rain forest spreads and becomes lusher, it produces more moisture.[1] As a rain forest produces more water this reinforces the precipitation cycle, and the forest spreads and becomes lusher.

While pragmatic philosophy points to some opportunities for GVV to grow, GVV likewise contributes to and expands the practical imprint of pragmatic philosophy. This chapter will explore this relationship through the lens of GVV's three-fold aim: (1) showing that action is possible; (2) guiding those who have decided to act; and (3) promoting practices that build moral muscle memory.

Showing action is possible

One of the fundamental tools employed in GVV is the exercise titled "A Tale of Two Stories." First, the exercise encourages each participant to recall two separate instances from her career when she was asked to do something that conflicted with her values. Participants are then tasked with telling the story of both cases. The first story is supposed to narrate an example where the protagonist successfully voiced her values while the second story chronicles an occasion where she failed to do so.

Like GVV, John Dewey's moral philosophy takes as its starting point an actual person in a specific situation. It is grounded on experience and not on principles. For Dewey, moral reasoning does not begin with rules that are then applied to situations, but rather with people experiencing distinct situations in unique ways. This designation of experience as the "indispensable starting point" for Dewey's moral philosophy is, according to Gregory Fernando Pappas, what makes it truly "original and revolutionary" (Pappas, 2008, p. 1).

This starting point which Dewey terms the "postulate of immediate empiricism" is basic to his entire body of thought, not only to his moral philosophy (Dewey MW 3:158 quoted in Pappas, 2008, 20). The postulate's notion is that things "are what they are experienced as" (Dewey MW 3:158 quoted in Pappas, 2008, 20). Much like Peirce and Wittgenstein's claim that human thought is limited to its linguistic boundaries, Dewey asserts that we know the world only through our experience of it and not through any special intuitive power that can grant access to a definitive view of reality.

The emphasis that Dewey places on everyday decision-making is a factor that is common among pragmatist thinkers, beginning with Ralph Waldo Emerson. In 1837, Emerson proclaimed, "I embrace the common, I explore and sit at the feet of the familiar, the low. Give me insight into today, and you may have the antique and future worlds" (Ralph Waldo Emerson, quoted in West, 1989, 12). Following a similar line of thought, Charles Peirce, who first defined pragmatism (largely in distinction to modern philosophy), insisted that philosophy should use everyday language since its purpose is to guide conduct and shape habits.

Although pragmatism has many branches, Cornel West asserts that it has common roots in "future-oriented instrumentalism that tries to deploy thought as a weapon to enable more effective action" (West, 1989, p. 5). In short, pragmatic ethics is about developing methods of practice and habits that enable people to act more effectively in their everyday lives. This suggests that pragmatic philosophy can benefit GVV practitioners by identifying various schemes and approaches to taking action in various situations that people face.

Pragmatic philosophy can also serve as a counterbalance to those whose principle-based approach may prevent them from seeing how action can be possible. While principles play an important role in Dewey's thought, helping us to navigate some situations effectively, he insists that their application is limited. Principles are tools that we might choose to use in the situations that we encounter. For Dewey, viewing principles or any particular ethical theory as embodying universal truth can have the unfortunate effect of blinding us to the range of options we may have at our disposal. It also can dampen our creative impulse and the development of new habits that may lead to a better alternative course of action. As Pappas puts it, "Ethical theory can be like a tool for moral education. Like our best maps, it can orient us, but we must do our own traveling" (Pappas, 2008, p. 64).

At first glance, having to do "our own traveling" with respect to navigating morally challenging situations can seem like a very lonely and difficult undertaking, but further consideration shows its value to GVV in describing a self that is capable of action. "Experience is primarily a process of undergoing," Dewey explains, "the organism has to endure, to undergo, the consequence of its own actions" (Dewey quoted in West, 1989, p. 88). These consequences of our actions, however, can be positive as well as unfortunate – and the same is also true when we choose to do nothing.

Experience is not just something that happens to us, according to Dewey's account, it is also something that we co-create with others. Dewey asserts that "all conscious experience has of necessity some degree of imaginative quality" (Dewey, 2005, p. 283). In this sense, his empiricism is not limiting, but rather, incredibly empowering.

This is of special importance to GVV because people who are caught up in morally complex situations often feel either that there is nothing that they can do which will have the desired impact or that they have no choice other than to obey the dictates of their superiors (Pappas, 2008, p. 32).[2] In such circumstances, people feel frozen or trapped and find it difficult to speak up and act. Dewey's assertion of creativity and imagination as elements of experience, however, suggests that people have other options available and that part of maturing morally may involve the development of new creative habits that can be liberating.

While the idea of liberating oneself from a situation where we feel trapped probably sounds appealing to most people facing a thorny situation, how to go about this may not be apparent. One of the great benefits of GVV is that it provides an easy-to-understand exercise that can help to change how we view our capabilities and unleash our creativity to solve problems. Completing the "A Tale of Two Stories" exercise not only reminds participants that a range of choices is available but also helps them to relive an experience when they acted on their values. As Gentile says in the introduction to *Giving Voice to Values*, "This book is about acknowledging and enabling choice" (Gentile, 2010, p. xxvii).

Pragmatic philosophy can similarly expand not only our view of choice but also how we see ourselves in relation to the communities to which we belong. Dewey asserts that the troubled feelings people experience in situations characterized by values conflicts should be understood more broadly than as elements of an individual's consciousness. The meaning that people attach to what they encounter in experience is something that is learned and co-created socially in relationship with the various communities to which they belong. As Pappas puts it, the unrest that people feel in troubling situations "is the presence of a dominant quality of a situation as a whole" (Pappas, 2008, p. 103).

The problems embodied in a values conflict are not simply psychological or individual but are characteristic of the tangle of social threads that comprise the situation (Dewey, 1994, p. 109). This perspective could help to provide a gateway to a broader narrative for a person struggling with a values conflict. This new narrative situates them and others within a community and helps to alleviate the sense of isolation that they may be feeling. For similar reasons, GVV recommends that people identify allies and emphasizes the importance of peer coaching. Pragmatism's view of morals as social helps to further encourage this.

Values, much like languages, are learned in communities and are social despite any individual differences in understanding and usage. "Morals," Dewey asserts, "is as much a matter of interaction of a person with his social environment as walking is an interaction of legs with a physical environment" (MW, 14:219). Extending this metaphor, Dewey notes that while the "character of walking depends upon the strength and competency of legs," an individual's personal capability is only one factor in the situation (MW, 14:219). How a person walks changes if a person "is walking in a bog or on a paved street, upon whether there is a safeguarded path set aside or whether he has to walk amid dangerous vehicles" (MW, 14:219).

Dewey's point in employing this walking/landscape metaphor is not to suggest a relativist approach to morals, but rather to remind his reader that morals are relational and that social situations are interactive and characterized by change. GVV similarly recognizes the influence that organizational culture and policies can have on either fostering an environment that enables people to act on their values or the converse (MW, 14:219). Keeping a steady focus on acknowledging and enabling choice,

Gentile not only acknowledges the influence of culture but also stresses the importance of "identify[ing] positive conditions that we can strive to create" to play to our strengths (Gentile, 2010, p. 57).

Pragmatist ethics also has much to say about human limitations that is of value to how we think about GVV. For example, Peirce and other pragmatist thinkers suggest that suffering and conflict are signs that help to reveal the need to correct both social habits and the intellectual models we employ for understanding the world. More recently, Richard Rorty follows this line of thought, saying that a more fruitful way for expressing our limitations would be "by comparing our way of being human with other, better, ways that may be someday adopted by our descendants" (Rorty, 2016, p. 1).

Because humans are finite beings with imperfect knowledge, Rorty insists that all of our actions involve risk. He stresses that there is a "need for risky experimentation" (Rorty, 2016, p. 56). This need, Rorty argues, should not be ignored, but rather our finitude should be emphasized as an integral element of the theoretical maps we employ to navigate experience. Emphasizing social healing can further encourage people to act on behalf of a purpose larger than themselves.

This includes GVV. Human finitude means that we can never be certain that our actions and theories are leading us in the right direction. Our experience of the world is theory-laden and, to paraphrase the poet Robert Blake, our windows of perception always stand in need of cleansing. As Rorty points out, evading our finitude seems to be a common human tendency. With this in mind, GVV explicitly tells people that enacting our values effectively is not easy and that taking action involves risk even when you have the best available tools at your disposal. One consequence of taking risks, Dewey would remind us, is an opportunity to strengthen our moral competence by building positive habits. We are not born with positive social habits. Rather, like the fitness and skill level of an athlete, beneficial habits are cultivated through intentional practice. Taking a similar view, this is why Gentile continually emphasizes the importance of building moral muscle memory.

Values conflicts can be viewed as catalysts for growth. A "problematic situation," Dewey asserts, is the "controlling factor . . . in regulating as well as evoking inquiry" (Dewey LW 14:44, quoted in Pappas, 2008, p. 41). Dewey encourages us to consider this disruption as an opportunity to make a positive difference. The same feelings which trouble us and which are "tiresome, hateful, unwelcome," he insists, can best be read as calls for human creativity and as signals to greater human freedom (MW 14, 140). Charles Peirce termed deeply felt doubt that keeps a person from sleeping "pillow doubt." He did so to distinguish it from the philosophic doubt which Descartes promoted as a catalyst for progress. This latter type of doubt Peirce derided as "paper doubt."

Dewey and Peirce's point is that the angst felt by a person experiencing a values conflict is a social signal as well as an individual one. This understanding provides the person in turmoil with a way to re-frame the situation and their initial response as having important social value akin to someone who is woken by the smell of smoke. Pillow doubt is a call to action and an opportunity to make a positive difference.

Guiding people who have decided to act

GVV seeks to guide people who have decided to exercise their freedom and act to make a positive difference. For Dewey, freedom and action involve creative effort – they require deliberation. The purpose of deliberation is "to resolve entanglements in existing activity, restore continuity, recover harmony, utilize loose impulse and redirect habit" (MW 14, 139). Deliberation seeks to loosen habits and impulses that are harmfully connected and identify a better course of action.

GVV provides a roadmap and tools for developing new positive habits in the hope of enabling better courses of action. "The thesis here," Gentile writes, "is that if enough of us felt empowered – and were skilled and practiced enough . . . business would be a different place" (Gentile, 2010, p. xxiii). GVV asserts that much like an athlete who trains and practices to become more highly skilled at a sport, people can become more skillful at handling morally challenging situations in the workplace through deliberate effort and practice.

In Dewey's view, becoming more skillful in this area requires developing a greater facility for deliberation. For Dewey "deliberation is a dramatic rehearsal (in imagination) of various competing possible lines of action" (MW 14, 132). An imaginative exercise, dramatic rehearsal halts overt action and takes time to put the various conflicting habits, values, and impulses that comprise a moral predicament onto the stage of its thought experiment. This imaginative undertaking does not yet change the situation outside of the body. It affords an opportunity for determining how best to act, taking into account the potential and likely outcomes of various courses of action. This is a matter of repeatedly re-mapping the multiple relationships which are entangled within a particular situation.

A similar imaginative undertaking is recommended in GVV which can be viewed as a heteroglot type of dramatic rehearsal that encourages bringing to bear a wide variety of approaches and activities. GVV asks the following questions among others. What are the stakes involved and who are the stakeholders? What reasons and rationalizations should be considered? Who or what might influence key decision-makers? What resources might enable taking action? These kinds of questions, once considered carefully, can be integrated into GVV scripts, practiced in rehearsals, and then tested via peer coaching. This becomes a way to strengthen positive habits and move from deliberation to action.

The initial action is an important beginning, but its impact is difficult to predict. Dewey deepens our understanding of deliberation as an agile process that continues to evolve through human creativity as circumstances change based upon our actions and those of others. GVV provides concrete examples of these evolving dynamics. Taken together, these two resources provide excellent guidance for those who have decided to act. Neither creates a false expectation that acting effectively will be easy.

Dewey understands deliberation to be an enormously complex task. Each of these habits, values, and impulses present in a particular situation are not only connected to multiple social narratives, but also to various stakeholders for whom they have meaning. As we consider possible ways of acting on our values "we foreknow how others will act in part," Dewey asserts, and this "foreknowledge is the beginning of judgment passed on action" (MW 14, 216). Other stakeholders whom we consider within our thought experiment become an imaginary "assembly . . . formed within our breast which discusses and appraises proposed and performed acts" (MW 14, 216).

The extent to which this imaginary assembly can help determine a preferred course of action, however, depends to a great extent on the actual quality of these existing relationships. How well a person understands other stakeholders – especially their different impulses and habits – is a difference that can make a difference.

GVV also repeatedly asserts that genuine stakeholder engagement is a critical factor in reasoning and making better decisions. Emphasizing the importance of asking the question, "What are the stakes?" in a given situation is core to GVV. This leads to further questions about who the various stakeholders are and their respective motivations. On this point, Gentile reminds her reader that "research tells us that we are often incorrect when we assign motivations to others," often viewing our actions as driven by circumstances while we tend to attribute the actions of others to their characters (Gentile, 2010, p. 216). In reality, we have very limited insight into the constant swirl of situational factors with which others are dealing constantly, never mind their impulses and habits.

Dewey's understanding of reason and rationality is helpful here. "Rationality . . . is not a force to evoke against impulse and habit," he claims, but rather "is the attainment of a working harmony among diverse desires" (MW 14, 136). The value of reason is not in chaining our impulses or those of others. Instead, rationality enables us to recognize the impulses and habits at play in a situation, to get a sense of where these might lead, and to consider in partnership with others how a new harmony might be established.

Re-framing is a powerful tool used in GVV for helping to establish a new harmony among values and impulses that are at odds. Gentile tells the story of business students at the American University of Sharjah in the United Emirates whose friends had asked for help cheating on an exam. These students felt torn between wanting to maintain their personal integrity and being loyal to their friends. Loyalty, as Gentile indicates, can be reframed in multiple ways. What about loyalty to your other friends and classmates who are *not* cheating? What about your friends' loyalty *to you* when they ask you to help them cheat? "What we begin to see through reframing," says Gentile, "is that equating voicing our values with disloyalty to friends and equating loyalty with not voicing our values needs to be revisited" (Gentile, 2010, p. 68).

Pragmatic philosophy's focus on communities offers a valuable reminder that broadening our perspective can be a potent way of reframing our understanding of situations as dialogical. This encourages proactive listening that formulates and asks good questions to better illuminate the different motivational drivers at play among the various people involved. This is of particular importance because it helps to counter some common decision-making models that can be a hindrance to the proliferation of GVV.[3]

As John F. McVea has shown, Dewey's understanding of deliberation as dramatic rehearsal differs in some important ways from the decision-making models that are most common in business education. These models, which McVea terms "calculative deliberation," depict decision-making "primarily . . . as a process of maximizing or optimizing according to pre-determined goals" (McVea, 2007, p. 380). The distinctions that McVea draws between dramatic rehearsal and calculative deliberation underscore the benefits of considering GVV as a heteroglot type of the former (McVea, 2007, p. 378).

Dramatic rehearsal views our impulses and our emotional responses to situations as crucial elements in decision-making, whereas in calculative deliberation they are usually viewed as a hindrance that should be pushed to the side. GVV case studies repeatedly show that as Dewey's dramatic rehearsal suggests, the emotional responses of protagonists to the challenging situations they encounter often serve as the initial catalyst leading them to take action.

Mary C. Gentile tells the story of Frank, an executive whose company had recently selected him to become the new controller for a regional sales unit. The regional sales director was pressuring Frank to recognize a major order the company had received in the quarter before it would be actualized to increase the bonus of the sales team. Although Frank believed the right course of action was to recognize the sale in the quarter where it was actualized, he also felt impulses to be seen as a trusted colleague and a team player in his new role. By broadening his frame for viewing the situation in the broader terms of the risk to the organization, Frank was able to transform "an exceptional – and for him – an emotional problem, fraught with blame, into a predictable and organizational challenge that draws on his professional expertise in the design and implementation of internal controls systems" (Gentile, 2010, pp. 82–84).

From the perspective of dramatic rehearsal, Frank's initial emotional reaction is not replaced by reasoning, but rather blossoms into a plan of action supported by impulses, reason, and directed habit. Importantly, dramatic rehearsal also emphasizes that deliberation is a process of discovery. It is only through this creative activity that we begin to discern some of the risks and consequences involved with our potential courses of action. This, Dewey says, is because "in quality, the good is never twice alike. It never copies itself. It is new every morning, fresh every evening" (MW 14, 146).

Whereas calculative deliberation operates from the assumption that "alternatives, risks, and consequences are known or are estimable and are *exogenous* to the decision-making process," Dewey takes an alternate view (McVea, 2007, p. 379). Due to the uniqueness of every situation, the alternatives, risks, and consequences involved cannot be known before the act of disentangling the various impulses and habits at play. Discovering the different drivers at play, how they are related to each other, and the potential risks and opportunities are some of the fruits of deliberation.

Deliberation need not be the activity of an isolated individual, and in fact, there are good reasons to view this as a less effective way to work through potential risks and opportunities. The reason that GVV emphasizes the importance of peer coaching is that it provides us with additional perspectives and insights. By voicing a challenging situation out loud to others "we not only generate scripts and skills for ourselves, but we invite others to be part of our process" (Gentile, 2010, p. 221). We may also learn that our colleagues have faced similar challenges and learn from their actions.

This aspect of dramatic rehearsal as an emergent process adds another important element to how we might think about GVV. Sometimes when people experience moral confusion they come to believe that the challenge before them is beyond their powers, leading them to despair of finding an acceptable course of action. Here, however, Dewey can be read as providing a theoretical framework for normalizing the initial sensation that we lack the proper tools to handle a morally perplexing situation.

Because every situation is unique, having a sense that we are not yet equipped for resolving it should not be surprising, but rather should be expected. The purpose of deliberation that Dewey describes and which is embodied in GVV is to create additional tools as needed that can liberate us from this particular perplexity and undertake actions that lead to a new harmony.

Normalization is, of course, one of the seven pillars of GVV. Part of the reason that encountering values conflicts in the workplace can be so upsetting to us is that many people tend to view them as disruptions to their normal daily activities. From this perspective, when we encounter a values conflict, "it threatens to derail us" (Gentile, 2010, p. 72). As Gentile notes, viewing values conflicts as normal elements of social cooperation – which includes business – helps to ameliorate the "emotional charge and pressure" people may experience (Gentile, 2010, p. 75). It also makes actively responding to such challenges feel more normal for us.

Pragmatic philosophy reminds us that language is an indispensable element in navigating the world and its various challenging situations. Language holds a central position in the thought of pragmatists stretching from Peirce to Rorty. Peirce famously asserted that all thought is through signs, denying the possibility of a direct intuitive connection to reality which had been a linchpin of modern philosophy. While the linguistic turn among pragmatic ethics denies the possibility of knowing the world directly and unequivocally, it also provides a map for how we can better know and navigate the situations we experience.

While no one description of the world "tells us *the* way the world is," Rorty explains that "each one of them tells us *a* way the world is" (Rorty quoted in West, 1989, p. 191). For some people, the proposition that there are multiple valid descriptions of the world can at first seem disorienting. It can, however, also be liberating. Instead of looking for a universal world view that can guide all of our behavior, Rorty suggests that we are better served by taking seriously the other perspectives that we encounter. Likewise, GVV identifies multiple ways of enacting our values, based on our strengths and preferences as well as concerning particular circumstances and stakeholders. In other words, there is an explicit recognition that many ways to enact our values exist and it is beneficial to have as many arrows in our quiver as possible. From this perspective, success is characterized by growth, the development of positive habits, and increasing our capacity to act effectively on our values. It is important to note that acknowledging multiple valid descriptions of the world does not imply moral relativism any more than the existence of multiple maps of a single territory – e.g., a road map detailing highways, a topographical map showing elevations, and a climate map depicting annual rainfall – would imply that any of them is disconnected from the concrete reality they each seek to communicate.

On a practical level, expanding our capacity to act effectively often begins with the sharing of stories which is and should remain a fundamental part of GVV workshops. This type of dialog is not only how we come to influence others and the social environment, but how we are changed as well. As Dewey explains, "Our thoughts of our own actions are saturated with the ideas that others entertain about them" (MW 14, 216).

Social saturation works in multiple directions, and we are all marked for better or worse with its stamps. We hold memberships in several groups, we are actors in multiple narratives, and we move about the world guided by many maps. How we move about, how we act impacts both us and our social environment. As Dewey says, "Morals is as much a matter of interaction of a person with his social environment as walking is an interaction of legs with a physical environment" (MW 14, 219). The potential to help reshape the social environment and make it a bit more navigable is perhaps GVV's highest hope.

Promoting practices that build moral muscle memory

The previous section highlights the need for creativity. New predicaments require the development of new approaches, new tools, and new habits. Showing that other options are available to be discovered or created is one of the immense benefits of GVV as is its openness to other bodies of knowledge. This openness is precisely what will enable GVV to grow through recognizing and adopting other forms of dramatic rehearsal and integrating new ones as they emerge. GVV's continuing ability to integrate other forms of dramatic rehearsal to its repertoire, to use tools from a range of disciplines, and to encourage the creation of new strategies is a great strength.

Perhaps the most fruitful connection to be drawn between pragmatist ethics and GVV is their shared focus on habit formation through practical exercises. GVV hails practical exercises as key to moral maturity. They are the vehicle for building positive habits that become second nature. "Rather than experiencing that deer-in-the-headlights feeling when we confront values conflicts," Gentile explains, "our muscle memory can kick in and the emotionality of the moment is reduced" (Gentile, 2010, p. 10).

While there are multiple ways for GVV to grow in the near future, the opportunity most relevant to the dialog with pragmatist ethics is to consider how other forms of dramatic rehearsal might be usefully employed within GVV.[4] Next we briefly outline two sets of practices – scenario planning from the field of communication and expressiveness exercises from theater – which we believe will add significant value to GVV. Table 2.1 lists schemes and approaches in pragmatic philosophy that have corresponding approaches in GVV.

It is worth noting that GVV already embodies several elements – story telling, framing, scripting, rehearsal, persuasion, stakeholder engagement – that demonstrate its strong connections to communication and theater. Given these long-standing associations, employing additional exercises from these disciplines should be relatively seamless. The two representative exercises that we outline should be read as signaling others from communication and theater that could hold similar promise for GVV.

The first of these exercises, scenario planning, is a strategy development method used by organizations to rehearse the future. Scenario planning, which is often employed in strategic communication and corporate communication MBA courses, does not seek to predict the future, but

Table 2.1 Corresponding approaches in pragmatic philosophy and GVV

Schemes and approaches from pragmatic philosophy	Corresponding ideas and actions in GVV
Co-creation and imagination	Acknowledging and enabling choice
Deliberation as dramatic rehearsal	Pre-scripting and rehearsal
Experience as the catalyst for deliberation	Beginning with a person in a concrete situation
Morals and moral conflicts are viewed as social	Identifying allies and seeking peer coaching is key to resolving dilemmas
Beneficial habits are cultivated through intentional practice	Scripting and rehearsal help us to build moral muscle memory
Deliberation is action that redirects habits	Intentional practice and effort build empowering habits
Mapping the various entanglements of impulses and habits involved in a moral predicament is a key step in deliberation	Identifying stakeholders and their dominant reasons and rationalizations is core to GVV
Rationality's value is in creating a working harmony among diverse desires	Reframing can help establish a new harmony among values that are at odds
Emotional responses are important signs that should impact our decision-making	Emotional responses can help to catalyze action
The unique qualities of every situation can lead to an initial state of moral confusion	Normalizing the experience of moral conflicts helps us to respond better

rather, through an imaginative exercise make better decisions in the present. As such, it is a specialized example of Dewey's concept of dramatic rehearsal.

The benefit of scenario planning for GVV is that it can help people involved in complex situations to determine how best to use their time and energy. The first step in scenario planning is to identify the major factors present in a situation that could impact the success or failure of a proposed course of action. The next step is to rank each of these factors according to two different criteria: (1) the relative magnitude of their potential impact on the success or failure of the proposed course of action; and (2) the level of uncertainty associated with this factor. For example, proposed energy regulations that are highly restrictive would be a very impactful factor for a company planning to open a new power plant. If the passage of these regulations depends on the results of an upcoming election cycle, this factor may also be highly uncertain.

This second step aims to identify two factors that like the preceding example are not only critically important but also are highly uncertain. These two factors are then combined to create four different scenario conditions that then become the focus of the strategic planners who will then develop alternate action plans for each of these potential states-of-affairs.

While scenario planning in organizations is a communal, imaginative, and structured form of deliberation it can likewise be employed by individuals or small teams of advocates. For people employing GVV, it could help them to disentangle the key factors that could impact a major decision someone is in the process of making. Instead of trying to disentangle every strand at once, disciplined scenario planning focuses time and energy on only two factors – the two that are most critical and most uncertain. While there is a risk that other critical factors might be overlooked, this structure has the benefit of keeping the decision-making process from becoming frozen by cognitive overload.

One of the chief issues for people facing morally challenging situations is getting overwhelmed by the complex factors that may be at play. Using scenario planning's criteria and its process can help determine the most crucial and salient factors in their situation and direct their scripting efforts. For GVV practitioners who have decided to act on their values but are struggling to determine where to begin due to the complexity of the challenge they face, scenario planning may provide beneficial guidance.

Expressiveness exercises from theater offer GVV practitioners a different type of dramatic rehearsal and skill development. To paraphrase the poet Robert Burns, even our best-laid plans can often go awry. The fault is not always in our plans – sometimes it is in our performance and how we have gone about the work of preparation skill development.

One area of skill development and preparation that gets overlooked by many business professionals is expressiveness, "the ability to express feelings and emotion appropriately by using all means of expression . . . to deliver one congruent message" (Halpern & Lubar, 2004, p. 129). The aptitude to express emotions in a way that is impactful and authentic is important to GVV because it enhances our facility for influencing others. According to leadership and theater consultants Belle Linda Halpern and Katie Lubar, most business people planning to deliver a message spend the vast majority of their preparation time focused on *what* they plan to say and next to no time practicing *how* they will communicate their message (Halpern & Lubar, 2004, p. 133).

Many people assume that if they can get the words right, the message will be effective. Academic studies, however, consistently show that the emotion expressed by a communicator through vocal tone and body language has a significant impact, concerning both audience impact and perceptions of the speaker's credibility (Sy, Côté, & Saavedra, 2005, pp. 295–305).[5] A pragmatist might point out that we know this from experience. For example, the loud and angry vocal tone of a teenager shouting "I'm sorry!" at their parent likely has an emotional impact that challenges the credibility of the teenager's words.

The good news – for teenagers and practitioners of GVV – is that vocal expressiveness can be improved through practical exercises. Theater has developed multiple drills for enhancing this skill. While knowing your lines is "table stakes" for an actor, it is not the hallmark of outstanding performance. Vocal expressiveness, how a person uses her voice in delivering her message, makes an enormous difference not only in *how* a message is heard but also in *what* message is received.

This fact is not only relevant for actors, but also for GVV practitioners who seek to create energy about the ideas they are proposing within their organization. What authentic feelings and emotions are they intending to convey or evoke in performing the scripts they have created to respond to their situation? How skilled are they at expressing these feelings and emotions? Which feelings and emotions would benefit from further practice?

Once areas for improvement are identified – either through self-assessment, peer coaching, or a combination of the two – individuals can practice the performative portions of their scripts with a particular focus on conveying feelings and emotions. Halpern and Lubar suggest the following exercise. First, the performer divides their script at each transition point. Next, they identify the main feeling or emotion they want to convey in each section. Then they perform the script out loud in front of a coach with the intent of using their vocal tone, pacing, and volume to express the feelings and emotions they are trying to convey (Halpern & Lubar, 2004, pp. 156–157).

Another exercise that Ed uses in his course, Leadership and Theater: Ethics, Innovation & Creativity, is to have participants read monologs out loud multiple times in peer groups.[6] Eventually, he takes the script away, challenging students to recite from memory. This has two positive effects. Removing the script not only helps speakers focus on the core story elements of the monolog but also it frees them to express the emotions that they associate with the story in their own words.

Each of these exercises is a physically actualized instance of Dewey's concept of dramatic rehearsal. Performing out loud, however, makes dramatic rehearsal more of a communal exercise where we have added peer coaches to the "assembly . . . formed within our breast which discusses and appraises proposed and performed acts" (MW 14, 216). The ability to develop the skills that define responsible leadership within a supportive community is one of the great benefits of higher education and strong company cultures that should not be taken for granted.

Fostering the growth of pragmatist ethics and GVV

We believe that GVV has a bright future both in MBA education in general and at our school in particular. The purpose of the Darden School is to improve the world by inspiring responsible leaders through unparalleled transformational learning experiences. Ethics at Darden has a long tradition beginning in the 1960s with the establishment of the Olsson Center for Ethics and the Olsson Chair. Over the last 50 years, ethics has become a core discipline at Darden on par with accounting, finance, operations, communication, organization behavior, and others. The school has a required and graded ethics course in its core, and a slate of electives, at least one of which the majority of MBA students take. Also, since the early 1990s, Darden has had a PhD program in business ethics, aimed at training a new generation of scholars who are equally at home in the social sciences and humanities.

GVV is a perfect fit for the Darden environment. The researchers at Darden have focused a great deal of their attention on figuring out what to do with difficult ethical issues where the answers are not very clear or have to be invented with creative (moral) imagination. GVV's focus on developing moral competence through practice and habit development complements this work and extends the application of the frameworks developed at Darden. Stakeholder theory, moral imagination, collaboration, and understanding emotional and moral ambiguity are hallmarks of the Darden research platform that have been informed in part by the turn to the pragmatists in philosophy as outlined in this chapter. In the last five years, we have seen the expansion of experiential learning in many parts of our curriculum and we expect this trend will continue given the value it creates. Experiential learning is the quintessential method of pragmatic education – it is a dramatic rehearsal that can be effective even if the instructor is unaware of the philosophical underpinnings. Once again, GVV is a perfect fit for these ideas.

Going forward we want GVV to have a permanent home at Darden, as well as living in so many organizations around the world. Darden's Institute for Business in Society, the focus of our current approach to put business and ethics together, will continue to support research and teaching on GVV and extend its development in all areas of business ethics theory and practice. Some integration of GVV has already begun both in courses being taught at the MBA level and in the executive education area. Darden Executive Education recently began offering a self-paced, digital GVV course designed to enable professionals to gain skill at acting on their values in the workplace.

We look forward to a robust pragmatist future where GVV helps Darden and the University of Virginia to remain a leading and forward-looking institution committed not only to thinking about business ethics but also to empowering people to more capably act on their values.

Notes

1 It is estimated that large rain forests such as the Amazon can produce as much half of their own precipitation.

2 As Pappas (2008) asserts, for Dewey all situations can contain moral aspects, but the cases which he terms "moral" are those where a person is struggling to determine a course of action amidst multiple moral claims and social pressures.

3 To be clear, we see the same ideas embedded in GVV with a slightly different emphasis. The argument here is that pragmatic philosophy adds an additional and harmonious voice in a unique tone to the GVV chorus and that this makes for even more powerful music.

4 For example, GVV has already grown in some important ways, creating tailored programs for other professions – in law, medicine, nursing, the military, NGOs, and various industries, etc. – and this expansion promises to continue.

5 This empirical study shows that moods signaled by a leader impacts both individuals and groups within an organization.

6 More information about this course is available online at http://it.darden. virginia.edu/leadershipandtheater/index.html.

Bibliography

Dewey, J. (1967–1990). *The collected works* (Jo Ann Boydston, Ed.). Middle Works, Volume 14, *Human nature and conduct* (Carbondale, IL: Southern Illinois University Press). Following the standard convention for references from *The collected works*, this volume is cited as MW 14 within this paper, along with the relevant page numbers.

Dewey, J. (1994). *The moral writings of John Dewey* (James Gouinlock, Ed.). Amherst, NY: Prometheus Books.

Dewey, J. (2005). *Art as experience*. New York: Perigee.

Gentile, M. C. (2010). *Giving voice to values: How to speak your mind when you know what's right*. New Haven, CT: Yale University Press.

Halpern, B. L., & Lubar, K. (2004). *Leadership presence*. New York: Avery.

McVea, J. F. (2007). Constructing good decisions in ethically charged situations: The role of dramatic rehearsal. *Journal of Business Ethics, 70*, 375–390.

Pappas, G. F. (2008). *John Dewey's ethics: Democracy as experience*. Bloomington, IN: Indiana University Press.

Rorty, R. (2016). *Philosophy as poetry* (Michael Bérubé, Ed.). Charlottesville, VA: University of Virginia Press.

Sy, T., Côté, S., & Saavedra, R. (2005). The contagious leader: Impact of the leader's mood on the mood of group members, group affective tone, and group processes. *Journal of Applied Psychology*, 90(2), 295–305.

West, C. (1989). *The American evasion of philosophy*. Madison, WI: University of Wisconsin Press.

3

GIVING VOICE TO VALUES AND THE LISTENER'S PERSPECTIVE

Jerry Goodstein

Introduction

In the Giving Voice to Values (GVV) case, "Better Wrong Than Right? Delivering the 'Bad' Market Research News (A)," (Gentile & Goodstein, 2010) members of a product marketing team in a high technology company are faced with the kind of challenge at the very heart of GVV. The product team wants to convince their manager, Larry Rogers, to make what they believe is the right choice – that is, to not intentionally manipulate the market research data the team had collected. The company was considering introducing two potential new product modifications for a high selling communications device. Larry's team had spent time collecting market data on consumer preferences for these modifications. Larry wanted to change the results so that the market research would show that customers preferred one new product modification over the other, despite the fact that the actual data showed consumers preferred the other product modification. Changing the results would support the product feature Larry knew Sean, his demanding, strong-willed boss preferred. Larry hoped to avoid what he knew would be an inevitable confrontation with his contentious boss.

The case adopts the traditional GVV perspective and puts students in the roles of members of his product team, who feel strongly about not changing the data and presenting the true results of their research to Larry's boss. At the end of the case, students are asked a series of critical questions to help them approach Larry: What arguments could they make and what support could they offer Larry that would enable him to change his direction? Students learn in "Better Wrong Than Right? Delivering the 'Bad' Market Research News (B) and (C)" that the team members did meet with Larry and were able to convince him to present the true market research results to his boss. Ultimately Larry's boss still decided to go with his preferred course of action.

In the teaching note that accompanies these cases, students are asked to consider Larry's perspective and think about why Larry might have changed his mind. What might have prompted him to listen to his team? What influenced him to change his mind and follow the advice of his team? The teaching note points out a number of factors – the quality of the relationship between Larry and his team, their mutual trust and respect, the intensity of emotion conveyed by team members – that compelled Larry to *listen* closely to his team, to acknowledge and respond to their deep concerns, and ultimately to change his mind.

In this chapter I want to flip the traditional GVV focus to direct greater attention to those in Larry's position, the intended audiences of those voicing their values, what I refer to in this chapter as *listeners*. Arguably one of the most significant developments in the teaching of business ethics over the past 15 years has been the emergence and growth of GVV. Created by Dr. Mary C. Gentile over a decade ago, Gentile added a new dimension to business ethics education where the focus is not on the traditional question of "What is the right thing to do in this situation?" but rather "Assuming you know the right thing to do . . . how can you get it done?" Since GVV's inception Gentile and her colleagues have created a variety of curricular materials (e.g., cases and teaching notes, published articles, books) that have been instrumental in introducing GVV to business schools and corporations around the world.

A defining characteristic of GVV is the emphasis on voice and adopting the perspective of what I refer to in this chapter as *voicers*. Voicers are encouraged to consider what they want to say, to whom, and how, as well as developing a well thought out implementation plan that goes beyond the "speaking" role to include key steps such as data gathering, re-framing, building allies, and considering the necessary interventions based on the specific situation and context. These questions play a central role in the development of a script and action plan that will be as persuasive and convincing as possible when presented to pivotal stakeholders in a given situation and context. GVV encourages voicers to consider carefully these stakeholders and to try to understand what concerns they might have, their points of resistance, and what enablers voicers can draw on. An important goal for GVV is for voicers to motivate listeners to seriously listen to and consider the values-related issues voicers are raising.

To date, there has not been as much attention within GVV to the role of listeners in GVV interactions and considering how to empower and motivate listeners. As I discuss in more depth next, the role of listeners has been emphasized more in the organizational training context, and in particular working with senior level leadership. What this experience working with senior leaders in corporations and universities has shown is that skilled, motivated listeners who listen carefully and acknowledge and respect voicers' underlying values, are able to foster effective two-way communication where voicers can truly be heard.

What if these leaders, and all those potentially in listening roles, adopted a similar stance as Gentile advocates with regard to voicers when she asks, "Assuming you know the right thing to do . . . how can you get it done?" That is, for listeners, what if the question becomes, "Assuming you want to listen and respond effectively to those voicing their values, what can you do?" Once we flip perspectives in this way, and ask this new question, we can give added emphasis to those times when we will be called upon to listen to others voicing their values to us, particularly if we are in managerial/leadership roles. We can recognize and seize these moments as true GVV opportunities for honest conversation and dialogue that can empower both voicers and listeners.

Integrating the listener's perspective more directly into GVV can be enhanced in two primary ways. First, contributors to GVV can draw on relevant literatures, in particular work in the field of communications on active listening, to bring to GVV important insights on listening effectiveness that emerge from this literature. Second, the listener's perspective can be further developed within GVV through building on what is already in place. Gentile (2016) has offered some initial thoughts and insights on what she has called "Listening for Values."

There are opportunities to revise/expand existing curricular materials, as well as develop new materials that emphasize the listener's perspective (e.g., cases, videos, readings). Those teaching and facilitating GVV in classrooms and workplaces could draw on these curricular materials to help GVV participants explicitly adopt the listener's perspective and work with participants to develop their listening skills in the GVV context. I discuss these various avenues of development in more detail next.

"Listening for values" and GVV

In articulating the importance of the role of listening within GVV Gentile (2016, p. 108) argued that

> listening for values has been a key component of GVV from the very start. The very protocol of questions and analysis that lie at the heart of the GVV process for crafting effective scripts and action plans require us to ask and answer the question, 'What is at stake, or at risk, for all affected parties with regard to the values conflicts at hand?'

Gentile framed her arguments from the perspective of voicers, suggesting that to effectively voice one's values, one must also make a "commitment to listening for values in others."

Gentile, however, also recognized the importance of this commitment to listening for values particularly for those in management and leadership positions. Gentile gained insights on the listener's perspective through her direct experience working with senior leaders to implement GVV in academia and the corporate sector. A key area of focus for the middle and senior level managers Gentile worked with was on identifying examples of situations where they were able to listen most effectively when their direct reports raised issues. For example, some leaders noted that they appreciated when they were not put on the defensive by their direct reports. Others mentioned that they were able to listen and respond more effectively when issues were presented in a more direct and concise manner and there was an acknowledgment and respect for the time pressures and challenges faced by leaders. When approached in these ways by voicers, senior leaders were able to be better listeners, to pay attention to the issues being voiced, to listen in a more open manner, and to communicate to staff their commitment to seriously consider and respond to these issues.

Gentile drew on these conversations to offer a number of important insights directed explicitly to the role of listening within GVV. First, she emphasized the importance of the listening environment/context noting that it is critical for leaders to

> maintain an organizational culture that encourages and enables and supports voicing values . . . and to provide opportunities to pre-script, rehearse and peer coach effective ways to hear and respond to the efforts of others (often lower level) employees when they raise values issues – that is, to *listen* for values. If and when employees do raise values questions, the manner in which their manager receives the message sends powerful signals about whether this sort of behavior is genuinely welcome (Gentile, 2016, p. 109).

Second, Gentile was able to see the relevance and importance of scripting for listeners, as well as voicers. As the leaders Gentile worked with discussed ways they could listen more effectively to the values-related issues being voiced by their direct reports, these leaders discovered that not all these issues were necessarily unique. At one university, for example, senior administrative leaders were able to identify common conversations and issues faculty might raise, for example uncertainty around the clarity on tenure standards. These leaders discussed the possibility of identifying some of the most important values-based issues and pre-scripting and rehearsing their responses in ways that fit the context and values of their institution. Through practicing and rehearsing how one might listen and respond in advance of a conversation, managers and leaders can lower their defensiveness and stay more open and engaged, even when difficult issues are raised that could cause these leaders to shut down and stop listening. Gentile (2016, p. 110) noted,

> Just as 'rehearsal' and peer coaching is a useful strategy to develop the muscle for voicing values effectively, so too these can be useful

approaches to building the patience, self-management and communication 'scripts' for hearing these messages in ways that signal true receptivity.

This kind of preparation and pre-scripting can ultimately help these leaders focus and feel more comfortable with listening attentively to what voicers are truly saying and learning from these conversations, rather than trying to refute or challenge what voicers are saying.

Advancing the listener's perspective in the classroom and workplace

How then might others working with GVV, either in the classroom or workplace, integrate the perspective of the listener into GVV? One place to begin is by building on current cases and methods within the GVV curriculum. As noted earlier, the focus for most GVV case discussions is on voicers and their development of a script (independently or with peer coaches) for voicing their values. In developing these scripts voicers are asked to consider the stakes involved in the situation, to confront relevant reasons and rationalizations, recognize both enablers and barriers to voicing their values, and ultimately develop their "most persuasive case." Those assigned to the roles of peer coaches are tasked with helping voicers develop their scripts and rehearse what they plan to say.

One might imagine a complementary set of activities occurring in parallel in classrooms, for example, utilizing the same GVV cases. Faculty could divide a class so that some students are in the traditional roles of voicers (e.g., Larry's team), responsible for developing and delivering their scripts of what to say and to whom. Other students would be assigned to take on the role of listener (e.g., Larry). For those in the role of listener, the primary focus would be on preparing for meeting with and listening to voicers. Instead of the traditional GVV script, listeners could prepare a GVV listening script grounded in the principles of active listening, an important domain of scholarship developed over a number of decades.

Active listening

The concept of active listening was first developed by Carl Rogers (1951, 1975). Lloyd, Boer, and Voelpel (2017, p. 509) summarize the practice of active listening "as an appreciating and nonjudgmental way of perceiving and responding to an individual." Lloyd et al. (2017, p. 509) suggest the importance of active listening for voicers: "Attentive listeners foster an atmosphere of safety to speak openly, create intimacy, and elicit positive perceptions of the listener." Research supports the importance of active listening in motivating employees to speak up, encouraging two-way communication, and inviting greater speaker self-disclosure (Lloyd et al., 2017). Management scholars also recognize active listening as a core skill of effective leaders/managers (see Lloyd et al., 2017).

Active listening involves a number of important skills or competencies associated with effective listening. These skills involve listeners understanding, remembering, interpreting, evaluating, and responding to the messages being communicated to them (Brownell, 1994). Critical to the development and application of these listening skills are: adopting an orientation of paying attention to what is being communicated, withholding judgment, and showing patience and curiosity in clarifying and reflecting the listener's understanding of the communication (Hoppe, 2006; Patterson, Grenny, McMillan, & Switzler, 2002). Asking questions is particularly important to effective active listening (Murphy, 2019, p. 147):

> Open and honest questions don't have a hidden agenda of fixing, saving, advising, or correcting. . . . It allows people to tell their stories, express their realities, and find the resources within themselves to figure out how they feel about a problem and decide next steps.

Patterson et al. (2002) highlight a number of additional "power listening tools" (summarized by the acronym AMPP – Ask, Mirror, Paraphrase, and Prime) that may be of particular relevance for fostering safe, open conversations in emotionally charged situations. A direct way to engage voicers is to ask questions such as "I'd really like to know what is on your mind," that indicate you are listening closely and are genuinely interested in understanding what the person is trying to say. Mirroring can be important when a listener senses one is trying to control their emotions and you want to convey that you can see how the voicer might truly be feeling, for example, "You say you're not worried, but you seem tense." Another way to signal to the voicer that you are listening and trying to understand is to paraphrase what the voicer has said, summarizing their words using your own. Finally, there may be times when you feel that someone has more to say, but are holding back because they don't feel it is safe to speak. Priming involves creating a more comfortable space for someone to open up. Patterson et al. write (2002, p. 152), "sometimes you have to offer your best guess at what the other person is thinking or feeling. You have to pour some meaning into the pool before the other person will do the same." One might, for example, ask a priming question such as, "Are you concerned that what you say might harm your supervisor's reputation?"

Developing this listening script is consistent with an "active listening strategy" (Hoppe, 2006) where listeners are able to be more proactive and undertake a kind of rehearsal in advance of having a conversation with voicers:

> When you can plan ahead for a discussion or meeting, work out your active listening strategy ahead of time just as you would think through the content of the meeting. What is your goal? How will active listening help you achieve your goal? What barriers might get in the way and how might you proactively address these barriers?
>
> (Hoppe, 2006, p. 25)

To help those adopting the listening roles prepare their active listening strategies, faculty can create curricular materials based on existing research and best practices (such as the readings highlighted earlier). Some of these best practices include:

- Preparing to listen in a non-defensive, respectful way that invites the voicer to be open
- Preparing to listen and respond in a way that is "appreciative" in nature – thanking the voicer for bringing to light particular issues
- Asking for clarification when needed
- Requesting more time when needed to consider and respond to the ideas/issues voicers have expressed
- Having listeners ask themselves (and ultimately share throughout the organization) how those voicing their values might communicate with them in ways that would make it easier for them to hear and respond appropriately

- Inviting *voicers* to offer *their* ideas about what effective listening means to them and thereby building in their direct participation in identifying ways that would make it easier for them to hear and respond appropriately

As with the current emphasis on voice, these materials could summarize in a concise and direct way practical, actionable insights on listening effectiveness.

GVV and the listener's perspective in the classroom

What would active listening look like in teaching GVV in the classroom context? Returning to "Better Right Than Wrong? Delivering the 'Bad' Market Research News (A)" at the opening to this chapter, students adopting Larry's role could be asked to address a series of questions to help them prepare their listening strategies:

- What are your goals in listening to your team (e.g., communicating to your team that you respect them for approaching you)?
- What issues/concerns might you anticipate your team expressing to you (e.g., your team's commitment to acting with integrity in presenting the true and unaltered market research findings)?
- Can you prepare in advance for listening to and responding to these concerns openly and non-defensively? How might you put into practice some of the "power listening tools" highlighted by Patterson et al. (2002) (e.g., asking/inviting team members to share their concerns and paraphrasing at different points to reflect your understanding of what your team is communicating to you)?
- What barriers might get in your way (e.g., concerns about Sean's response, wanting to hold firm with your initial decision) of listening openly and responsively to your team members?

Preparing for these kinds of questions can serve as a kind of rehearsal for listeners that increases the likelihood of effective communication between speakers and listeners.

After allowing some time for the various parties to prepare and rehearse, including the possibility of peer coaching for voicers *and* listeners (see

Gentile, 2010), faculty could take these GVV cases one step further and have voicers (e.g., Larry's team members) and listeners (Larry) put into action the scripts and listening strategies they have prepared and rehearsed. This might be followed by a debriefing discussion where participants share their reactions to the conversations. As part of the debriefing discussion, faculty might ask students to consider a set of questions directed to the role of listening within GVV. Questions could be framed from the perspective of voicers and listeners and focus on a specific case, as well as broader contexts: Voicers might be asked to think about and respond to questions such as:

- How well do you believe Larry listened to you? Why or why not? If not, could you have done anything to encourage greater listening?
- How much time do you spend listening to and trying to understand the perspectives and concerns of your audiences, as compared to the time spent preparing what you were going to say and do?
- How effective were you in listening to the values-related issues raised by your team? What enabled you to be effective? What would have helped you to be more effective?
- When a colleague expresses their concerns to us, how can we diminish the defensiveness that sometimes blocks us from truly hearing what the underlying issue is? How can GVV-style "rehearsal" and peer coaching help with this?

Finally, in recognizing the importance of the listening environment in fostering a context for effective listening and the encouragement of voice, faculty might ask students questions such as:

- What potential barriers in the workplace might undermine the quality and effectiveness of the listening environment?
- What organizational practices could be put into place to support more effective and consistent expression and listening to values-based concerns?

In the end, an important insight revealed in the "Better Right Than Wrong? Delivering the 'Bad' Market Research News (A)" teaching note is the importance of listening not only to what is said, but paying attention while listening to the emotions conveyed and body language, for example:

> In discussing this incident with Larry, he shared that what influenced him to present the true market research results was not only *what* his team said to him, but *how* they communicated their concerns to him. The intensity of their emotions conveyed how much they cared about upholding the integrity of the market research results and their trust in Larry to make the right decision.

Beyond the adaptation of existing GVV cases, faculty could develop new cases for classroom discussion that specifically emphasize the perspective of the listener. This shift in emphasis might mean faculty developing cases by working more directly and closely with individuals at management and senior leadership levels and asking them about their experiences as listeners in responding to issues brought to them by their direct reports (or other employees). Listeners could reflect on when they were able to listen effectively in an open way without shutting voicers down, as well as share times when they did not listen effectively. These experiences could be developed into GVV cases, along with teaching notes and complementary readings to accompany the cases, that give greater attention to considerations of listening effectiveness and the development of active listening strategies, including opportunities to pre-script, rehearse, and peer coach effective ways to hear and respond to efforts when voicers raise values issues.

GVV and the listener's perspective in the workplace

There are likely to be significant opportunities as well to integrate these listening-oriented cases and supplementary materials into workplace ethics training, as well as the classroom context discussed earlier (see Bedzow & Waldron, 2021 for an example). This kind of training has been integrated into a number of existing corporate management and leadership development efforts whether focused on ethics and/or communications skills (Goodstein, 2021). As GVV continues to expand beyond the classroom and into workplaces across the world, there are likely to be more opportunities for listening-oriented training to complement efforts to empower voicers. Gentile (2016), for example, worked with trainers at one organization who were able to come up with a novel way to work with managers. These trainers asked managers to give them examples of times (without identifying specific individuals) when their direct reports were effective in raising values conflicts with them. These examples served as resources for then developing a list of listening tactics for managers to draw on when engaged in GVV conversations, "tactics that will have credibility because they were identified as appropriate and welcome by more senior managers in the same firm" (Gentile, 2016, p. 109).

Workplace training discussions such as these can provide a foundation for enhancing managers' listening effectiveness in these situations, and for developing some "best practices" to share among managers. In turn, managers can provide guidance to employees on how to best communicate values-related issues in ways that will help managers listen and respond with greater understanding and empathy. These efforts can serve an important role in developing a culture that supports both voice and listening (Lloyd et al., 2017).

One additional area of innovation is the use of GVV online training modules, currently offered through the Nomadic and Coursera platforms, in workplace settings. These online modules have been introduced in a variety of corporate settings and provide an efficient and effective platform for ethics training for employees and managers across multiple regions/units throughout the world. The modules feature small vignettes/scenarios that are framed from the perspective of those who are asked to voice their concerns/issues. Nomadic has recently introduced into their GVV training a module focused on "Listening for Values" that offers trainees the opportunity to learn more about active listening in the workplace.

Ultimately this kind of active listening at the individual level can enhance the broader context and culture for both listening and voicing. Brownell (1994, p. 3) writes, "Strong listening environments are characterized by a concern for the individual employee and his or her values, needs, and goals." One of the most important influences on listening environments is the listening orientation of top management. Strong listening environments reflect a willingness of top management to listen to employees and employee perceptions that supervisors are interested in their input and will listen to the issues and concerns they might raise (Bass and Avolio, 1994; Drucker, 2004; Morrison, 2011). When leadership and supervisors are perceived as "willing to listen to sensitive issues, employees may infer that the organization cares about its employees' concerns" (Dutton, Ashford, Lawrence, & Miner-Rubino, 2002, p. 359).

There are of course barriers to active listening that can weaken listening environments. Developing the kinds of active listening skills highlighted earlier is not easy for employees, supervisors, or more senior leaders. External pressures and limited time can intensify emotions and get in the way of effective listening. In addition, management attributions of employees may undermine active listening; "If supervisors attribute the behavior [employee voice] to cooperative, other-focused motives, they are likely to respond much more favorably than if they attribute it to self-interest" (Morrison, 2011, p. 389). Understanding the barriers that undermine a strong culture of listening, as well as the enablers that reinforce active listening throughout the organization, are important components of GVV education in the workplace, as well as in the classroom.

Conclusion

If GVV were to more fully reflect the listening perspective outlined in this chapter, what might this mean for the future of GVV? First, in the same way that GVV has empowered voicers by enhancing their skills and repertoire of tools (e.g., developing scripts), a greater emphasis on active listening also has the potential to empower listeners by enhancing their listening skills and expanding their repertoire of tools (e.g., developing active listening strategies). With more skillful voicers and more skillful listeners, there might be an opportunity for the kind of two-way communication that advances more effective responses to values-based concerns and issues raised within organizations.

Second, an emphasis on active listening within GVV is likely to make voicers better listeners, more attentive to others' values and their issues and concerns. Currently, within GVV voicers are encouraged to consider the values and circumstances of their audiences/listeners in developing a convincing and persuasive script for framing and sharing their concerns. A natural extension of this orientation would be for voicers to think more explicitly about how they might present their concerns and issues in ways that are responsive to the needs of their listeners. And it will be important as well for voicers to listen closely to the responses of those to whom that have expressed their concerns/issues, and to adapt their strategies and their scripts to what might emerge as an evolving and mutually adaptive dialogue between voicers and listeners.

Third, with GVV participants engaging in conversations about how to become better voicers and listeners, there is an even greater opportunity for GVV to influence the development of workplace cultures that support voicing values and emphasize the importance of active listening. Organizational leaders in particular play a critical role in developing organizational practices and identifying, communicating, and reinforcing organizational values (e.g., commitment to integrity, respect for individuals) that align with the goals of GVV and explicitly encourage voice and active listening at all levels of the organization.

For over a decade GVV has encouraged individuals to trust their values, to honor their sense of knowing the right thing to do when these values are challenged, and to adopt an action orientation through expressing their voice and their values. As more and more individuals in classrooms and workplaces around the world are empowered through GVV to voice their values, perhaps now is the time for GVV to empower listeners as well.

> There is no magic formula for listening for values just as there is no universal answer to the question of how to voice them. Circumstances and relationships will dictate different approaches. But the key lesson here is that we cannot express our values effectively if we do not listen to what matters to the persons we are trying to influence; and we cannot expect our employees to express their values-driven concerns if we typically 'kill the messenger.' And in the end, one of the best ways to build the muscle and the skill and the confidence to accomplish both of these goals is through practice and an intentional attention to sharing what has worked in the past.
>
> (Gentile, 2016, p. 110)

Developing GVV in ways that promote greater attention to the role of listeners and the importance of effective listening, can open up new, imaginative possibilities for GVV in the future and throughout the world.

References

Bass, B. M., & Avolio, B. J. (1994). *Improving organizational effectiveness through transformational leadership*. Thousand Oaks, CA: Sage.

Bedzow, I., & Waldron, H. (2021). Giving voice to values in health professions education. In J. Goodstein & M. C. Gentile (Eds.), *Giving voice to values: An innovation and impact agenda* (pp. 87–100). London: Routledge Publishing.

Brownell, J. (1994). Creating strong listening environments: A key hospitality management task. *International Journal of Contemporary Hospitality Manage ment, 6*(3), 3–10.

Drucker, P. F. (2004, June). What makes an effective executive? *Harvard Business Review, 58–63.*

Dutton, J. E., Ashford, S. J., Lawrence, K. A., & Miner-Rubino, K. (2002). Red light, greenlight: Making sense of the organizational context for issue selling. *Organization Science, 13*, 335–369.

Gentile, M. C. (2010). *Giving voice to values.* New Haven, CT: Yale University Press.

Gentile, M. C. (2016). Listening for values. *Humanistic Management Journal, 1,* 107–111.

Gentile, M. C., & Goodstein, J. (2010). *Better wrong than right? Delivering the "bad" market research news (A).* Case OB-1139. Retrieved from www. GivingVoiceToValues.org

Goodstein, J. (2021). Implementing giving voice to values into the workplace: Insights from the experience of four organizations. In J. Goodstein & M. C. Gentile (Eds.), *Giving voice to values: An innovation and impact agenda* (pp. 144–164). London: Routledge Publishing.

Hoppe, M. H. (2006). *Active listening.* Chapel Hill, NC: Center for Creative Leadership.

Lloyd, K. J., Boer, D., & Voelpel, S. C. (2017). From listening to leading: Toward an understanding of supervisor listening within the framework of leader-member exchange theory. *International Journal of Business Communication, 54*(4), 431–451.

Morrison, E. (2011). Employee voice behavior: Integration and directions for future research. *The Academy of Management Annals, 5*(1), 373–412.

Murphy, K. (2019). *You're not listening: What you're missing and why it matters.* New York: Celadon Books.

Patterson, K., Grenny, J., McMillan, R., & Switzler, A. (2002). *Crucial conversations.* New York: McGraw Hill.

Rogers, C. R. (1951). *Client-centered therapy: Its current practice, implications, and theory.* Boston, MA: Houghton Mifflin Harcourt.

Rogers, C. R. (1975). Empathic: An unappreciated way of being. *The Counseling Psychologist, 5*(2), 2–10.

4

INTEGRATING GIVING VOICE TO VALUES ACROSS BUSINESS FIELDS AND FUNCTIONS

Daniel Arce

Introduction

I have been a professor for three decades. About a third of the way into my career, which includes a great deal of teaching microeconomics to EMBAs and managerial economics to undergraduates, I had a metamorphosis. It was not physical, like the character Gregor Samsa in Kafka's (1915) classic novella. Instead, it was more akin to acquiring an ability to differentiate reality from dreaming. Before, I was like the protagonist without a name in Julio Cortázar's (1964) short story, "La Noche Boca Arriba," who is confused as to whether he is sedated in a hospital operating room following a motorcycle accident, or if he has been drugged and laid out on a slab and is about to be sacrificed in an Aztec ritual in pre-Columbian Mexico. [Spoiler Alert!] As it turns out, the motorcycle accident is the dream and the sacrifice at the hands of the Aztecs is the reality. In my "dream," I used textbooks that treated the instability of cartels as a problem to be overcome. Similarly, the formation of auction rings (bidder cartels) was a question of getting incentives right – in terms of the sharing rule among ring members – so that the item is won at a deflated price and no member has an incentive to cheat on the ring. I also found intellectual merit in Holman Jenkins' (2006) argument that back-dating options is a misunderstood alternative for augmenting executive compensation because it is merely a substitute for adjusting the vesting period, expiration date, number of options, and so on.

By contrast, the reality is that consumers are harmed by the increased prices resulting from tacit cooperation among firms. Taxpayers suffer if an auction ring suppresses the revenue the government receives in a spectrum auction for mobile service providers (e.g., the 3G spectrum auction in Germany). Backdating options (declaring an alternative date than that of issuance) is fraud, which is different from discounting them (granting options that are in the money).[1] Beyond economics, valuing diversity and hiring for diversity does not ensure that all employees are treated respectfully. Another example is employees of defense contractors who design and manufacture products that, if used correctly, result in the deaths of others. Moreover, these products can fall into the wrong hands.

Why is it the case that these sides of the story are neglected in business education, particularly in textbooks? Asking this question led to my metamorphosis because to see reality for what it is requires awareness of the ethical context of business decision-making and the ability to offer advice about what to do from there. Ultimately, I chose Giving Voice to Values (GVV) as a way to ground my courses in reality. In what follows, I discuss my path to GVV, why I chose it, how I use GVV, teaching tips, student reactions to GVV, and the assessment of GVV for accreditation. Future directions are discussed in the conclusion.

Background and motivation

Wanting to incorporate ethics into my courses, I took the first logical step – surveying the treatment of ethics in the existing managerial economics textbooks. Unfortunately, the treatment of ethics is effectively absent in these textbooks, as I document in my 2004 *Journal of Business Ethics* article (Arce, 2004). A decade and a half later, these textbooks are no better on this account, even though in the interim two financial crises largely attributable to unethical managerial behavior have occurred.[2] By contrast, a significant exception exists in finance. Since at least 2006, Ivo Welch has included a freely downloadable web chapter for his textbook, *Corporate Finance. An Introduction*, which is ranked by CNN, Forbes, and INC, as one of the 100 Best Corporate Finance Books of All Time.[3] Welch prepares his readers for the online chapter with the following proviso, "The chapter is 'not' representative of the remainder of the book. . . . . However, I believe that the subject is important – and too often simply ignored by us finance professors – so this chapter will remain freely available." At the same time, Welch maintains that there is often "no clear answer either to the questions posed in this chapter, or as to what should go into an ethics chapter to begin with." Playing Devil's Advocate, one wonders if it is similarly acceptable to conclude that there is "no clear answer" to the financial questions posed in the "representative" chapters in Welch's textbook. In contradistinction, how does one go about promoting ethical answers to a firm's financial concerns?

As I did not find much in the way of integrating ethical awareness, concerns, and solutions into the economics that I was teaching to undergraduates and EMBAs, I decided to try a hand at it myself. Arce (2004) provides several illustrations of how moral reasoning augments economic decision-making. At the same time, I was troubled by one of the issues raised by the paper; namely, how do you know that the behavior observed is motivated by ethics or instead by self-interest? Using a simple two-player game I demonstrate that whether or not a firm voluntarily recalls a product may be determined by the type of regulator they are facing.[4] That is, if a firm feels that it is facing an activist FDA or NTSB, rather than a passive one, then even a firm that would rather not recall its product can be observed to be "voluntarily" recalling it. So, the firm, whose underlying preferences are not at all socially concerted, is observed as acting ethically. Conversely, if faced with a more laissez-faire regulator, no recall takes place.

A case in point is Johnson & Johnson (hereafter, J&J). The firm's voluntary recall during the Tylenol scare of 1982 is a classic business ethics case. In particular, the recall is seen as epitomizing the J&J credo. But J&J is the same firm that conducted a "stealth" Motrin recall in 2009. Tablets in eight-packs sold primarily at checkout counters were found to be dissolving improperly. Instead of announcing a recall, J&J hired an outside contractor to pose as regular customers and purchase the affected stock at over 5,000 retailers. What explains the difference in J&J's behavior with respect to Tylenol versus Motrin? Is it possible that J&J felt that they faced different regulatory administrations in the two cases, one activist and the other laissez-fair?[5] The Motrin imperfection could lead to "adverse events," whereas the poisoned Tylenol pills could cause death, so perhaps this difference provides the explanation. Or did J&J's ethics change?

Another example from J&J exemplifies the operationalization of ethics within an organization. It may be hard to believe in this day and age, but during the late 1960s and early 1970s J&J cross-promoted its baby oil, which contains no sunscreen, for the purposes of obtaining a, "healthy tan."[6] In the early 1970s, during a meeting to review this strategy, the newly appointed product manager of baby oil at J&J was asked, what is meant by a "healthy tan," and could he prove that tans were, indeed, healthy (Nash, 1988, pp. 97–98; Nash, 1990, pp. 83–85). In examining the nascent medical literature on the long-term consequences of tanning, the product manager realized there was no way to prove that tanning was *not* harmful.[7] The cross-promotion strategy was abandoned at great cost to the product manager and J&J.[8] In contrast to the Tylenol case, which was publicly known at the time, knowledge of this decision is not widespread. Such an action is consistent with the notion of character being what you do when no one else is watching. It is also an example of the importance of ethics versus regulation, as the FDA did not regulate sunscreen until 1974. Regulations are typically reactive as their necessity is often understood only after the fact. Ethics, however, guide you irrespective of whether regulations exist or not.

In Nash's (1990) narrative of this event, the product manager is surprised by the question, "what is meant by a 'healthy' tan." Consistent with the J&J credo, the manager judiciously examines both the *stakes* involved in abandoning the cross-promotion strategy ($5 million in lost revenue) and also the existing evidence on the healthiness of tans. In weighing the pros and cons, the manager does not conclude that there may be no correct answer because this is not an acceptable deliverable. Moreover, the business rationales for the cross-promotion are acknowledged and treated as legitimate points needing to be addressed. In addition, the product manager achieves the ethical alternative by altering his perspective. Instead of answering what is meant by a healthy tan, he asks whether it can be proved that tanning is not harmful.

This vignette contains the rudimentary steps for operationalizing ethical action at the workplace, something that is often missing in business ethics courses, which tend to emphasize ethical awareness and the identification of ethical principles present in a case. Here, awareness certainly takes place – in the form of the question about healthy tans. But then the usual focus of business ethics education is flipped. The emphasis is on operationalizing what is recognized as the right course of action in a particular situation rather than debating right versus wrong.[9] The manager first acknowledges the vested interests and *reasons and rationalizations* opposed to ethical concerns about tanning. Baby oil is a mature market with slow growth. Cross promotion represents an avenue for renewed growth. *Levers* are needed to promote the ethical concerns over these alternative interests. To this end, the manager obtains preliminary medical studies on the effects of tanning. This requires substantial effort – there was no Google Scholar available in the 1970s. As is the case for any strategic question involving a conglomerate, finding a solution is never easy or definitive.

I have purposely used the language of GVV – *stakes, reasons and rationalizations, levers* – in the two preceding paragraphs because for me GVV represents a fully articulated paradigm for placing the operationalization of ethics on equal ground with the functional areas of business. MBAs learn how to "do" accounting, economics, finance, marketing, operations management, and even leadership. With GVV they are provided with a rubric that allows for "doing ethics" in a business context. To wit, ethical concerns within the firm can be addressed by answering the following four questions. One, what is at *stake* for the key parties, including you and those who disagree with you? Two, what are the main arguments that you are trying to counter? That is, what are the *reasons and rationalizations* that you need to address? Three, what *levers* can you use to influence those who disagree with you? Four, what is your most *powerful and persuasive response* to the reasons and rationalizations you need to address? To whom should the argument be made? When and in what context? Together, these questions and their answers are called the *GVV script*. How I use this script in my own classes is the subject of the next section.

Operationalizing ethics in the classroom

When teaching managerial economics or MBAs, I do my best to steer clear of topics that appear in textbooks primarily because they are interesting to economists.[10] My attitude is that the course is all about operationalizing economics for business decision-making. In addition, MBAs' horizon for learning imposes further constraints on the subject matter. For example, Kreps (2019, pp. vii–viii) observes that, for MBA students, "the group ethic is that ideas that do not pay back in the first 5 months on the job are suspect and those that might not pay back in the first 5 years are a complete waste of time."[11]

While I am not completely won over by this argument, it is true that GVV fits within its constructs. Much of business ethics education emphasizes (in)famous cases such as the 1982 Tylenol recall. By contrast, GVV starts with ethical concerns that are likely to arise within an MBA's learning horizon. Moreover, in GVV cases the principal does not have to be the CEO. Hence, the stakes are likely to be much lower and most, if not all, students can agree on what is the right thing to do. The beauty of GVV is that the four questions constituting the script allow for almost any situation with ethical content to be treated as a variation on the theme.

In order to illustrate how GVV can be introduced efficaciously, Slides 1–4 come from the actual PowerPoint deck that I use to introduce GVV without stepping outside the subject matter of my course. I think of it as my "one hour introduction to GVV." In the first slide I introduce GVV in a general way, following the points articulated in Gentile (2010). In the second slide students are given a mini case. The specifics here include background information about Waffle House, which is a chain of diners that operates primarily in the gulf coast states of the US.[12] The local area of a particular Waffle House has been hit by a natural disaster such as a hurricane. Note that readers need not use the Waffle House case for their introduction to GVV. The four slides can be adjusted to any curriculum. My suggestion is to alter the slides so that they correspond to a fundamental concept in your class so as to leverage awareness. Here, that concept is market equilibrium and supply and demand. In the third slide the ethical context is laid out. Students who understand supply, demand, and market equilibrium have sufficient intuition to make a prediction regarding the effect of the disaster on the diner's prices. In the fourth slide it is made unambiguously clear that the manager has resolved to maintain the pre-disaster prices. GVV is post-decision-making and I have found it to be worthwhile to reiterate that the purpose of the exercise is not to debate the merits of the manager's decision. Instead, the purpose is to apply the GVV script in order to help the manager make an argument that operationalizes their ethics.

SLIDE 1

Doing ethics: Giving Voice to Values (GVV)

- Focus is POST Decision-Making: your answers to these cases are meant to give practice to articulating your values. How do you raise the issue in an effective manner; what do you need to do in order to be heard; how to correct an existing course of action when necessary.
- Emphasis is NOT on application of ethical reasoning models to business dilemmas. No philosophical ethics: Utilitarianism, Kant (categorical imperative ⇔ suppose everyone behaved like that), Virtue Ethics, Rawls (veil of ignorance), rights vs. justice, etc.
- Emphasizes the importance of defining your own sense of purpose broadly and explicitly. It is important to clarify your own values.
- Allows you to expand your comfort zone for voicing your values in front of your peers. It is useful to become familiar, if not comfortable, with the inevitable risks that come with values conflicts; that is, to *normalize the stakes*.
- Allows you to recognize the false dichotomy between unquestioning moral idealism and the suspension of any moral obligation at the workplace.

SLIDE 2

The case: Waffle House Restaurants

Reggie Smith is the manager of a Waffle House Restaurant, which is a chain of diners in gulf coast states. The region where Reggie works has just experienced a local disaster (hurricane, tornado, volcanic eruption, flood, earthquake, etc.). Power is out almost everywhere but he can keep his restaurant open, owing to the emergency generator the restaurant always has on-hand to keep the lights on and the ability to switch fuels used to power the grill by means of a several-day supply of gas in tanks.

The grill is the only thing that can be used to cook with at the moment. This means a limited menu, constructed by keeping in mind what is easiest to prepare and what people want most. The limited menu decision has far-reaching implications, as FEMA has a "Waffle House Index" to measure the severity of a disaster. According to the index, Green corresponds to a full menu; Yellow means a limited menu (power from a generator and low food supplies); and Red corresponds to a closed restaurant. Reggie knows FEMA will be calling soon. The information he provides will be consistent with Yellow.

SLIDE 3

The issue at hand: should Reggie change prices?

Reggie anticipates volume of more than 2–3 times what is normal. What do the laws of supply and demand predict will happen to prices under these circumstances?

Owing to the limited menu he is going to have to write the available items and their prices on a blackboard. He has the latitude to change prices, particularly if costs have dramatically changed. He currently has food on hand and Waffle House has a policy of restocking from surrounding restaurants that are outside the disaster area. He does not expect prolonged supply disruptions because his primary supplier also provides food to hospitals (this choice of supplier is by design). At the same time, it is more costly to keep the lights on with a generator and run the grill out of gas tanks. Although it is not mandatory, it is recommended to check with HQ if considering a price change.

SLIDE 4

GVV is post-decision-making

Resolved: Reggie believes that in order to show post-disaster solidarity with the local community **he should not change prices whatsoever**.

Break out into your groups. Your group needs to provide 5 answers each for questions 1–3. In answering these questions take the broader perspective of the context of NOT raising prices on necessary goods in the immediate aftermath of a natural disaster.

1   What's at *stake* for the key parties, including those who disagree with you? What's at stake for you?
2   What are the main arguments that you are trying to counter? That is, what are the *reasons and rationalizations* that you need to address?

3   What *levers* can you use to influence those who disagree with you?
4   What is your most *powerful and persuasive response* to the reasons and rationalizations you need to address? To whom should the argument be made? When and in what context?

Students are then asked to break out into groups in order to formulate answers. I give them no more than 30 minutes to do so. After the group session is finished, one member from each group presents their answers to the class as a whole. Feedback is solicited from those not in the group, with particular attention paid to how realistic the group's primary argument is. Slide 5 presents a summary of stepping-off points that have been used as scripts for holding prices constant after a natural disaster.

SLIDE 5

What *levers* can you use to influence those who disagree with you?

- Not raising prices is the social norm. This is why people are so outraged when prices are raised substantially. Such exceedingly rare practices are consequently labeled as price gouging.
- Not raising prices is a form of "social insurance" that many firms are willing to supply as part of their "license to operate" during normal times.[13]
- The evidence suggests that consumers ration themselves at the disequilibrium (non-market-clearing) price, rather than formal rationing by the firm. Consequently, the analogy to a binding price ceiling is false. Self-rationing implies that the demand curve shifts back to the left, implying that a price increase need not be inevitable.
- Solidarity: we are in this together. Waffle House can provide empathy and support that boosts the morale of the affected community. Waffle House should not be seen as taking advantage of customers during a natural disaster. Our prices are not only paid by customers, but they are publicly observable by others and so provide a signal of our solidarity with the community.
- Future revenues: we will lose the goodwill of the community if we increase our prices. No price increase will create a locus of loyalty

once the crisis is over, but a price increase could have the opposite effect. In the long-run, a price increase during a natural disaster
might even shift our demand curve to the left.

- Is the consumer base able to afford a price increase in the aftermath
of the disaster? The most economically vulnerable will not be able to
compete on the basis of price with those with higher incomes.
- This is a situation where the Golden Rule is meant to apply.

I have found that this exercise is sufficient for students to be capable
enough to be given a GVV case on every group assignment/problem set
from then on. Each group is asked to provide five answers to the first
three questions in the script, and a single word-processed page addressing
the fourth point. The GVV question in the assignment counts as much
as any other question. By judiciously selecting cases that correspond to
the material in the rest of the group assignment, GVV is fully integrated
into the course without any significant detour from the subject matter.
Hence, the usual objection to integrating ethics within the curriculum –
that there is already not enough time to cover standard topics – is a moot
point. In this way, GVV becomes part and parcel to the course, being
conjoined with other topics in the syllabus.

For example, one case I use in my course (Arce & Gentile, 2016c)
explores the ethical dimension of profits versus layoffs. Sometime later, a
former student who was exposed to the case became involved in the decision to close one of the retirement homes in the network of homes they
managed. GVV led them to significantly broaden their consideration of
the stakeholders involved. Consequently, the closing was postponed so
that past employees and families of former residents could be notified.
Then the corporation arranged to have a retirement ceremony for the
retirement home, with past and current stakeholders in attendance. A
video of the ceremony including footage of past activities and personal
remembrances was also distributed. I received a copy with a note from the
student nearly two years after they took the course.

One of the appeals of GVV is that the cases are free and they cover a
broad spectrum of fields. Even so, students appreciate the opportunity to
engage timely events. Consequently, I often use the Weekly Review on
Ethics from the *Wall Street Journal* so that students apply GVV to current

events. The feed comes out via email and is based upon articles appearing in the WSJ during the week. Any professor can sign up for the feed. Access to the articles requires a personal or institutional subscription. The most common remark that I receive about GVV in my course evaluations is that students find it to be directly applicable to the "real world." Keeping things current reinforces their appreciation of GVV.

Due to the fact that most of my teaching is lecture-driven, when starting GVV I was apprehensive about what to do if students do not engage. Two strategies eased my apprehension. First, as is the case when teaching anything, it pays to be prepared. For example, a quick Google Scholar search on Ethics + Disaster + Prices yields a plethora of research to cull talking points from for the earlier example on disaster pricing. Faculty can also do this in preparing a preliminary key for assignments based on GVV cases or WSJ feeds. Most importantly, be confident that students will have something to teach each other *and* you. Students' talking points and answers have long replaced my original notes for GVV cases and WSJ feeds.

Second, I follow Headlee's (2017) advice on having conversations that matter. Begin by recognizing that good conversations are not necessarily easy. So again, be prepared. Anticipate that many of the reasons and rationalizations will come from your course's subject matter. This is a reliable ice-breaker. Also, admit to yourself that some students may be better at this than you are. For an economist without formal training in business ethics, this is easy to do. Plan to leverage students' comparative advantage. Be mindful by acknowledging students' points without being judgmental. Listen rather than lecture. Neutrality facilitates participation and the building of a GVV script.[14] It is also different from asserting that there is no correct answer. The GVV deliverable is *the most persuasive argument*. GVV is also designed to sidestep the practice of ethics-as-sophistry to justify almost anything (Gentile, 2010). To this end, be firm that you are not going to discuss the merits of the ethical decision made by the principal in the case. The decision has already been made. Finally, be authentic because you are asking your students to do so as well. Just as is the case for teaching anything else, you will have to teach a course that integrates GVV at least three times before you learn less than your students do.

Assessment and student reaction

Assessment is particularly tricky because, in my experience, what accreditors mean by assessment is not the common understanding of the term. At times I have given students the option of describing the components of a GVV script as a question that they can choose to answer on a final exam. When I do so, it is without warning so that students cannot prepare for it. Yet this option inevitably turns out to be the most chosen question answered, and more than 90% of the students earn a perfect score. From this perspective, I am confident that GVV builds "ethics muscle memory," as claimed by Gentile (2010). My own characterization is that GVV promotes the operationalization of ethics by osmosis. At the same time, my experience is that accreditors are not particularly open to holistic claims. Fortunately, the GVV script and associated responses – generated by either your reading of the associated literature or by collecting students' responses – is an exemplar of the GVV learning objective. In addition, Ingols (2011) provides a rubric for grading GVV case assignments that is also useful for evaluating student cohorts.

Many accreditors (and state legislatures) are also moving towards requiring documentation of the marketable skills associated with a degree. Students exposed to GVV know how to effectively address and resolve ethical difficulties in the workplace. The GVV script is much more tangible than requiring students to sign an MBA code of ethics. Understanding how to operationalize the GVV script is a valuable asset because ethics is an unavoidable dimension of organizational behavior. GVV puts the "doing" into business ethics.

I have gauged student reaction to GVV in a couple of ways. First, no student has ever complained to me about the integration of GVV into my courses. Nor have they done so in the comments section of my university's end-of-term teaching assessment, or on the midterm teaching evaluation that I personally design to contain specific questions about GVV.[15] As I wrote the inaugural economics and finance cases for GVV, and implemented them into my courses soon thereafter, I am referring to hundreds of students. Second, the many comments that I do receive indicate that students are appreciative of GVV. Pragmatically, students understand that during their career they will make decisions with ethical consequences. Professors also know this is true because the universities and colleges in which we work are not immune to situations where GVV can serve as a guideline for reaching an ethical resolution. As mentioned earlier, students appreciate that GVV is designed to be operationalized in "the real world."

Future directions

I am sorry to say that economists themselves do not always see it this way. Even though I have yet to meet the executive who has used calculus to make a real-world decision, I have economist colleagues in business schools that have explicitly expressed a preference for more calculus (i.e., "rigor") over meeting the AACSB's ethics mandate within their courses. This is a false tradeoff, which is explicitly why I created the game-theoretic addendum to the GVV case on *Product Safety and (Preemptive) Recall* (Arce & Gentile, 2016b). It also ignores that fact that I can predict with certainty that every one of my students will need to operationalize their ethics during their careers, whereas many will never use calculus to make a business decision. Yet it is still the case that more must be done to create a comfort zone for GVV (and ethics in general) in mathematically grounded areas of business education.

Two efforts in this direction are Aragon (2011) and Stevens (2018), which capture the zeitgeist of the theoretical literature on how social norms and intrinsic preferences matter for the functioning of firms and markets. The findings in this literature demonstrate – often in mathematically rigorous fashion – that ethics does, indeed, matter in positivist economic and financial models. In particular, ethical agents may make the firm more profitable as compared to classically opportunistic agents. Yet even if the means exist for ethical employees to self-select according to an organization's mission, no prescriptions are given as to how such agents are to get the job done. This is the entry point where I believe that GVV has the potential to gain traction in math-based business disciplines.

For example, in the aftermath of the Great Financial Crisis, US banks holding TARP funds were restricted from offering performance-based pay to executives. It is no surprise, then, that these banks moved quickly to pay back their TARP loans. Rather than being self-serving, the rationale given was that the pay restrictions severely hampered banks in the market for talent. But what type of talent are we talking about? The truth is that the banks were restricted to the types of contracts that the theoretical literature has shown to be conducive for attracting managers who regard themselves as stewards. By contrast, an opportunistic manager bridles under such pay. If a bank offers incentive pay to its opportunistic CEO, would you rather be the CEO, a shareholder, or, heaven forbid, a debtholder? Does your answer change if the CEO is instead a steward? So here, rather than theory providing reasons and rationalizations, theory and GVV can be combined as levers to address the reasons and rationalizations for returning to incentive-based pay. Hence, GVV is a means for facilitating organizational change consistent with behavioral-based modeling in economics and finance.

Notes

1 The latter may not provide the intended incentive but it is not illegal *per se*. Gentile (2016) provides a GVV case on backdating options.

2 The editions of the textbooks surveyed in 2004 were published before or during the new economy/dot.com crisis, ENRON, Sarbanes-Oxley, etc., so they had no opportunity to address the associated crisis. The current assessment considers editions of the texts published long after the Great Financial Crisis and the associated ethical lapses in the private and public sectors.

3 https://bookauthority.org/books/best-corporate-finance-books. Accessed 10 September 2020.

4 See also Chapter 5 in Freeman and Gilbert (1988). The associated analysis is also presented in the Addendum to GVV case UBA-OB-1166 (Arce & Gentile, 2016b).

5 Johnson & Johnson ultimately paid fines to multiple states for the phantom recall.

6 The sun protection factor (SPF) was not introduced until 1974. Baby oil actually accelerates the burning process.

7 Emphasis in Nash (1990).

8 The manager eventually came upon an acceptable cross promotion for baby oil (removing cosmetics) and had a fruitful career at J&J.

9 The corresponding GVV case is Arce and Gentile (2016a).

10 An example is the long-run average cost curve. Frank (2010) concurs.

11 Here, Kreps is referring to his experience with MBAs at the GSB in Stanford.

12 See Arce (2011) for the fully elaborated case.
13 The "license to operate" is a term from Friedman (1970).
14 Neutrality also includes body language.
15 Specific student comments about GVV can be found in Arce (2013).

References

Aragon, G. A. (2011). *Financial ethics: A positivist analysis.* Oxford: Oxford University Press.

Arce, D. G. (2004). Conspicuous by its absence: Ethics and managerial economics. *Journal of Business Ethics, 54*(3), 261–277.

Arce, D. G. (2011). Giving voice to values in economics and finance. *Journal of Business Ethics Education, 8,* 343–347.

Arce, D. G. (2013). Giving voice to values in the economics classroom. In M. C. Gentile (Ed.), *Education for values-driven leadership: Giving voice to values across the curriculum* (pp. 17–29). New York: Business Expert Press.

Arce, D. G., & Gentile, M. C. (2016a). *Product safety and (preemptive) recall.* Case UVA-OB-1166. University of Virginia, Darden Business Publishing.

Arce, D. G., & Gentile, M. C. (2016b). *Addendum: Product safety and (preemptive) recall.* Case UVA-OB-1166. University of Virginia, Darden Business Publishing.

Arce, D. G., & Gentile, M. C. (2016c). *Profit maximization and layoffs.* Case UVA-OB-1167, University of Virginia. Darden Business Publishing.

Cortázar, J. (1964). La Noche Boca Arriba. In *Final del Juego.* Buenos Aires: Sudamericana.

Frank, R. (2010). Principles of microeconomics. In S. W. Bowmaker (Ed.), *The heart of teaching economics* (pp. 3–23). Northampton, MA: Edward Elgar.

Freeman, R. E., & Gilbert Jr., D. R. (1988). *Corporate strategy and the search for ethics.* Englewood Cliffs, NJ: Prentice Hall.

Friedman, M. (1970, September 13). The social responsibility of the firm is to increase its profits. *New York Times Sunday Magazine,* pp. 32, 33, 122, 124, 126.

Gentile, M. C. (2010). *Giving voice to values: How to speak your mind when you know what's right.* New Haven, CT: Yale University Press.

Gentile, M. C. (2016). *The backdating scandal: Who am I trying to persuade?* Case UVA-OB-1123. University of Virginia, Darden Business Publishing.

Headlee, C. (2017). *We need to talk: How to have conversations that matter.* London: Little, Brown Book Group.

Ingols, C. (2011). Assessing students' knowledge through *Giving Voice to Values*: From individuals to cohorts. *Journal of Business Ethics Education, 8,* 358–364.

Jenkins, H. (2006, July 12). Backdating revisited. *The Wall Street Journal.*

Kafka, F. (1915). *The metamorphoses* (Stanley Comgold, Trans., 2013 ed.). New York: Modern Library.

Kreps, D. M. (2019). *Microeconomics for managers.* Princeton, NJ: Princeton University Press.

Nash, L. (1988). Johnson & Johnson's credo. In *Corporate ethics: A prime business asset* (pp. 77–104). New York: The Business Roundtable.

Nash, L. (1990). *Good intentions aside: A manager's guide to resolving ethical problems.* Boston, MA: Harvard Business School Press.

Stevens, D. E. (2018). *Social norms and the theory of the firm: A foundational approach.* Cambridge: Cambridge University Press.

5

GIVING VOICE TO VALUES IN EDUCATING ETHICAL LEADERS

Lessons learned and ideas for the future

Christopher Adkins and Jessica McManus Warnell

Faculty continue to seek effective approaches for developing values-based leaders, especially as accreditation bodies elevate ethics in their standards and organizations seek leaders who can create ethical workplaces. The Giving Voice to Values (GVV) curriculum, with over 1,175 pilots (and growing) at educational institutions (undergraduate, graduate, and executive education) and business and nonprofit organizations on all seven continents, offers an engaging, pragmatic, and flexible approach to developing ethical leaders at the undergraduate, graduate, and professional education levels. Having been early adopters of the GVV approach within business schools, we seek to share our experiences and propose ideas for the future, organized in three parts: first, a brief review of the adoption and integration of the GVV curriculum from our experiences at two universities;[1] second, our reflections on the challenges, lessons learned, and opportunities associated with scaling the impact and deepening the integration of GVV within the business school curriculum; and third, emerging ideas in both teaching and research that could extend the GVV approach both within the university and across institutions.

While we both are currently professors in the management faculty at the Mendoza College of Business at the University of Notre Dame, we have had different experiences over the last decade in teaching and integrating GVV. Chris has championed the GVV approach since its inception, first through his work at William & Mary and now as an instructor for the undergraduate, graduate, and executive levels of business education and through his direction of the Notre Dame Deloitte Center for Ethical Leadership (NDDCEL). At Notre Dame, Jessica developed and taught the first GVV undergraduate elective business school course and introduced the GVV tenets into her teaching of the required undergraduate course in business ethics. Together we have led the expansion of the required undergraduate course at our business school to incorporate the GVV methodology. In addition, we have collaborated with colleagues to provide co-curricular engagement through orientations and workshops for graduate students and sessions for executive audiences.

Our past success with GVV inspires us to consider the future of GVV at Notre Dame and for our colleagues at other universities. While recognizing the challenges of curricular innovation and interdisciplinary collaborations, we see GVV as an adaptive framework that can engage colleagues from diverse disciplines for a variety of courses and programs. Also, we see opportunities for conducting empirical research on the impact of GVV within the university and in early work experiences. Our goal is to share the best practices and lessons learned from our experiences, and propose future directions to sustain and strengthen GVV in the next decade.

Part 1: two b-school stories of early implementation of GVV

While we now both teach at the University of Notre Dame, we first connected at a gathering of early adopters of the GVV approach. Both of us were teaching undergraduates, Chris at the College of William & Mary and Jessica at the University of Notre Dame. At the time, resources for teaching business ethics were primarily aimed at graduate students, often with organizational dilemmas and societal challenges facing senior leaders. Also, the learning objectives were focused primarily on developing ethical awareness and analysis, rather than planning for action. GVV offered a pragmatic approach to build upon our existing coursework in ethical analysis, as well as personal approach that leveraged one's own values and skills through practice and collaboration. Lastly, GVV offered cases and exercises that engaged undergraduates to reflect on their present and past, identifying the internal and external factors that have influenced their likelihood of voicing their values. Each of us had begun piloting the GVV approach, Chris within a required course, and Jessica with a new elective. In this section, we will briefly discuss our approaches in implementing GVV at our respective business schools.

The required course approach: adopting GVV at the College of William & Mary

When Chris arrived at the College of William & Mary, the undergraduate business curriculum did not include a formal approach to integrating business ethics. Rather, ethics was integrated informally across the curriculum, with faculty encouraged to integrate ethics into their class discussions, and connect to their specific disciplines. One required course did offer an opportunity for integrating GVV. Every new business student enrolled in a one-credit course called Business Perspectives and Applications that addressed ethical issues, communications, teamwork, and integrative business decision-making, to be completed in their first semester (usually in their third or junior year). The challenge with any short course is what to include considering the limited time available. This course offered an additional challenge of needing to address not only ethics, but teamwork, communications, and decision-making (and often each of these themes has their own course).

As Chris redesigned the course, he recognized that GVV offered a flexible framework to integrate all of these themes. Ethics would be the primary focus of the course, including a foundation in traditional ethical approaches (virtue-based, consequentialism, deontology) to decision-making. GVV cases would be used to help students to develop strategies and scripts to a variety of situations they would face early in their career. Students would work in teams of five, and collaborate on the cases inside and outside of class. During class sessions, students would sit in team clusters, allowing the large class discussion to easily move to small-group, team discussions. Such discussions would strengthen teamwork and interpersonal communication by providing everyone the opportunity to practice voicing both their analyses and plans for action. Each team also prepared a presentation on a case where they developed multiple scripts for voicing their particular values in that scenario.

Working in teams reinforced the GVV themes of the importance of allies and support, peer coaching, and multiple approaches to voicing. Throughout these discussions and presentations, each team would apply both traditional ethical approaches and the Reasons & Rationalizations framework. GVV emphasis on thinking about "what's at stake" for all the stakeholders, then finding "levers" for influence would enhance integrated decision-making. (Adkins, 2011; Adkins, Gentile, Ingols, & Trefalt, 2011; Gentile, 2010)

The course also integrated the foundational GVV exercise, "Tale of Two Stories." This reflection offered a personal starting point for the course, where students reflected on and articulated when and how they had voiced their values effectively. Students would bring their stories to class, and share with their team their story of when they had expressed their voices. Such conversations normed the class discussion to focus on ways to voice or engage in moments of challenge, rather than emphasize ways we struggle or disengage when challenged. This opening exercise was then followed by a sequence of GVV cases, beginning with situations where college students were protagonists (on-campus challenges or intern challenges) before moving to cases about early and mid-level professionals (Adkins, 2011; Adkins et al., 2011; Gentile, 2010).

Designed to build from students' past experiences, personal values, and strengths, the GVV approach was well-received by students, and provided a pragmatic approach to ethics before pursuing their summer internship experiences. Also, by having this course in their first semester, GVV provided a lens for looking at ethical issues in other classes. A primary challenge, however, was ensuring that this approach would extend beyond this introductory class. Also, the one-credit design of the course significantly limited the scope and depth of content and skill development. Both of these challenges will be discussed in the next section, after exploring Jessica's adoption of GVV at Notre Dame.

The elective course approach: creating a GVV elective at the University of Notre Dame

At the Mendoza College of Business, ethical leadership has been at the core of our college's mission since its inception. The framework is three-fold:

individual integrity, organizational effectiveness, and societal impact, each focused on "growing the good in business." In 2008, Dean Carolyn Woo invited Mary C. Gentile to visit Notre Dame, and connected Jessica with Mary during her visit. Soon after this meeting and learning more about the GVV approach, Jessica proposed and taught the first dedicated Giving Voice to Values elective course developed specifically for undergraduate business students. In this next section, we discuss course development and pedagogy, as well as reflections on the student experience, in the hope of providing guidance and inspiration to other instructors seeking to create a GVV elective (Warnell, 2011).

At Notre Dame, every business student is required to take an introductory course in business ethics, usually in the sophomore or second year of their studies. Similar to William & Mary, this course was one-credit, yet dedicated solely to ethical decision-making by exploring the rich philosophical, behavioral, and organizational approaches to ethics. With the course being taught by several different faculty members, Jessica recognized that integrating GVV into this introductory course could prove difficult as each faculty member was not familiar with GVV, and had already experienced the challenge of covering ethical analysis within the limits of a one-credit course.

Creating a GVV elective offered a pilot approach to test and develop the content with students. Students could choose the elective course after completing the required foundations course, with the purpose of facilitating the progression from *knowing* ethics to *doing* ethics. Ideally, the introductory course motivates this critical next step of exploring and "trying out" practical implications of ethics ourselves, and through consideration of personal and others' experiences, within organizations and professions. By creating a course that follows the introductory course, Jessica focused on a "post decision-making" approach with the purpose of providing students with a toolkit of strategies, skills, and scripts that reflected their particular values and voice.

This course, like other electives in the business school, is seven weeks long with two 75-minute sessions per week, and enrolls between 15 and 25 students each semester that it is offered. It is primarily discussion-based, and incorporates an emphasis on collaborative exploration of existing GVV and self-generated real-world scenarios faced in internships, part-time work, and other early career experiences. The final assignment involves the development of a GVV case and teaching note of the students' own scenario. Those cases of the highest quality in the course have been included in the GVV teaching collection and are available widely. GVV cases and exercises (such as "Tale of Two Stories"), as well as role-playing, provided students with the opportunity to practice ethical decision-making within the contexts of college, internships, and early career challenges. Consistent with the GVV methodology, role-playing exercises depart from traditional, adversarial role playing that often characterizes such class activities and instead focus on scripting responses to scenarios, action planning, and peer coaching, with an emphasis on collaborative skill building.

Course evaluations reflect student enthusiasm for the course, perceived alignment with the college's mission of "growing the good in business," and appreciation for immediately useful and "real-world" focus on ethics in action at work. Student comments include descriptions of the course as "dynamic," "[a course with a] comfortable classroom environment that encourages discussion," "practical," "relevant," "pertinent," and "engaging" (Warnell, 2011). The discussion focus and peer-coaching approach were positively received, with one student noting, "The insights from my fellow students have been the most rewarding part of this class. I have been really impressed" (Warnell, 2011). No students provided negative course feedback or indication of dissatisfaction – several students remarked that the only negative about the course was that it was not required of all of their classmates.

While the elective course was successful, Jessica faced the challenge inherent in any elective course: the course only impacted those who were willing to choose such an experience. The challenge of scaling GVV will be addressed in the next section as we explore our lessons learned as early adopters of GVV.

Part 2: challenges and opportunities in adopting, integrating, and scaling GVV

The previous section provided two examples of how faculty might adopt GVV into their business schools, with an emphasis on course design and pedagogy. We each began with our own enthusiasm for GVV's innovative approach, but we recognized that our own interest would be insufficient when shaping curriculum or culture within a business school; one needs support from senior leaders and fellow faculty, as well as a track record of success once given the opportunity to pilot new approaches. In this section, we will discuss the lessons learned from our experiences, with a particular focus on the opportunities and challenges one is likely to encounter in adopting, integrating, and scaling GVV.

Finding resources, leadership support, and faculty allies for launch and scaling

Innovation in any organization often requires finding the necessary resources and allies. As highlighted earlier, Jessica had the support of her dean, as well as strong alignment with the organization's mission. She also had a supportive group of colleagues committed to teaching business ethics. At the same time, her colleagues were focused on ethical thinking within the limits of the one-credit required course. Rather than focus on integration within an existing course, she sought to develop proof of concept by piloting a GVV elective course. Funding and departmental support were essential in taking this approach. For Chris, he was given the opportunity to redesign a required course, yet had to incorporate several important themes within a one-credit course: ethics, teamwork, communications, and decision-making. With the support of his dean, Chris was encouraged to elevate ethics as long as these other themes were addressed as well. As described earlier, the GVV approach could be adapted to integrate all of these themes, and thus received continued support in future semesters.

While we both found support for the adoption of GVV within our business schools, scaling and integrating GVV beyond a particular course or a specific faculty member proved to be a primary challenge. One typically scales through expansion of the curriculum or integration into existing curriculum. Expanding requires additional funding for new courses and faculty costs (both of which can be difficult to find), as well as an increase in course credits toward the degree. Grant opportunities may be available for new course development, but even if awarded such funds for course design, one needs the funding to sustain the delivery of the new course. In the face of such challenges, one might look for opportunities to integrate within the existing curriculum.

One opportunity is to identify courses that align with GVV's values-based decision-making, and then update or replace existing course content with GVV content (exercises, readings, or cases). Ethics, leadership, and organizational behavior courses may come to mind, but considering the depth and breadth of GVV curricular materials, there are a variety of resources that are easily available and relevant to faculty across diverse disciplines, contexts (accounting, finance, marketing, strategy, analytics, operations, HR), and teaching at different levels where undergraduate, MBA, or executive education. Jessica and Chris have encouraged faculty in this way, both through private conversations and by hosting seminars where faculty could learn about the approach. While there has been some interest and some have adopted a case or two, experienced faculty often have cases they prefer or wonder what they might eliminate if they were to adopt GVV. In addressing such concerns, we have found it helpful to emphasize that integrating GVV into a class does not always require using GVV cases or exercises. One can approach existing cases with a GVV mindset: assuming that one wants to voice one's values in the case, how might one voice effectively? In this way, faculty can extend case discussion beyond analysis to action planning, so students can practice the strategies and scripts for effective response. For example, this approach proved quite effective for a faculty member teaching a course in conflict resolution. Instead of replacing existing cases with GVV cases, she applied the GVV framework of "Reasons and Rationalizations" and "Enablers and Disablers" to these situations.

In retrospect, and as we think about opportunities to find allies and deepen the integration of GVV at Notre Dame, one approach that may prove helpful is to engage a team of faculty interested in strengthening the theme of voicing values across the curriculum. This team of faculty could be composed within a course team or department or major program, or could be cross-disciplinary, depending on the theme to be addressed (such as values-based leadership or diversity and inclusion). This could shift the conversation from "How might *you* integrate voicing values in your course?" to "How might *we* integrate voicing values in our department or our college?" This would create a sense of shared purpose and community, as well as positive norming for course innovation. Also, the emphasis on voicing values (rather than ethics) may make it easier for faculty to see connections to their courses and cases. While one can envision faculty teams collaborating within one university, faculty also could connect across universities. For example, economics faculty using GVV from several universities might collaborate on best practices and case development. For example, GVV has been shared at professional association conferences like the American Accounting Association, the International Leadership Association and the Academy of Management, where faculty from a variety of institutions can come together to discuss how to use the pedagogy/curriculum in their teaching.

Align with organizational and societal interests, including accreditation, assessment, and global standards

As ethics scandals continue to emerge in business, business schools often are asked how their curriculum addresses the ethics education. In both of our situations, our deans could point to our courses as examples of the commitment to develop ethical business leaders. Our courses were also essential in the AACSB accreditation process, where business schools must demonstrate the educational effectiveness of their curriculum, including a specific focus on ethics. At both Notre Dame and William & Mary, Jessica and Chris worked with the accreditation teams to identify ethics learning objectives and assignments that aligned with our GVV efforts and met accreditation goals. At Notre Dame, the AASCB Assurance of Learning assessment includes performance dimensions related to identifying, evaluating, and applying key terms and concepts in ethics. Jessica and Chris's considerations of these objectives and outcomes, informed by the GVV approach, allow for rubric development that aligns with a central goal of learning assessment. Future iterations of the accreditation process will continue to be informed by the critical focus on behavioral ethics that GVV provides.

Meeting accreditation requirements is essential, but GVV can contribute to the mission of business schools to develop ethical leaders and elevate the commitment of business for the social and global good. In our particular context at Notre Dame, the Mendoza College of Business's "Grow the Good in Business" framework is one part of a rich tradition of business schools around the world acknowledging the critical role of ethics in business education. Such approaches are aligned with the focus of such global efforts as the United Nations' Principles for Responsible Management Education (PRME) initiative, through which business schools communicate progress and share best practices toward prosocial goals. These and other efforts can strengthen the mechanism – business school – through which our emerging leaders develop. GVV offers a pragmatic curriculum for reaching the goals and developing these leadership skills.

Integrate and elevate GVV in co-curricular programs and executive education

One approach that we did not discuss in Part 1 was the opportunity to integrate GVV through orientations or other co-curricular programming, particularly at the graduate level where orientations and other co-curricular programming in leadership development are common. Over the last several years, Jessica has had several opportunities to engage non-business students in the GVV approach through engagement with various graduate programs at the University of Notre Dame, including a seminar for students enrolled in the university's Ethical Leaders in STEM leadership program. After hearing Jessica present her work with GVV at an academic and practitioner conference, Jessica was invited by an associate dean of the graduate school to share the GVV approach with this group of multidisciplinary graduate students engaged in a year-long invitation-only professional development program. After developing the undergraduate course at William & Mary, Chris was invited by the faculty leader of the MBA Leadership Development program to integrate GVV throughout the yearly programming, including a half-day session where students completed the Tale of Two Stories exercise and applied the Reasons and Rationalization framework to an ethical challenge faced by a mid-level manager.

Upon joining Notre Dame, Chris approached both the dean of the College of Business and dean of the MBA program about incorporating GVV within the MBA orientation, as well as within the MBA required course in ethical leadership. Both were supportive, as GVV offered a pragmatic focus on developing skills for voicing one's values, and recognized how the orientation and ethics courses offered an ideal context for cultivating such skills. GVV complements philosophical and behavioral approaches to ethics, using engaging exercises and cases that build on the MBAs' past experiences and prepare for them for common mid-career ethical and leadership challenges. In addition to class sessions, students are required to attend an ethics lecture series (facilitated by the Notre Dame Deloitte Center for Ethical Leadership). With Chris as Executive

Director of this center, he has selected a number of business leaders who have incorporated GVV in their own organizations. In one case, the leader described how she used the Enablers and Disablers to advocate for herself and her team in a difficult moment with her supervisor. In another case, the leader shared how the GVV strategies of asking questions and enlisting allies helped uncover shared value in a challenging negotiation with community leaders. Students benefit from seeing that GVV extends beyond business schools and hear firsthand of the impact of GVV in supporting voice in the workplace and in cultivating ethical organizations.

Lastly, Jessica and Chris have been incorporating GVV in the design and delivery of executive education sessions, both through Notre Dame programs and with corporate and non-profit organizations. In our experience, senior leaders appreciate the emphasis on ethical action (rather than just analysis), and recognize the value of appreciating multiple stakeholders, finding levers for influence and creating shared value, and planning for action that aligns both performance and purpose. GVV offers a number of short cases that are well-suited for such training sessions.

Part 3: ideas for expanding and strengthening GVV in universities

As we seek to strengthen our effectiveness in educating ethical leaders at the University of Notre Dame, we wish to build on our successes, learn from our challenges, and explore new ways to scale and deepen the impact of our efforts. We see GVV as a key component of these efforts. In this concluding section, we will discuss several ideas for expanding GVV that may be helpful to our colleagues in their own universities, and ideally spark GVV collaborations across universities.

Extending GVV beyond the business school

In the last three years, GVV has played an important role in strengthening our ethics curriculum in the undergraduate and MBA programs in the Mendoza College of Business. We expanded our one-credit required ethics undergraduate course to 1.5 credits, creating more time in the course to incorporate GVV cases and exercises. As described briefly earlier, Chris uses the GVV framework and cases in our required MBA ethics course, and has integrated GVV into the speaker series so both undergraduate and graduate students can learn how business professionals integrate GVV in their workplaces. We have found that such speaker series offer an ideal venue to attract and engage students and faculty from beyond the business school. To broaden the appeal, we have advertised the speaker series beyond the business school community, and focused on broader topics of sustainability, economic inequality, and diversity and inclusion. We also involved speakers who have used the GVV approach in their work on these topics, so students could see how leaders apply GVV in organizations.

Going forward we believe the time is right to expand these efforts by elevating the theme of gender equality in the workplace. This theme is timely for all of our students, and can engage faculty and students of all disciplines and majors. We also seek to engage alumni as speakers in the classroom sessions and speaker series so students can benefit from the lived experiences of Notre Dame professionals who are voicing their values at work. GVV offers a positive and pragmatic framework for such sessions, beginning with the idea that we all have voiced our values, and would like to do so more often (Gentile, 2010). With the support of corporate partners, we can scale the visibility and impact of GVV to more students.

Contributing to the vast collection of GVV cases to reflect the myriad applications of the approach also includes providing material for students just beginning their academic and professional careers. With students in her undergraduate course, Jessica developed several cases reflecting undergraduate business student life in diverse contexts including internships, student club activities, athletics, dorm life, and part-time work. The cases are available in the GVV collection [www.GivingVoiceToValues.org and http://store.darden.virginia.edu/giving-voice-to-values]. These cases allow for undergraduate students to see themselves clearly in these dilemmas, unlike traditional case studies focusing on leadership decisions of senior executives which may feel aspirational but are certainly distant for college students studying business. Many opportunities exist within a variety of disciplines to develop the dilemmas and challenges that arise in class discussions and assignments into teachable cases. Cultivating these cases generates material that students and faculty within the university and beyond can find meaningful and useful. Using student-generated cases in the classroom extends the peer coaching component and signals the iterative and progressive nature of developing an ethical institutional culture within the university and beyond.

We also envision engaging instructors across the university to share best practices in developing values-based leaders and strengthening students' competence in voicing their values. While GVV would be one of the approaches highlighted, we would learn what others are finding effective, and thus foster a culture of collaboration around this shared purpose. Student affairs professionals would be included in these conversations so they can learn how faculty are supporting students on the theme of voicing values, and they can share how their programs with the faculty.

Developing peer coaches

In facilitating GVV conversations in our classes, we have found that the peer coaching questions [offered in the Appendix of *Giving Voice to Values* (Gentile, 2010) and at Darden Business Publishing (http://store.darden. virginia.edu/giving-voice-to-values)] provide a powerful script for helping students think through their responses and voice more effectively. Such coaching happens informally in these conversations, yet we can see how one might formalize the role of GVV peer coach. For example, students who have completed a course or module in GVV might apply to become a GVV Peer Coach, and then be trained on effective facilitation of GVV conversations and coaching their peers to develop strategies and scripts for voicing their values. These peer coaches would then work with students and/or student teams within or outside of classes to help them with the GVV class assignments. The peer coaches could receive course credit, or be compensated as teaching assistants. In addition to supporting their peers and strengthening the student culture, peer coaches could speak of this distinctive experience in their job interviews. It is quite rare to have a new hire who has the training and practice of coaching their peers in voicing their values.

Research opportunities

As more universities employ the GVV approach, we see an opportunity for research collaborations on the impact of various GVV applications. Some are using GVV extensively within a course, others as stand-alone modules, others within orientations and leadership development programs. It would be valuable to better understand the effectiveness of such approaches as faculty consider what options will lead to optimal and lasting impact. Research studies assessing the impact of GVV compared to non-GVV courses could be conducted, both within one's own university as well as across several universities. Some work has been published in accounting education and more is in the works; a current list of publications is available at www.GivingVoiceToValues.org.

In addition to using samples of current students, we see the opportunity to follow up with young professionals who experienced GVV in their education, and examine how GVV has shaped their voice in the workplace. Offered through the GVV Business Ethics and Corporate Social Responsibility Collection series of books, Jessica's *Engaging Millennials for Ethical Leadership: What Works for Young Professionals and Their Managers* (2015) presents best practices and research highlights of effective, ethical leadership development for young professionals. The book includes insights from students studying the approach, and from those managing this generation of businesspeople. Coverage of the book has led to invitations to speak with various corporate audiences on the topic of millennial management toward ethical leadership. Future research may extend this topic to include the generational cohort ascending to business practice today, and various other applications of the GVV approach to personal and organizational effectiveness. Articles in journals including the *Journal of Business Ethics* and *Global Perspectives on Accounting Education*, and other books in the GVV collection, offer opportunities to explore and build on scholarly engagement with the curriculum.

Conclusion

An essential element of the new ideas in Part 3, as well as the successes in Part 1 and lessons learned in Part 2 of this chapter, are rooted in the GVV idea of finding allies. For the two of us at Notre Dame, we must extend our thinking beyond courses and curricula and college, with the goal of finding new partners who share the commitment of developing values-based leaders. We can begin by identifying and inviting colleagues into a community of best practices in developing the next generation of ethical leaders. The good news is that the GVV approach is accessible to faculty of diverse disciplines and adaptable to various course and program designs. Moreover, GVV can help close the skills gap between areas of emphasis for traditional business school curricula and skills the market for employees demands (AACSB, 2019). By enhancing the ability to move from decision-making to ethical action, the GVV approach can provide a mechanism for developing the skills demanded by today's employers and the commitment required to lead within the complexity of today's business environment.

Note

1 For more information on how other schools and organizations have used GVV, see www.GivingVoiceToValues.org and/or contact: GentileM@darden. virginia.edu.

References

AACSB BizEd. (2019, January–February). Integrates survey data and makes case for needed changes in b-school curricula. *Lea Weiss*. Retrieved from https://bized.aacsb.edu/articles/2019/january/the-case-for-soft-skills

AACSB Blog/Top Stories. (2019, January 8) What do employers want from business schools? *Marco de Novellis*. Retrieved from www.aacsb.edu/blog/2019/january/what-do-employers-want-from-business-schools

Adkins, C. P. (2011). A pathway for educating moral intuition: Experiential learning within the giving voice to values curriculum. *Journal of Business Ethics Education*, 8(1), 383–391.

Adkins, C. P., Gentile, M. C., Ingols, C., & Trefalt, S. (2011). Teaching "how" – not "whether" – to manage with integrity: Undergraduate and MBA application of the "Giving Voice to Values" curriculum. *Management Education for Integrity*, 107–133.

Gentile, M. C. (2010). *Giving voice to values: How to speak your mind when you know what's right*. New Haven, CT: Yale University Press.

Warnell, J. M. (2011). "Ask more" of business education: Giving Voice to Values for emerging leaders. *Journal of Business Ethics Education*, 8(1), 320–325.

Warnell, J. M. (2015). *Engaging millennials for ethical leadership: What works for young professionals and their managers*. New York: Business Expert Press.

6

GIVING VOICE TO VALUES IN HEALTH PROFESSIONS EDUCATION

Ira Bedzow and Heidi Waldron

Giving Voice to Values (GVV) is a post–decision-making, action-orientated approach that can be utilized in medical education for the purposes of teaching medical ethics and cultivating professional identity formation. As a method of instruction that starts with the premise that a person wants to give voice to his or her (professional and personal) values and that practice will make the person more successful in doing so, GVV provides a strong foundation for medical students to recognize and affirm their sense of meaning and efficacy as they develop into competent and professional physicians. Moreover, through its pragmatic approach, which recognizes that people are more prone to act ethically when they find it easier to do so, GVV provides students with the means to learn how to approach real-world problems in ways that mitigate potential tensions between other stakeholders and that utilize levers in systems-based practice.

This chapter will explore how the GVV approach is utilized in two different medical schools on two different continents to train students to engage professionally in their respective healthcare settings. The principles of GVV are highly relevant to other health professions that also prioritize the development of students' ethical, communication, and professional competencies. While every course will be unique, particularly with respect to how educational theory and a given school's individual learning objectives, priorities, and resources inform course design, incorporating GVV principles into healthcare curricula supports the common patient-centered priorities of such training. The following two medical school examples can serve to show how GVV can be effectively implemented in different educational settings. Before doing so, however, we will first introduce the challenges of medical ethics and professionalism education in the current healthcare environment.

Challenges in healthcare that GVV addresses

The GVV methodology addresses three major challenges that medical students face in learning how to act professionally in a healthcare environment. It addresses how a person can build skills and confidence to communicate his or her values to others in situations of values conflict; it provides a way to learn how medical ethics principles can be put into practice; and it allows students to build on their own personal identity when integrating professional norms and ethics into their professional identity.

Communication

Tensions in the health workplace are natural and expected – it is a place that brings together different healthcare professionals, all of whom care deeply and want to help patients, yet, because they come from different health professions, members of the care team may have different goals for care and different values and frames for approaching care. Moreover, the collaborative care teams work to treat patients who are unwell and vulnerable, which oftentimes means that they must engage in shared decision-making with people who may not understand the complexity of those decisions or may be unable to speak for themselves. Patients also have different cultural perspectives and personal priorities that the healthcare team must understand and incorporate in a way that ensures that care is patient-centered. Emphasis on collaborative care, shared decision-making, and cultural competency reflects a shift in healthcare delivery that has occurred over the past generation. Previous generations of healthcare have been much more hierarchical and paternalistic, where the physician has led the health team in directing care in a doctor-driven manner. While the flattening of the healthcare hierarchy has made it easier for medical students, as well as students from other health professions, to communicate their values, they must nevertheless develop the skills to do so effectively.

As a means to teach communication skills, GVV strengthens each individual's ability and confidence to skillfully raise concerns, advocate for personal and professional values, and maintain relationships even in complicated situations. These skills give students the means to give voice to their own values and advocate for their patient's values, and foster understanding and respect for the perspectives of others, which contributes to effective teamwork and more harmonious workplaces. This creates better environments for staff, as well as for patients and families receiving care.

Putting ethics into practice

In addition to training students to communicate more effectively, the GVV methodology also provides a practical means for students to learn how to act on medical ethics principles. Many medical ethics courses provide students with medical ethics principles and concepts, such as informed consent. They also introduce students to different theories for ethical analysis, such as principlism, consequentialism, and deontology. As such, students become familiar with what might be at stake in different clinical settings and learn how to analyze ethical questions for the sake of evaluating answers to medical ethics questions in general and in the abstract.

However, awareness of ethical concepts and analysis of ethical questions, while necessary, is insufficient to prepare students for clinical practice. By changing the question from "What should be done in this case?" to "How can one act on their values in this case?" GVV cases encourage students to consider how they would act, given their level of knowledge, their position on the healthcare team, the other stakeholders, and the organizational ethos and policies by which they practice medicine. When considering all of these factors, students learn to understand how medical ethics concepts are operationalized, i.e., what they mean in practice and not only in theory. They also learn to consider how medical ethics principles may mean something different to different people and in different circumstances. Many cases of values-conflict in the clinical setting stem from situations where people have differing interpretations of the same medical ethics concept. Patient autonomy is such an example, where one might conceive of it in terms of respecting the decisions that patients make, while another conceives of it in terms of ensuring that patients are truly informed to make a decision. Moreover, when anticipating rationalizations that students may have themselves or from other potential stakeholders, and in providing persuasive reasons to act on students' suggestions, students can become more attuned to when ethical theories are being used to think sincerely about possible solutions and when they are being used to rationalize acting in ways that do not in fact live up even to shared values. All this is to say that the GVV method of case examination provides vicarious experience for students to learn how to act, in addition to recognizing the importance of awareness and analysis.

Building on one's sense of self

Third, the GVV methodology can serve to help students develop their own professional identities and build the competencies that are associated with professionalism. Professionalism has become a major learning objective in medical education, but it is both challenging to instruct and to assess. The difficulty stems from the fact that professionalism is much more than simply showing up on time and not acting inappropriately. It demands that students develop their own sense of self as a doctor – including the realization that their own goals and desires may come in conflict with what is expected of them as professionals. By starting with the personal question, i.e., "What would I do if I could act on my values to resolve the tension of this situation?" the GVV methodology makes it easier for students to see themselves as professionals. The frame shift allows them to reflect on their own priorities and challenges, rather than view what professionals should do from an "armchair" position. The training of the GVV method also provides ways to assess the motivational component of professionalism, since exercises ask students to evaluate their action strategies and decisions from the perspective of their own personal-professional profile. Such an evaluation demands that students learn to hold themselves accountable to what they say they believe and value. It also provides them with the means to internalize professional values through opportunities where they can act on them as part of their own value set.

Two examples of GVV in medical education

Given the benefits of the GVV methodology to teach medical ethics and to provide opportunities for students to develop their professional identities, each of us has incorporated GVV into our respective school's curriculum. Next are descriptions of how we have included GVV in our respective schools. The first subsection describes how GVV has become part of the formal medical ethics course at New York Medical College (NYMC), an American medical school. The second subsection describes how components of GVV have been included in different areas of the communication training at the Fremantle School of Medicine at the University of Notre Dame Australia (Notre Dame).

The NYMC GVV-Medical Ethics Course

At New York Medical College, the GVV–Medical Ethics Course is designed as follows: the course begins with an introductory lecture, which provides students with a background into medical ethics and into GVV. It explains to students the components of ethical decision-making and moral action, the nature of professionalism and its relationship to ethics, and how the GVV methodology shifts the frame of ethics from what is the right answer to how one can act on one's values.

Students are then asked to complete a personal-professional profile, where they articulate not only the values that they hold dear but also the personal factors that they must take into account when devising a moral action strategy, such as questions of personal and professional goals, risk aversion, communication styles and preferences, loyalty and self-image. Students refer to their personal-professional profiles throughout the course in order to reinforce their own professional identities, as well as to gauge whether they will realistically implement their action strategies given their self-appraisal.

After the introductory lecture, the remaining sessions consist of different types of case studies. Over the entirety of the course, the cases will cover practical examples for many of the topics that medical ethics courses address, such as tensions in the patient–physician relationship, issues regarding beginning-of-life and end-of-life care, confidentiality, and duties to report. Also included are topics that are relevant to clinical practice and working on a healthcare team, but are not often included in traditional medical ethics courses, such as confronting a superior, speaking to colleagues about their patients' complaints, and talking to members of other healthcare professions when conflicts on the collaborative care team arise.

The case studies are of two different types. The first type describes an ethical question and informs the students of what the protagonist of the case wants to do in order to act on his or her values with the chosen decision being the most ethically appropriate response to the dilemma. The case includes a section describing who the key stakeholders are and what is at stake for them, what arguments or rationalizations the protagonist is likely to encounter, and what strategies he or she can use to counter opposing arguments and/or plot a course of action for addressing the situation. The assignment for these types of cases is for students to prepare an action plan and script for the protagonist. The main pedagogical objective for these cases is for students to learn and develop skills for moral action. They are truly post-decisional in the GVV sense. These cases teach the students to look at the particular situations at hand, to discover organizational enablers and barriers, to consider personal strengths and weaknesses, and to devise action plans that can be evaluated for efficacy. By emphasizing implementation, students can focus fully on developing those skills required to strategize on how to act successfully.

After students have successfully evaluated their action plans, the sessions end with a facilitator-led discussion about the ethical justification for the protagonist's decision. This scaffolds learning between case types one and two (discussed in more detail later) and allows students to engage with ethical principles to understand why the protagonist's decision is the correct moral choice for the situation. Through this discussion, students define the terms or concepts used in the scenario, evaluate how the various factors of the moral question relate to the protagonist's decision, and discuss the moral and legal assumptions on which the conclusion relies. When discussing the moral explanation for the decision that the protagonist made, students consider how applying various ethical frameworks can lead to differing conclusions. Carefully guided discussion about the processes involved in ethical deliberation actively counteracts the idea that ethical frameworks can be used to rationalize any answer or that ethics is relative. Instead, using post-decision cases that start with the most ethically correct conclusion allows students to confidently practice the skills of ethical deliberation without fear that they will arrive at a wrong conclusion.

For the second set of cases, students do not prepare an action plan and script for a protagonist. Rather, they must imagine themselves as one of the stakeholders in the case who must decide what the ethical decision is and how to act on that decision given his or her own personal capabilities and professional capacities. As one of the stakeholders, their assignment is to imagine how they would want to act in the situation and to prepare a script and/or action strategy for themselves. As such, it builds on the previous set of cases. By being asked to see themselves as stakeholders, these cases show that value conflicts are natural components of interpersonal, collaborative action and that students should appreciate their own views on a matter so that they do not simply defer to consensus. At the same time, students should also become aware that effective resolution comes from engaging other stakeholders and not ignoring them.

The methodological assumption for putting these cases second is that only after students learn to appreciate what is involved in successful moral action and develop skills to do so will they incorporate these considerations into the decision-making process. By reversing the order of "decide then act" in the first set of cases by having students focus primarily on the acting part and then discussing what went into the deciding part, students are better equipped to see the relationship between these two components, instead of seeing them as two independent points in a sequence. Moreover, once students gain experience developing action plans and scripts, they will gain confidence and feel that they have a real actionable choice when presented with a moral challenge, which will make it more likely for them to make ethical decisions when presented with the second set of cases.

Student scripts and explanations of their action strategies are assessed through formative, narrative assessment. Formative assessment refers to the type of assessment that guides future learning by providing reassurance, promoting reflection, and shaping values. It is different from summative assessments, which are intended to make an overall judgment about competence. One of the purposes of the formative assessment is to provide students with concrete comments to help them reflect on their scripts and action plans in a way that allows them to develop and integrate faculty insights into later action. Narrative assessment allows the formative assessment to take part as an active conversation between faculty and students, so that students are not only aware of how they might have met expectations or not, but also how they might be able to improve in the future.

Through this course format, students are able to build skills and confidence to communicate their values to others in situations of values conflict. They work together in small groups and present action strategies to each other, applying the same tools in different contexts to practice their skills. The format also provides a way to learn how medical ethics principles can be put into practice, both through their strategies and through the debrief discussions. Finally, by using the GVV methodology, the course makes the cases personal so that students build on their own personal identity when integrating professional norms and ethos into their professional identity. It will take some time to witness the longer-term impact that incorporation of GVV approach into the medical ethics course has on students' development of professional competencies and identity. However, the generalized student responses to the reframing of medical ethics teaching through the perspectives and pedagogy of GVV are a greater sense of confidence and self-efficacy to act on their values in a way that is meaningful both personally and clinically.

The University of Notre Dame Australia, Fremantle School of Medicine Communication Skills Training

Communication is regarded as a fundamental skill that underpins the delivery of patient-centered care. Communication Skills Training (CST) opportunities are embedded across the four-year post-graduate medical doctorate based in Fremantle, Western Australia. In common with medical courses worldwide, educators and students face the challenge of a crowded curriculum with students expected to develop substantial knowledge and skills over four years. GVV principles were embedded alongside existing simulation-based CST approaches to enhance the abilities of students to respond in ethically challenging situations and to accelerate development of professional identity. Specifically, existing role-plays were modified so that scenarios address discrete ethical concepts, with a focus upon post-decision-making actions, and briefing discussions explore varied stakeholder perspectives and values. This shift in emphasis is particularly beneficial, as there was no significant increase in the time allocated to CST, and yet the pedagogical changes provide opportunities for students to reinforce their understanding of how values link to ethical principles and the skills they use to provide clinical care.

Most medical courses aspire to train doctors who demonstrate attributes including compassionate communication and ethical behavior. GVV facilitates exploration of ethical concepts in the context of existing communication skills curriculum. Students are guided to apply their communication skills in ethically challenging situations. Furthermore, GVV provides support to the clinicians who deliver CST training to students, by explicitly highlighting how values affect communication. Experienced clinicians often have an implicit understanding that values underpin clinical and patient decision-making. The GVV framework makes these values evident to learners who lack the clinical experience to recognize how values underpin dynamics in doctor-patient-family-team communication.

The following paragraphs highlight the synergistic effects of embedding GVV alongside traditional CST. Notre Dame uses the Calgary-Cambridge guide to the medical interview as its foundation to teach communication (Kurtz, Silverman & Draper, 2016).[1] The Calgary-Cambridge guide is an approach to teaching medical interviewing skills that presumes that, even if the context and details of clinical interactions change and the content of the communication varies, the process skills for good communication remain the same and can be evaluated independently. In line with the premise of GVV that previous experiences can inform current and future action strategies, the school's communication training provides a bridge that scaffolds learning between students' existing conversational or disciplinary skills to develop skills that are specifically applicable to medical situations.

Experiential learning, and particularly simulation, is used to practice and consolidate communication skills especially in the two preclinical years. The GVV approach shares many similarities with simulation roleplay strategies, such as scripting and rehearsing responses and receiving feedback from mentors; these factors facilitated a seamless integration of the two methods into curriculum. The following paragraphs describe first, pre-GVV CST strategies, followed by explanations of how GVV was embedded using examples of selected CST activities.

Students regularly practice peer role-plays using clinical illness scripts at weekly workshops focused on developing history, examination, and procedural skills. Scripts define a doctor-patient interaction where students play one of the roles, serving as a vehicle to consolidate learning of clinical features of disease as well as embody the communication attributes required for future practice. A doctor facilitates and provides students with feedback about both clinical matters and skills development. One of the important roles of this doctor is to observe the doctor-patient interactions and encourage students to consider alternative ways to communicate. In this context, according to GVV framework, the doctor is a respected and respectful mentor (hereafter referred to as a clinical mentor) who coaches the student to script and rehearse specific communication phrases and reinforces effects through repeated deliberate practice.

Both preclinical years also have a specialized workshop series scheduled over three weeks that targets defined communication skills relevant to students' level of training. These workshops have medical interview role-plays with actors or real patients rather than peers to portray the patient role, which increases the authenticity and challenge for students. First year workshops focus on skills such as building rapport, which are not reliant upon possessing specialized clinical knowledge. In contrast, second year workshops focus on advanced skills such as managing conflict and dealing with angry patients, to prepare students for the transition to hospital-based learning.

As an innovative way to pave the way for GVV, a series of instructional videos was created collaboratively featuring academics from the university, real patients, and health professionals from various hospitals across the city of Perth (Waldron, 2017).[2] The GVV inspired videos demonstrate the importance of listening carefully to patients recount their clinical story so that students learn to recognize important features of the clinical presentation as well as to appreciate how a patient's values influence shared decision-making about care. Stage-appropriate videos are used in lectures describing Calgary Cambridge communication strategies immediately prior to the specialized workshop series in the first and second year.

After watching the videos students report heightened understanding of how ethical principles, such as autonomy, apply in regular clinical practice and recognize that clinical communication can support or diminish patients' experiences of healthcare. For example, one scenario follows a mother who shares her experiences about the delay in reaching a diagnosis for her daughter's cancer, which she attributes to the attending doctor dismissing her concerns. While her daughter subsequently received and responded to chemotherapy, the sharing of their situation illustrates the importance of listening. The viewer sees the emotional impact of a near-miss situation, where a disastrous outcome was narrowly avoided. However, the videos do not portray a reductionist approach to complex clinical scenarios; instead, there is a range of stakeholder perspectives presented through interview commentaries that speak to the challenges of busy hospitals and the many urgent demands faced by staff. These elements segue into role-plays used during the subsequent workshops, including an "apology" scenario.

Common student responses to the GVV videos are empathy towards patients, appreciation of collaborative care, and motivation to refine their communication strategies and skills. The combination of videos and subsequent workshops prompt students to think about how they could act differently by focusing on what they might do in similar situations if they were to act on their professional values of care and patient-centricity. Students are also prompted to consider the varying perspectives, pressures, and values held by varying stakeholders in given scenarios – in this case: patient, family, team colleagues, and self.

The "apology" role-play from the second year CST workshops highlights how GVV enhances and reinforces simulation-based skills training to consolidate students' confidence to act in alignment with their values. The student who role-plays the doctor must offer an apology to a simulated patient, who is role-played by an actor. One of GVV's premises is the idea of normalizing and calibrating expectations. In particular, the methodology asks students to recognize that ethical challenges are commonplace in the work environment, so that they can shift their focus from being shocked when values-based conflicts occur towards more adaptive action-orientated responses. These concepts are introduced using blended learning strategies. The open disclosure framework for medical errors, a national procedural guideline, is outlined in the lecture that precedes the workshop. During the lecture, video is shown where respected clinicians acknowledge that mistakes are commonplace and occur at all levels of medical experience. The lecturer and video experts suggest strategies for how one can respond appropriately in the event a mistake occurs.

Students then participate in simulation workshops, with the "apology" scenario enabling students to combine their theoretical understanding with the practical experience of giving an apology. The blended learning format juxtaposes professional expectations, through the medical errors guidelines and expert commentary, with the personal challenge of actioning an appropriate apology.

In preparation for simulated role-plays, it is best practice to conduct a pre-brief, where facilitators (clinical mentors) and actors discuss intended learning outcomes. With incorporation of GVV into CST, pre-briefs include discussion about teaching techniques to promote deeper exploration of values and effective action-focused communication. GVV's post-decision-making stance focuses attention on action rather than ethical deliberation, and is achieved through the way scenarios are constructed and enacted. During student pre-briefing for each role-play, clinical mentors insist that certain actions are taken. In the apology scenario they guide students, directing "You have decided to apologize to this patient: how would you go about it? What might you say?" Before commencing the role-play, students collectively consider ways the situation could be handled and how different approaches might be perceived by patients, including whether the patient might interpret that a rationalization rather than an apology is being offered. The clinical mentor encourages students to consider barriers and enablers that could alter how effectively they communicate their intended message, including the physical layout of the doctor's room and body language used. The GVV approach encourages students to consider the varying values of stakeholders, including patient and doctor, when formulating an effective communication response script. Practice of skills in a simulation role-play may occur multiple times, which sets this process apart from real clinical practice. If the student is uncertain about how to progress, they can seek the advice of their peers and the clinical mentor to develop alternative scripted responses. Scripting then repeating the interaction allows the student to experience different consequences. Repetition also allows the actor to embody differing patient perspectives and values to provide students with a spectrum of experiences and insights.

The role-play is followed by facilitated discussion and performance feedback from both the clinical mentor and the actor. The focus upon stakeholder perspectives and values distinguishes the GVV approach from traditional clinical role-plays. An important question posed to the student is "How did managing that situation feel?" This can lead to exploration of the student's values and sense of self, and whether they felt their actions were coherent with these. The opportunity to practice and informally appraise these essential skills in a simulated scenario using a post-decision-making framework removes some of the negative emotional connotations that would naturally occur if this were a real-life situation. Discussion about the student's experience as a role-play participant allows consideration of developing professional identity and the factors that shape this evolving sense of self. When faced with such role-play situations, students often report that it seems initially straightforward. However, after participating with an actor who has been trained to convey authentic emotions, including intense anger, students often reflect that they rely upon using the full range of their communication skills to respond to their patient's concerns. This challenges them to deeply consider the efficacy of their approach and the reality of varying perspectives held by patients and colleagues. In recognizing the complexity of clinical practice, many students express that they feel highly motivated to continue refining their communication skills.

By integrating GVV methodology into traditional simulation-based CST, students have greater opportunities to develop communication skills that acknowledge the relevance of values during clinical interactions. The post decision-making, action-focused emphasis of GVV increases the immediacy and impacts of existing simulation practices. Through experiential role-plays, students explore tensions common in clinical settings and consider the varied perspectives, values, and ethical consequences for patients, families, the care team, and themselves. Students predict possible challenges and develop scripted responses utilizing supportive peer discussion and clinical mentor advice; this enables repetitive practice of active communication to resolve tensions. Debriefing following simulation, led by mentors and actors, provides valuable feedback about effectiveness and emotional impacts of the interactions, which supports the shaping of students' skills and sense of professional self.

Conclusion

Even though the two schools incorporate GVV in different ways, both schools share the belief that the GVV methodology can be used to train physicians to be better communicators and more effective professionals who learn to internalize the values of the profession. A physician's ability to provide quality care to patients hinges upon his or her clinical skills and personal capabilities to act within the culture of a health system that faces many pressures, including time, legal, and budgetary constraints. GVV provides a powerful way to help students develop skills that empower them and builds their confidence to communicate their values effectively and respect the values of their patients and co-workers, even in the most challenging health scenarios. We believe that this will lead to improved patient satisfaction, safety metrics, and clinical outcomes once students graduate as professional physicians.

As professionalism increases in priority in medical education and inter-professional education becomes an expected standard across health professions education, there will be a greater need for curricula that can provide opportunities for students to build skills and confidence to communicate their values to others and for students to build on their own personal identity when integrating professional norms and ethos into their professional identity. GVV clearly prepares medical students for their future roles as health professionals. The skills students are practicing in NYMC and Notre Dame are relevant for health professionals in the workforce: using communication skills to resolve values conflicts, translating ethical theory into tangible action, and building a robust sense of professional self. Time pressures in the workplace have a similar impact as that seen in the university setting, with clinicians often finding it hard to create time and space to schedule ongoing professional development. This is despite the recognized benefits of focusing attention on communication, ethics, and professionalism across all levels of expertise, from students to experienced clinicians. The GVV framework offers an efficient way to maximize training time and build relevant, effective skills.

Notes

1 Kurtz, S., Silverman, J., & Draper, J. (2016). *Teaching and learning communication skills in medicine* (2nd ed.). London, England: CRC Press.

2 Waldron, H. (2017). *Communication videos for healthcare setting: Supporting health professionals and patients to voice their values.* Research and Education in Ethics Grant. Mary Philippa Brazill Foundation. Melbourne, Australia.

7

GIVING VOICE TO VALUES IN SUPPORT OF A MISSION TO EDUCATE AFRICA'S NEXT GENERATION OF ETHICAL LEADERS

Rebecca Awuah

Introduction and background

In 2008, after vigorous debate, students at Ashesi University in Ghana voted into force an examinations honor code, committing to take tests and exams without proctors, upon their honor. They opted to sign the following statement at the end of each test or exam: "I pledge on my honor that during this examination I have neither given nor received unauthorized assistance, nor have I seen any violations of the Exam Code of Conduct."

The code stipulates that, if any student fails to sign the statement after a test or exam, the course instructor will follow up to investigate the credibility of the exam. Since 2008, each incoming year group has held discussions and voted on whether to join the honor system, making an affirmative choice to uphold a high standard of ethical behavior, and to hold their peers to the same. More recently, students have initiated an effort to extend the honor system beyond the classroom and into the social realm.

Not long after the students' historic 2008 vote, I had the opportunity to attend the Global Business Ethics Symposium at Bentley University, USA, and to hear a presentation on "Giving Voice to Values" by Dr. Mary C. Gentile. Listening to Dr. Gentile's presentation, it struck me that the Giving Voice to Values (GVV) approach directly addressed the most common concern students had voiced in deliberations on the honor system: doubt in their ability to speak up if they observed a classmate or friend doing the wrong thing. While students expressed confidence in their own ability not to cheat, they believed that some of their classmates might, and wondered if they could trust themselves to speak up about it.

One finding from Dr. Gentile's research stood out as particularly relevant to the concerns of Ashesi University students. According to Gentile, research suggested that many individuals describe having had conversations with a colleague, a trusted friend, or a family member, etc. – essentially talking through what they may say and do – before speaking up and acting in alignment with their values (Gentile, 2010a). This form of "rehearsal" is captured in GVV when students write scripts and rehearse responses to cases involving a protagonist in a values conflict situation who has determined his or her values position and would like to speak up and act. Could rehearsal, through writing scripts, action planning, and practice, help students feel more confident in their ability to navigate the volatile territory of reporting instances of honor code violations?

Additional concepts and vocabulary that Dr. Gentile touched on that day, such as enablers and disablers for voicing values and reframing reasons and rationalizations (these concepts will be discussed in more detail later), struck me as useful tools with which students could formulate action plans for speaking up. By unpacking the factors behind failures to uphold academic integrity – such as loyalty to friends, fear of ostracism, fear of disappointing parents, time pressure – students could formulate more nuanced action plans, even ways to dissuade their colleagues and friends from making the choice to cheat in the first place.

Beginning in September 2011, GVV was implemented as a five-week seminar taken by all students during their first semester on campus. The course has become part of the "Ashesi experience" and precedes each year group's discussion and vote on whether to join the honor system. Beyond strengthening students' ability to uphold academic integrity on campus, Ashesi University's implementation of GVV sought to achieve a number of other institutional and pedagogical objectives.

First, GVV was implemented to rally the entire community around the university's mission to "educate the next generation of ethical leaders in Africa" by including a broad range of stakeholders in the facilitation and delivery of the curriculum. Second, GVV was implemented to support the leadership mission of the university by framing skills in ethical action as fundamental to effective leadership. Third, the implementation of GVV was guided by pedagogical models already woven into the educational philosophy of the institution, namely experiential learning theory, the cognitive theory of growth mindsets, and the ethos of contextualizing the curriculum to the Ghana and Africa context.

Purpose of the chapter

The remainder of the chapter will examine how GVV has been implemented to meet these institutional and pedagogical objectives. The result is a high level of integration between ethics education, the leadership mission of the university, and the local context, which other institutions may be interested to follow. The chapter will proceed as follows. First, the need for ethical leadership in Africa and current approaches to ethics education on the continent will be examined. This will be followed by an overview of Ashesi University's leadership curriculum, how ethics is incorporated into leadership learning, and the gap GVV aims to fill. Next, a detailed overview of the five-week GVV course will highlight how the institutional and pedagogical objectives mentioned earlier are met. Finally, the chapter will conclude with a discussion of broader institutional impacts and new directions.

The need for ethical leadership in Africa

In Africa, more than one in four people who access public services pay bribes with a disproportionate share of these bribes being paid by the poor (Pring & Vrushi, 2019). The status quo of corruption that exists in many African countries constrains growth in both the private and public sectors (Burger, Kopf, Spreng, Yoong, & Sood, 2012). The effects of corruption include environmental degradation when resources are extracted illegally, extending the duration required to complete development projects, loss of tax revenue to the state, and the impact on policy making when clientelism leads to policies not in the public interest (Kurer, 1993).

Although government and private sector accountability measures and safe corruption reporting channels for citizens have been shown to reduce corrupt practices in government (Pring & Vrushi, 2019), sustainable change requires that individuals at all levels and in all sectors of society wrestle with the ethical dimensions of corrupt practices, and take action within their spheres of influence.

Individuals in positions of leadership have a particularly important role to play in shifting the status quo away from corrupt practices. Leaders influence others through their articulated visions of change and through the visibility of their everyday actions. In sub-Saharan Africa, about 9% of young adults enroll in tertiary education (2017 estimate, UNESCO Institute for Statistics, 2020) and many of those who complete their university degrees will take up positions of leadership within the private and public sectors. The civic purpose of the university demands that African universities tackle issues surrounding corruption and make a concerted effort to prepare the next generation of leaders for the continent to "do better."

Ethics education in Africa

Within higher education in Africa, ethics is typically taught in the context of the professions: medical ethics, legal ethics, business ethics, etc. (Rossouw, 2011). In addition, many private higher education institutions are faith-based and address ethics from a religious and moral perspective. Although didactic teaching approaches are common in African universities, faculty are increasingly using cases, Socratic teaching, and other active learning methods in their ethics courses (McLaughlin & Pfister, 2018).

Ethics courses within the context of the professions are important because they expose students to professional codes of conduct, help them perceive the ethical dimensions of situations unique to their professions, and provide them with analytical tools for ethical reasoning and arriving at judgments. However, as Mary C. Gentile and others have pointed out, this approach leaves out an important set of skills, particularly in the fight against corruption – namely, what to do when one observes or is asked to do something fraudulent or unethical (in effect, becoming unwittingly saddled with some degree of complicity), and how to effectively speak up and act against it.

By adopting an integrated approach to ethics education, which includes GVV, ethics in the context of the professions, and other components, such as honor codes and programs in values-driven leadership, African universities can better prepare the continent's future leaders to engage in the difficult task of shifting the status quo away from corrupt practices.

Overview of Ashesi University and the core leadership seminar series

Ashesi University was founded in Ghana in 2003 as a private, not-for-profit, non-denominational undergraduate institution with a core mission to educate a new generation of ethical entrepreneurial leaders for Africa. The university began with 30 students and three majors in 2003 and has grown to over 1,000 students and six majors today, namely business administration, management information systems, computer science, and three engineering majors. The curriculum is a unique hybrid that blends a liberal arts core, which aims to prepare students broadly to deal with complexity, diversity, and change, with professional majors and, importantly, an emphasis on the African context.

Tied to the university's leadership mission, every student takes four seminars in leadership as part of the core curriculum. The first seminar, *Leadership 1: What Makes a Good Leader?* examines the concept of leadership and its practical manifestations. Evaluating leadership in different contexts and from different perspectives underlies the bulk of the discussions. This includes analyzing leadership decisions and actions using frameworks of ethical reasoning such as consequential, rule-based, communitarian, and care- or virtue-based approaches. The seminar also asks students to take stock of their own leadership potential.

Leadership 2: Rights, Ethics and the Rule of Law and *Leadership 3: The Economic Organization of a Good Society*, both seminars taken in the second year, examine political and economic leadership, respectively, and how these impact a nation's development. The fourth and final seminar, *Leadership 4: Leadership as Service*, is taken during the third year and encourages students' sense of social responsibility and commitment to serve. Developing students' sense of themselves as leaders is an important objective of *Leadership 4*.

The five-week GVV seminar was introduced in 2011 and precedes *Leadership 1*. *Giving Voice to Values* takes place during the first semester of the first year and *Leadership 1* during the second semester. Although the initial sequencing was tied to supporting incoming students in upholding the examination honor code, GVV nicely sets up two key propositions of *Leadership 1*: that good leadership is ethical leadership, and that leadership skills, including reasoning, judgment, and action, can be taught.

Students take GVV in groups of about 20. Each section of the course is co-facilitated by an Ashesi University staff or faculty member and a recent graduate completing their National Service year as a teaching assistant on campus. In addition, alumni who have been working for more than three years join the seminars to interact with first year students and share their experiences of values conflicts encountered in the Ghanaian workplace. Since 2011, members of staff, including the Directors of Career Services, Finance, Human Resources, Admissions, and University Development, have co-facilitated sections of the course along with faculty from diverse disciplines. The participation of staff and faculty from different disciplines reinforces the notion that speaking up and acting on one's values is not an exclusively academic pursuit, but a set of skills relevant to any profession.

The next section will give a brief overview of the pedagogical frameworks that guided the implementation of GVV at Ashesi University – experiential learning theory and the cognitive theory of growth mindsets – followed by a week-by-week overview of the topics and activities of the five-week seminar, with particular attention to the contextualization of the curriculum to the Africa and Ghana context.

Pedagogical frameworks

The growth mindset

A starting assumption for GVV is the belief that skills in ethical action can be developed through effort and practice (Gentile, 2010b). The belief that knowledge, skills, and personal qualities can be cultivated through effort is known as the *growth mindset*, and research by Carol Dweck and others (Hong, Chiu, & Dweck, 1999; Dweck, 2006; Blackwell, Trzesniewski, & Dweck, 2007) has shown that the growth mindset is associated with increased motivation for learning and resilience in the face of setbacks. At Ashesi University, the GVV seminar begins several weeks after the theory of mindsets and the cognitive science of brain plasticity are introduced during new-student orientation. Therefore, the starting assumption of GVV – the belief that skills in ethical action can be developed through effort and practice – can build naturally on the theory of mindsets.

Research has shown that implicit theories about the malleability of human characteristics, such as intelligence, personal qualities, or skills, "create a framework for making predictions and judging the meaning of events in one's world" (Yeager & Dweck, 2012, p. 303). When a person believes human characteristics are fixed, (called the *fixed mindset*), there is little reason to put effort into changing them. On the other hand, if a person has the growth mindset – believing that human characteristics can change – their motivation to work toward desired outcomes increases. In the context of GVV, if we believe that those asking us to do something that goes against our values can change, it feels more worthwhile to analyze the rationalizations behind their actions and to consider strategies for persuading them to do otherwise. Gentile emphasizes that most people are pragmatists and would like to do the right thing if personal consequences are not too high and/or if they think they could be effective. Reinforcing the malleability view within GVV makes students more open to attributing an unethical request to factors other than the person is simply "unethical" and may lead to greater motivation for putting new skills in ethical action to use.

The experiential learning cycle

Another objective of placing GVV in the first semester of college is to set up an iterative process of making meaning about values and ethical action over the four years of university. According to Kolb (1984), humans learn from experience in a four-step cycle: (a) concrete experience, (b) reflective observation, (c) abstract hypothesis, and (d) active testing. Zull (2002) describes how the four regions of the neocortex most involved in human learning can be roughly mapped to Kolb's experiential learning cycle. Crucially, the physical sensations of an experience – the processing of sight, sound, touch, and smell, and the physical sensations resulting from emotion – stimulate the meaning making process (Zull, 2002).

The GVV curriculum begins by tapping into students' concrete experiences with ethical reasoning, judgments, and action prior to attending college. By bringing to the fore prior experiences, students' current understandings of the moral dimension of their world can form the basis of reconstructing and adding to its meaning. As the seminar progresses, roleplaying initiates cycles of learning from the experience of speaking and acting out responses to GVV cases. Finally, conflict situations that occur naturally in the university setting, particularly in the context of an honor code, are opportunities to set in motion further cycles of learning from experience.

The second step in Kolb's experiential learning cycle, reflective observation, is how the brain begins to make meaning from the physical sensations of an experience. Reflective observation is an integrative process, which involves remembering, associating, making connections, and rerunning and analyzing experiences (Zull, 2002). GVV activities and discussions facilitate reflective observation when students further probe their experiences in light of new vocabulary and frameworks, such as enablers and disablers and common ethical dilemmas. When students compare their experiences to others and identify patterns and generalize, they are engaging in Kolb's third step, abstract hypothesis. Abstract hypothesis is concerned with generating abstractions through the manipulation of images and language and creating new mental arrangements which can be drawn upon to develop plans for action. When students can easily imagine themselves and picture their own context in cases and discussion prompts, reflection and experience are more likely to inform understandings of the ethical issues and positions, and hence, approaches to speaking and acting that are realistic.

The final step in the experiential learning cycle, active testing, involves the motor brain. Zull emphasizes that a person must *do* something with new learning, both to test understanding and to solidify new mental arrangements. The final seminar in Ashesi University's rollout of GVV has small groups of students acting out scripts to several GVV cases. Without these final rehearsals, ideas about ethical action could remain inert and hypothetical, and the course might risk leaving students with the feeling that speaking up is just a matter of applying the right strategy, and that, somehow, one always will. Practice through acting out scripts plays double duty – closing the loop on one iteration of learning from experience and, hopefully, stimulating many more.

Giving voice to values at Ashesi University

This section gives a week-by-week overview of the topics and activities of the GVV seminar with special attention to the ways in which the key institutional objectives mentioned in the introduction are met.

These include strengthening students' ability to uphold academic integrity on campus; rallying the entire community around the university's mission to educate ethical leaders in Africa; and adhering to the tenets of mindset theory, the experiential learning cycle, and the imperative of contextualization.

Week 1

The first week of GVV introduces the idea that the course is not about debating what is right or wrong in any particular instance, but about teaching skills in ethical action – how to speak up and be heard when your values are in conflict with what someone has asked you to do. This is done through a "Go to Your Post" activity (Silberman, 1996). Posters with the following texts are placed at the four corners of the classroom: *Do Unto Others As You Would Have Them Do Unto You, Honor Thy Mother and Father, Question Authority,* and *Save the Planet.* Students are instructed to choose a poster and discuss their choice with others. One person from each group shares a short summary of the group's discussion. Typically, one or two students will want to "debate" about which choice is "best." This is a perfect opportunity for the instructor to politely interrupt and point out that the activity demonstrates that we all *have* values, whether they come from our family, culture, religion, generation, or elsewhere, and then clarify that GVV is *not* about teaching and debating values. Instead, it is about *ethical action* – skills that will help us more effectively speak up and be heard when our values conflict with what we observe or what someone asks us to do.

Ashesi University alumni return to campus for this first meeting, and following the Go to Your Post Activity, the seminar instructor conducts an interview with an alum framed around their Tale of Two Stories. Alumni are prompted to share a time when they spoke up in a values conflict situation and a time when they did not, from their work experiences or their student days. The interview models Tale of Two Stories reflective questions such as, what motivated you to speak up and act? How satisfied were you with the outcome? How would you like to have responded? What would have made it easier to speak up or act? How might you act in accordance with your values if faced with a similar situation again? There is usually time for a brief Q & A with the alum before the session ends with students assigned to reflect on their own Tale of Two Stories which they will share in small groups during Week 2.

The format of the first session accomplishes several key goals. First, the Go to Your Post activity differentiates skills in ethical action that will be taught in the course from reasoning about values and ethics, which students may be expecting based on the course title or past experiences. Second, the alumni interviews draw on the real-world experiences of alumni with values conflicts in the Ghanaian workplace. This brings an important element of contextualization to the conversation. Third, many alumni reach out to join the seminar and share their experiences. The opportunity keeps alumni connected to the university's ethics mission and the tools of Giving Voice to Values. Fourth, the interviews model the process of reflective reasoning, and show alumni growing in their conviction and courage and in their ability to speak up effectively.

In addition to conflicts at work, returnees have shared stories of values conflicts they experienced in Ashesi – within the hostels, in the classroom, when they themselves cheated or covered up for a friend and faced the consequences, conflicts within group work and extracurricular programs – and even conflicts within their families. Whether or not they chose to speak up in these situations, whether or not they were satisfied with the outcomes, alumni are able to share important lessons that have guided them going forward.

Week 2

In the second week, students come to class prepared to share their own Tale of Two Stories. Working in small groups, each person shares a time when they spoke up in a values conflict situation and a time when they did not. Each group then creates lists of enablers and disablers derived from the stories – personal qualities, experiences, or contextual factors that either supported a choice to speak up or made such a choice seem difficult, impossible, or not worthwhile. These lists are then shared with the larger group and patterns are identified, such as enablers or disablers that are common to many situations, unique to an individual or circumstance, within or beyond a person's control, or something like friendship, which can be both an enabler or disabler depending on the situation. The session ends with students reflecting on why it may be useful to identify enablers and disablers in situations where they would like to speak or act on their values.

The Tale of Two Stories written assignment in preparation for the discussion on enablers and disablers brings to the fore students' prior concrete experiences with ethical reasoning, judgments, and action, and engages students in reflective observation. Reflective observation is enriched when the discussion shifts to the larger group, where students refine the images and meanings attached to their experiences in light of the broader patterns in people's choices to speak up and the consequent range of outcomes, laying a foundation for constructing higher-level abstractions that can be applied to future values conflict situations.

A good example of this type of image refinement occurs in the large group discussion of enablers and disablers. Initially, many students will consider "the way I was raised," their religion, or cultural factors as enablers in the story where they chose to speak up and act. The facilitator points out that they had the same religion, parents, and cultural background in both instances, but in one case they chose to speak up and in the other they didn't, so "what else could be at work here?" Students reflect again on their stories and dig deeper to identify other elements in each experience that could have encouraged or dissuaded their decision to speak up.

The in-class discussion of students' Tale of Two Stories and of enablers and disablers is itself a concrete experience that seems to trigger an "a-ha" moment that makes it "stick" for students. When final year students or alumni are asked what they remember from GVV, "enablers and disablers" are often recalled first. Zull (2002) emphasizes that reflective observation can take time – similarly, the GVV experience seems to be one that percolates and resurfaces for further reflection over time.

Week 3

Week 3 has three related objectives. The first objective is to help students identify reasons and rationalizations people give when acting unethically, particularly in familiar and "everyday" situations. The second objective is to help students recognize the common ethical dilemmas embedded within those reasons and rationalizations. And the third objective is to introduce the concept of reframing as an approach to formulating persuasive counterarguments.

The session begins with a large group discussion about a circumstance of unethical behavior that students will likely have experienced individually or within a family context or be keenly aware of through current events. Cases vary from year to year but in the past, police bribery and the issue of medical doctors withdrawing emergency services as part of a strike action have been used. Students are asked to take on a role and participate in a thought experiment: if they want to persuade an uncle who is police officer or a mother who is a medical doctor that their actions go against strongly held values, what can they say and do? How can they be persuasive?

Students write their first mini script for a short GVV case in Week 3. The case involves a values conflict situation for a newly hired young admissions officer in a university in Ghana. A senior staff member is exerting pressure to admit an applicant whom they have financially supported through their education. As in all GVV cases, the protagonist knows their ethical position and would like to speak up and act.

Students are tasked to work with one or two colleagues to consider enablers and disablers for the young admissions officer, reasons and rationalizations the admissions officer might confront, and how the admissions officer could use reframing to formulate an effective approach to speaking up. Integrity in college admissions is a persistent issue in Ghana, as is the difficulty of a younger person challenging an older person in a work setting (age always appears as a disabler in the Week 2 discussion), so most students view this scenario as a realistic one.

Week 4

Week 4 addresses the tasks of analyzing what is at stake for individuals involved in values conflict situations and aligning an approach to acting and voicing values to the personality, style, and sense of purpose of the primary actors. Students work in small groups to analyze and write a script for a more detailed case in Week 4. Conflicts in Week 4 cases might include disagreements about allocating funds within a student club or challenges with group work in a project-based course.

Week 4 cases contain more detail about characteristics of the individuals such as personality traits and personal and professional goals. This is an opportunity to reintroduce the malleability concept from mindset theory.

Ashesi students often associate the ability to speak up with extroversion, which they typically view as a fixed personality trait. This perception surfaces during the enablers and disablers discussion in Week 2 when "being shy" ends up on the list of disablers. And it will come up again during *Leadership 1* when students are asked to evaluate the characteristics of good leaders with "outgoing" or "extrovert" being common responses. GVV attempts to counteract this view with the notion that, by exercising the parts of the brain that develop ethical arguments, and putting those arguments into words through scripting and rehearsals, people can become "smarter" and overcome self-talk such as "I'm just not good at this." By exposing students to protagonists with different temperaments and styles in the GVV cases, and from the examples of alumni and course facilitators, the curriculum aims to promote the view that the ability to speak up effectively is not associated with a particular personality trait.

At the end of the class, students are assigned a final case in groups of about five and instructed to prepare a five-minute roleplay demonstrating how the protagonist in the case could voice their values. The final set of cases was developed in collaboration with a former Dean of Students and comprises composite sketches of students involved in values conflict situations reported to counsellors and career services officers over the years. Scenarios include a student being asked to inflate prices during an internship, a student discovering that a close friend is cheating during an exam, and an individual faced with the challenge of speaking up when a friend is in an unhealthy relationship.

Week 5

During the final class meeting, students perform their roleplays and receive peer feedback. The seminar concludes with a short reflective exercise asking students to write about an "a-ha" moment from the past five weeks, which they are invited to share with the group if they wish. Finally, students are reminded that values conflicts during their time in university are inevitable and can be viewed as an opportunity to build "moral muscle memory" for speaking up through practice (Gentile, 2013, p. 11), and that, when unsure how to take action, they are encouraged to use the approach of "pre-scripting" – rehearsing how they may speak up and act with a trusted person such as a friend, family member, or mentor.

Institutional impacts and further directions

Since 2011, close to 1000 Ashesi University graduates have experienced the GVV curriculum, over 30 alumni have returned to campus to share their experiences in the workplace, about 25 staff and faculty have cycled through as facilitators, and nearly 40 graduates completing their National Service year as teaching assistants have co-facilitated the GVV seminar. Nearly all board members and many major donors have participated with students in writing scripts and acting out roleplays to GVV cases on annual trips to campus. This final section seeks to examine the impact on the institution of involving such a broad range of stakeholders in experiencing and teaching GVV.

Through numerous interviews, observations, and my own engagement with each of the stakeholder groups, I have identified institutional impacts on four levels. These include the level of students, the level of faculty and staff who teach the course, the organizational level, and finally, beyond the university. It is important to keep in mind that GVV is one component of an integrated approach to achieving Ashesi University's ethical leadership mission. The honor code, the core curriculum in leadership, the university's own leadership approach, and many ethics and integrity conversations that take place within the curriculum and co-curriculum all influence the degree to which the mission is achieved. My aim here is to provide some evidence and examples of the role GVV plays in supporting the larger mission; any specific outcome will certainly be confounded by many values, ethics, and leadership touchpoints experienced by each stakeholder group.

From interviews with those who work with students outside of the classroom – within student life, career services, and human resources – the GVV seminars in the first semester are where students begin the process of clarifying their own values, particularly around issues relevant to the university setting, such as academic integrity, relationships, and teamwork – values frequently tested in the transition from high school to university. Because GVV poses the question "*if* I were to take this position, how might I speak up and act?" students can fully participate and consider actions they may take even when they are not presently committed to a particular position. According to Ashesi University's Dean of Students,

It's easy for students to say that "I'm not going to do this." But it becomes more difficult when they have to take it a step further, to identify someone who is not doing the right thing. From that standpoint GVV helps tremendously. . . . And it's reinforced by alums coming back to share their personal experience, letting the students know that they are not alone in this.

The Dean of Students further notes that conversations with students around ethics violations shift once students have gone through GVV. Rather than starting with a debate about right and wrong, the conversation begins with a discussion of the student's own reasons and rationalizations regarding the violation. The Dean believes students are more accepting, though not happy, about penalties after going through GVV.

An academic violation that has come up several times over the years has to do with a student "signing" for a friend who is absent on the class attendance sheet. With class sizes of over 50, instructors often do not pick this up, but students do notice and have reported several such cases. The values dilemma for students is between helping a friend and upholding the notion of one's signature as evidence of identity and intent, and as a symbol of trust. In a broader culture of corruption and breached contract obligations, reframing around the value of signatures is an important conversation. And there are several instances when alumni returning to participate in GVV have described this issue when sharing their Tale of Two Stories. For example, one graduate explained that during his National Service year at a local government school, he decided to speak up about a practice of collusion by teachers to delay signing against their arrival time in the sign-in book, in effect covering for teachers who were late but able to sign against an earlier time. Late arrivals by teachers reduces instructional time and negatively impacts learning and is a serious problem in many government schools in Ghana. Over the years, students have reported a range of academic violations, including violations of the examination honor code, instances of plagiarism, and classmates copying the work of others.

Several staff and faculty who have taught GVV describe the course as giving students a "toolkit" for ethical action. The Dean of Students observed that over the four years, he saw students "learning about the tools, learning from putting them into practice, and developing a stronger sense of who they are and what they stand for by the time they approach graduation."

Impacts on faculty and staff who teach GVV are both personal and professional. In several interviews, preparing for teaching was viewed as an opportunity to re-examine past experiences in light of GVV content. "What do I want to bring to the table? Am I living the values I aspire to?" were questions one staff member asked herself as she prepared to teach. Professionally, themes around being patient with colleagues, realizing the importance of persuading people before expecting them to come on board with decisions and actions, and taking time to reflect and plan prior to difficult conversations were mentioned as benefits. The Dean of Students acknowledged that "some are just teaching it while some are clearly living it." But he also stated that employees "feel more vested in the mission and that they ought to speak up." Ashesi's former Human Resources Manager observed that GVV helps employees become fully integrated: "Employees join Ashesi in part because of the mission and ethical posture, but when they have the experience of teaching GVV it becomes easier to understand how to apply it in real life."

Another theme that emerged from several interviews was the opportunity for mentoring relationships that develop as a result of teaching GVV. The former Human Resources Manager mentioned students from her class coming to seek advice on ethics challenges faced during their internships. Another staff member described a former student coming to discuss an ethics violation case they were caught up in due to being aware of a cheating incident but not reporting it. It was a difficult and anxious conversation, but the student learned from the experience, and even agreed to share the experience in the staff member's GVV section the next academic year. Finally, professionally for faculty, GVV can lead to avenues for academic research. One such example is a book chapter written by a faculty member using the GVV framework to promote anti-corruption practices in Africa (Kudonoo, 2019).

Beyond Ashesi University, impacts can be seen as alumni navigate the ethical terrain of their professional and personal lives, in the values and ethics programs initiated by alums within their organizations, and through the university's outreach programs which have recently included workshops for organizations interested in implementing GVV.

Insight into the impact of the GVV curriculum on graduates comes from those who return to campus to participate in the seminars and who share their personal Tale of Two Stories with each new batch of first year students. Alumni stories capture the wide range of values conflicts they encounter and for which they have considered whether and how to voice their values: gender discrimination and sexual harassment in the workplace, observing financial impropriety, requests to cover for shoddy or uncompleted work, issues around unmet contract obligations, colleagues taking credit for the work of others, requests to fudge earnings or sales figures, request to pad the true cost of inputs passed on to customers, conflicts around gifts or other requests for special treatment by customers, requests for bribes from tax officials, work delays and other unspoken requests for kickbacks, to name a few. In a number of cases, alumni have spoken about ethics programs they have initiated within their own ventures and organizations. One example which specifically draws on GVV is alumna Yawa Hansen-Quao, who, as Executive Director of Emerging Public Leaders, a two-year fellowship program for emerging public sector leaders in Ghana and Liberia, has implemented GVV as part of the training for fellows. Her team is working on writing cases specifically for the public sector context.

Ashesi University hosts several outreach programs aimed at broadening its impact which include elements of GVV. The *Ashesi Innovation Experience* (AIX) is a summer program for high school students which includes scripting and roleplaying GVV-type cases as part of the program's youth leadership module. The Ashesi University *Deep Dive* is held over three days each October and brings together individuals from governmental, non-governmental, philanthropic, business, and academic institutions, from within and outside of Ghana, who wish to gain a deeper understanding of the university's work. After a brief introduction to the curriculum, visitors join current students in developing scripts and roleplaying GVV cases. Participants in Ashesi's Deep Dive have included university presidents and deans from top liberal arts colleges and historically black colleges in the US.

Finally, the *Education Collaborative* is a community of practice for education practitioners across the African continent hosted by Ashesi University. In July 2020, the Education Collaborative offered its first GVV virtual training for 20 participants from NGOs and education institutions in Ghana, Sierra Leone, and USA. As part of the virtual training, participants developed scripts in Zoom breakout rooms and presented their roleplays through video. This training supported the implementation of GVV in two low-cost private schools run by EducAid in Sierra Leone and for the Emerging Public Leaders fellowship program mentioned earlier, among other organizations. The Education Collaborative recently offered small grants of up to $500 for organizations who participated in the training to develop GVV cases relevant to their sectors and contexts. In addition, an effort is underway to develop a hybrid online course tailored to the African context. The aim is to make GVV accessible to a wider audience in Africa and to offer more faculty and staff at Ashesi University the opportunity to benefit from the content, even if they are unable to teach.

Conclusion

Although it was easy to recognize back in 2009 when I first heard Dr. Gentile speak at the Ethics in Higher Education Symposium at Bentley University, that GVV could be a useful tool for students in upholding Ashesi University's newly adopted examination honor code, what I realize ten years on is that GVV also became a means to rally a young institution around its larger mission of impacting ethical leadership in Africa. Having a strong ethical compass and knowing how to effectively steer oneself and others toward what is right is the vision not just for the students who learn and graduate from the institution, but for staff and faculty who work here, alumni, members of the board, and other stakeholders as well. Clarifying one's values, learning how to effectively speak up and act in accordance with one's values, and gaining the confidence to do so, is a process — a process that is supported by the tools of GVV, learning from the success and failures of putting them into practice, and importantly from the encouragement that comes from having many people involved in the project.

References

Blackwell, L. S., Trzesniewski, K. H., & Dweck, C. S. (2007). Implicit theories of intelligence predict achievement across an adolescent transition: A longitudinal study and an intervention. *Child Development, 78*(1), 246–263. https://doi.org/10.1111/j.1467-8624.2007.00995.x

Burger, N. E., Kopf, D., Spreng, C. P., Yoong, J., & Sood, N. (2012). Healthy firms: Constraints to growth among private health sector facilities in Ghana and Kenya. *PLoS ONE, 7*(2), 1–9. https://doi.org/10.1371/journal.pone.0027885

Dweck, C. S. (2006). *Mindset: The new psychology of success*. New York, NY: Random House.

Gentile, M. C. (2010a). *Giving voice to values: How to speak your mind when you know what's right*. New Haven, CT: Yale University Press.

Gentile, M. C. (2010b). *Starting assumptions for giving voice to values*. Retrieved from www.GivingVoicetoValues.org

Gentile, M. C. (2013). *Educating for values-driven leadership: Giving voice to values across the curriculum*. New York, NY: Business Expert Press. https://doi.org/10.1007/978-3-642-28036-8_136

Hong, Y., Chiu, C., & Dweck, C. S. (1999). Implicit theories, attributions, and coping: A meaning system approach. *Journal of Personality and Social Psychology*, 77(3), 588–599. https://doi.org/10.1080/15298860600823864

Kolb, D. A. (1984). *Experiential learning: Experience as the source of learning and development*. Upper Saddle River, N.J.: Prentice Hall.

Kudonoo, E. C. (2019). Personal responsibility and public accountability approach to anti-corruption education in Sub-Saharan Africa. In A. Stachowicz-Stanusch & W. Amann (Eds.), *Anti-corruption in management research and business school classrooms* (pp. 95–115). Charlotte, NC: Information Age Publishing.

Kurer, O. (1993). Clientelism, corruption, and the allocation of resources. *Public Choice*, 77(2), 259–273. https://doi.org/10.1007/BF01047869

McLaughlin, E., & Pfister, A. (2018). Equipping African medical students with ethical decision-making skills: A case-based method from Burundi. *Christian Journal for Global Health*, 5(3), 23–28. https://doi.org/10.15566/cjgh.v5i3.229

Pring, C., & Vrushi, J. (2019). Global Corruption Barometer – Africa 2019: Citizens' views and experiences of corruption (p. 64). *Transparency International, Afrobarometer*. Retrieved from www.afrobarometer.org/publications/global-corruption-barometer-africa-2019-citizens-views-and-experiences-corruption

Rossouw, G. J. (2011). Business ethics as field of teaching, training and research in Sub-Saharan Africa. *Journal of Business Ethics*, 104(1), 83–92. https://doi.org/10.1007/s10551-012-1265-y

Silberman, M. (1996). *Active learning: 101 strategies to teach any subject*. Boston, MA: Allyn and Bacon.

UNESCO Institute for Statistics (UIS). Retrieved July 15, 2020, from http://data.uis.unesco.org

Yeager, D. S., & Dweck, C. S. (2012). Mindsets that promote resilience: When students believe that personal characteristics can be developed. *Educational Psychologist*, 47(4), 302–314. https://doi.org/10.1080/00461520.2012.722805

Zull, J. E. (2002). *The art of changing the brain*. Sterling, VA: Stylus Publishing, LLC.

Part II

STRENGTHENING THE IMPACT OF GVV BEYOND HIGHER EDUCATION

8

GIVING VOICE TO VALUES IN THE LEGAL INDUSTRY

Carolyn Plump

Introduction

The Giving Voice to Values (GVV) framework established by Dr. Mary C. Gentile[1] is most often utilized in educational settings with business students. In 2018, I authored a book entitled *Giving Voice to Values in the Legal Profession: Effective Advocacy with Integrity.*[2] The purpose of the book was to encourage law students and law practitioners to utilize the GVV framework in legal practice. GVV holds tremendous promise for the legal industry. Too often a lawyer's singular focus on the confines of the law obscures the purpose and ethical implications behind such laws.

After a brief overview of the GVV framework, this chapter examines the traditional approach lawyers adopt when providing legal advice and resolving internal challenges, explains how contemporary times call for a broader approach to such matters, and examines real-life scenarios in which lawyers have successfully used a GVV methodology, often without even realizing it. By integrating the GVV framework into their legal toolkit, the next generation of lawyers can better advise clients and address organizational issues in a comprehensive, practical, and ethical manner.

GVV overview

Although it is rare to be able to immediately and completely change the actions of our peers or an organization, the GVV approach allows us to achieve incremental improvements and to strengthen our moral muscle by preparing scripts and voicing our values. Preparing effective scripts requires us to anticipate justifications we might encounter when we express our views. While these rationalizations can be complicated and varied, they are somewhat predictable, allowing us to prepare responses in advance to counter them. It is crucial to recognize such justifications before they act to silence us or permit us to disengage from the consequences of unethical behavior. Four of the most common rationalizations are: (1) standard practice/status quo, (2) materiality, (3) locus of responsibility, and (4) locus of loyalty.[3]

But simply anticipating reactions is not enough. We also must develop strategies for responding to these justifications. In the GVV context, strategies are a set of methods designed to accomplish a particular outcome. The precise outcome will depend on the particular situation, although all situations involve voicing our values in the workplace. "Voice" is a metaphor for many actions rather than about literal "voice" and can take a variety of forms including gathering data and research, reframing issues or presenting alternatives, asking probing questions to clarify positions, identifying key decision-makers, finding allies or working through others, reflecting back what others say, or building an action plan.

Before deciding on a strategy, it is also instrumental to consider the audience, reflect on one's communication style, gather data, chart a series of steps, and recognize risks. These factors guide us in determining the appropriate strategy. The four main GVV strategies are: (1) reframing, (2) bridging the gap, (3) building coalitions, and (4) listening. In the real-life examples that follow, we will examine the common justifications and consider each of the strategies.

Legal industry: the traditional approach for advising clients

Businesses hire attorneys to provide legal advice. Perhaps unsurprisingly, attorneys usually advise their clients on the parameters of the law alone.

This occurs for two reasons: (1) law school teaches students to focus on identifying legal issues and applying "black-letter" law to those issues, and (2) lawyers often conflate effective advocacy with winning at all costs. Because law students' and practitioners' primary focus is on what the law is rather than what it does, ethical considerations – if discussed at all – are often relegated to a minor sidebar or an afterthought following a public backlash or a private lawsuit. This pattern of advising clients solely on the legality of an action has led to troubling results as even a cursory review of the news will confirm.

Legal industry: an innovative approach to advising clients

The traditional approach in the legal industry has been: determine what the law is, find a way to fit what your client wants to do within the bounds of the law, and recommend that course of action. The following four reasons explain why lawyers would be well served to adopt a more innovative approach to counseling clients – an approach that requires lawyers to thoroughly consider and communicate ethical implications to their clients.

First, and quite simply, it is the morally just approach. Although the question of whether a particular action is legal must always be a consideration, it should not be the sole consideration. Laws and legal actions can be unethical. It is incumbent on attorneys to examine more than an action's legality to ensure ethical decisions. The profession can be, and must be, better than a mere recitation of existing laws. Given that lawyers are intimately involved with many aspects of business, they are in an optimal position to help shape business decisions and to ensure that ethical considerations become part of corporate discussions. Viewed from this perspective, the law can be a starting point for a more robust, comprehensive, and meaningful conversation that includes ethical considerations.

Second, given the exponential growth in corporate social responsibility (CSR) and transparency over the last decade, attorneys arguably have a duty to look beyond the black letter of the law. By finding ways to use their voices to influence how businesses act and to encourage clients to incorporate values assessments into their legal decisions, attorneys can provide opportunities for consideration of multiple stakeholders and nuanced decisions. Thus, a GVV approach helps align business decisions with CSR principles.

Third, there are significant costs for failing to anticipate or examine the consequences of unethical business decisions. For example, there are financial costs – litigation expenses, loss of customers, and harm to a company's brand. Unethical decisions also can cause a company to experience internal strife – difficulty in hiring or retaining employees, lower productivity, and harm to workplace culture. Finally, there can be intangible costs – damage to employee morale, harm to individual wellbeing, or a permanent stigma that follows an executive or an attorney.

Finally, stakeholders are demanding socially responsible decisions. Customers and clients want to conduct business with ethical companies and ethical people. They want to ensure their dollars are spent on companies that strive to ensure a positive impact on the world. While the American Bar Association's Model Rules of Professional Conduct contain guidelines that relate to ethical behavior there is still significant room for interpretation and not all ethical situations can possibly be addressed.

Legal industry: the traditional approach to resolving internal law firm issues

Law firms – like all organizations – experience internal strife. While lawyers are skilled at writing legal briefs, making cogent arguments in court, and advocating for their clients, they are not always equally adept at handling internal disputes or managing people. The traditional approach has been to wait until someone complains about an issue or brings a lawsuit before acting. Recent headlines reveal blue-chip law firms embroiled in disputes ranging from sexual harassment[4] to pay equity[5] and discrimination.[6] All can agree that reacting after the fact is not the most effective method. Often these issues are the result of smaller inequities or injustices that go unchecked or unchallenged for years, growing into substantial and intractable matters that harm firm culture, tarnish organizational integrity, and diminish the profession.

Legal industry: an innovative approach to resolving internal law firm issues

Even though lawyers initially may lack some of the skills to address internal issues, that does not mean they cannot learn them. This is where the

GVV framework proves useful. The same reasons it is important to adopt the GVV framework for advising clients apply to resolving internal matters. Further, consider the perception of a firm defending a client against pay disparity claims when it is itself entangled in a lawsuit involving such a claim. Stakeholders no longer tolerate this type of hypocritical behavior. The examples that follow provide insight into how firms can incorporate GVV to address their own internal issues.

Real-life examples of GVV in practice

To envision what voicing one's values in the legal industry might look like, we will consider six real-life situations.[7] These examples outline common issues that arise when advising clients or managing a law firm. Adopting a GVV approach helps lawyers consider the broader implications of the law.

The approaches the protagonists take in the following examples are neither perfect nor the only solution. Similarly, the approaches may not work in every situation. Instead, the purpose of including these real-life, imperfect examples is to demonstrate what acting on your values *might* look like and to provide assurance that it can be done.

Examples: advising clients

Scenario I: The Conflicted General Counsel
GVV Rationalization: Everyone Does It So It Must Be Okay
GVV Strategy: Bridging the Gap

Alexander Marino works for a large, multinational investment firm. One day while meeting with his team at the company's Midwest office, they discussed upcoming projects. One project involved work with a new client. The project involved appraising a portfolio for potential investment in a project. The team wanted to work on the project because the prospective client (Client) had an excellent reputation, massive capital reserves, and significant influence in the industry. Working on the project would undoubtably be lucrative and prestigious and expand the firm's client base.

There was, however, a complication – it had been widely reported in the news that the Client recently took a controversial position on a racially charged event. The international community responded with immediate condemnation of the Client's stance. The team worried, among other things, that working on the project may negatively impact the financial wellbeing of the company's portfolio if the media, clients, investors, and other stakeholders reacted negatively to the firm's new Client.

As the team debated the issue, they bandied about a variety of responses including: the practice is lawful; the connection between the representation of the new Client and the harm to the existing portfolio is too tenuous; and existing clients may never learn about the company's work. The response that garnered the most support was that other investment firms frequently partnered with or invested in projects where their clients faced allegations of human rights violations and other egregious charges. One team member claimed it was the norm in the industry and then joked, "If we turned away clients with controversial backgrounds we wouldn't have any clients." He ended with a comment that it was standard to consider only the terms of the project rather than the client's behavior. In GVV terms, this rationalization is known as the status quo response. The argument assumes that an action is acceptable simply because the majority of the people engage in it or because it is something that has been done for a long period of time. Many of us regularly fall prey to the allure of this rationalization.

As the company's Chief Legal Officer, Alexander had to make the final decision – a decision which not only had consequences for the current project, but also set a precedent for future projects. Although he knew he was uncomfortable moving forward with the new Client, he was unsure how to move forward given his unease about investing with the Client, his need to protect existing clients from any fallout, and his desire to retain the lucrative opportunity.

The next morning as Alexander entered the building, he looked up to see the company's mission etched on the stone façade in the atrium. He had walked past the inscription countless times without paying it much heed. Today, however, one of the words caught his attention. Integrity. The word resonated with him. The action his team proposed was not in line with the company's mission or his own integrity. He went back to his team and reminded them of the company's mission. He charged them with finding an alternate solution that would allow the company to maintain the firm's integrity. Ultimately, the team decided to refer the Client to an independent fiduciary to appraise the Client's portfolio. Although the company would lose the fees it would still receive a referral fee from the independent fiduciary and the Client would still receive excellent service. When the team pitched this idea to the Client, the Client was grateful for the firm's forthright disclosure and its loyalty to its existing clients.

The strategy Alexander utilized is one of four common strategies espoused by Dr. Gentile. The strategy is called bridging the gap. Bridging the gap refers to making a connection between a company's overall mission and the action you propose. By looking at the potential ramifications of his team's actions and realigning them with the company's mission, the team developed a new solution. The new solution was superior to the original plan and solidified the new Client's trust, protected existing client's interests, and aligned with the company's values. Simply operating on autopilot based on standard industry practices may be expedient, but it is rarely the best action.

Scenario II: When Cultures Collide
GVV Rationalization: Locus of Responsibility
GVV Strategy: Building Coalitions

In April 2019, the nation of Brunei announced it would implement strict new Islamic laws requiring, among other things, the death sentence for homosexual acts.[8] The action prompted immediate, widespread condemnation from the United Nations, international rights groups, transnational companies, and celebrities.[9] It also posed an ethical dilemma for companies doing business with Brunei and Sultan Hassanal Bolkiah.

One such instance involved Keira Coric, General Counsel of an international oil company. Given Brunei's substantial oil and gas reserves, Keira's company had significant financial interests in maintaining a good professional working relationship with Brunei. Yet it struggled with the new law and worried about shareholder and customer reactions.

Keira and her department held various in-house talks about how to proceed. During these sessions the team members uniformly denounced the law punishing homosexual acts with death. Nonetheless, many sought to distance the company from any responsibility for conducting business in the country by pointing to the fact that Brunei, not the company, instituted the practice. GVV refers to this common rationalization as locus of responsibility. Locus of responsibility refers to our sense of who we think should act in a situation or who is requiring us to act in a situation. It is commonly expressed by phrases such as, "It is not my problem" or "I'm just following orders." Individuals often employ this reason to abdicate responsibility by asserting they are not the appropriate ones to handle the situation or do not possess the requisite authority to remedy the issue. It often signals a certain amount of discomfort with the situation and an attempt to deflect taking action. It is appealing because it seems to "let people off the hook."

This rationalization can be particularly insidious because it allows people to opt for inaction rather than face difficult conversations and decisions. Despite the temptation to take the easiest route out and ignore the dilemma, Keira decided to act on her values. Before she could do this, she needed to consider how to present her concerns by considering her audience, determining the appropriate communication style, gathering additional data, charting incremental steps, and considering possible risks.

Her initial audience was her in-house legal team. It was a group of highly motivated, hard-working professionals. While she always encouraged their input, they would take their cues from her. She needed to be transparent about her misgivings and seek candid feedback. She decided the best way to elicit feedback on such a sensitive matter was to do so in person. She also knew her team needed data to consider all options. Accordingly, she gathered financial information on the company's contracts with Brunei (e.g., the amount of the contracts, when they expired, the projected financial impact of not renewing them), the cost of securing alternative oil and gas, the number of other oil and gas companies doing business in Brunei, and the potential impact to the company's brand and its various stakeholders. Keira envisioned a three-step process involving meeting with her team to decide on a strategy, recommending a course of action to the board, and communicating the decision (with input from the marketing department) to Brunei. The risks were substantial. It could mean the loss of millions of dollars in business, harm to the company's relationship with Brunei, and loss of jobs for her and her legal team depending on the backlash. She needed to be forthright with her team about all of these risks.

Confident in the knowledge she had a roadmap, Keira reconvened her legal team. The team engaged in a comprehensive discussion on the legal, financial, and ethical implications of continuing to do business with Brunei. Although no one had raised any ethical concerns in the team's prior meeting, the team whole-heartedly voiced concerns at this subsequent meeting. Keira attributed this to giving the team "permission" to incorporate such considerations into the decision-making process by voicing her values. If she had remained silent, she never would have known how many people held similar views but were fearful of expressing them.

After several days, the group settled on a plan of action. They knew from news reports that many groups had concerns about Brunei's policy. They also had data on the number of companies doing business in Brunei. They decided to collaborate with outside groups to determine how to move forward. GVV refers to this strategy as building coalitions. It centers on the idea of finding allies inside and outside one's organization to help further a cause. It can be a powerful strategy when the stakes of acting alone have significant risks or repercussions.

In this instance, it proved to be an effective strategy given the willing support of other oil and gas companies, businesses in the hospitality industry, political institutions and leaders, and celebrities. Keira's company helped organize the coalition. Given the substantial financial and political influence of the coalition, and the widespread public criticism, Sultan Bolkiah eventually announced a moratorium on the death penalty.[10]

While Keira was pleased with the result, she remained troubled that Brunei had not made changes to other strict punishments including whipping women convicted of lesbian acts.[11] Ultimately, she decided the company would honor its existing contracts, but would not renew those contracts or enter into any new contracts with Brunei going forward unless it changed various policies. To date, the oil company has not entered into any new contracts because of Keira's continuing concerns over Brunei's violations of international human rights.

Later, when reflecting on the outcome, Keira realized the Brunei coalition could be called on to help address other issues. This was another important consequence of voicing her values that had ramifications for future decisions. It also reminded her that success in one situation does not relieve her from acting the next time, and that voicing her values is a continuing process that takes practice.

Scenario III: Never Side Outside the Family
GVV Rationalization: Locus of Loyalty
GVV Strategy: Reframing

Micah Gallucci is a partner of a Northeast law firm. One of his clients, a Forbes 500 company, contacted him for legal advice about firing a high-ranking employee. The company's General Counsel was incensed that his employee provided a favorable reference to one of her subordinates seeking to leave the company for another position. The General Counsel was frustrated that the management employee took a position he saw as contrary to the best interests of the company by "helping" one of its employees leave the company. He felt the supervisor's action demonstrated a lack of loyalty to the company. He felt he had ample legal grounds to fire the employee but wanted Micah's opinion because the employee had recently requested family and medical leave.

If Micah limited himself to reciting the law, he would have advised the company that it had a legally sound basis for firing the employee – there was an objective reason for terminating her that had no relationship to her request for medical leave. Micah felt, however, that an approach that incorporated ethical considerations would result in a better decision. Having worked for decades with the General Counsel, Micah recognized the General Counsel's reaction that the employee was disloyal. GVV refers to it as a locus of loyalty argument. This rationalization assumes that loyalty to one group necessarily means disloyalty to another group. In this instance, the General Counsel saw the manager's loyalty to the departing employee as disloyalty to the company. Examples of this argument abound in popular media. In the Godfather II, Al Pacino's character Michael Corleone says, "Fredo, you're my older brother, and I love you. But don't ever take sides with anyone against the family again. Ever."[12]

Micah decided to adopt a GVV strategy called reframing to respond to his client's concerns. Reframing involves stepping out of your current view and embodying the opposing view, searching for common ground among the principles each side shares, and creating a new frame of reference rooted in shared principles. Micah asked the General Counsel to consider the supervisor's view. If she knew the employee was unhappy and was going to leave the company with or without the supervisor's help, helping the employee would allow for a departure on good terms. This could have various positive repercussions for the company: a smoother transition for the department without harm to morale; the employee's willingness to hire and to train a replacement; possible future referrals of business from the departing employee; avoidance of litigation (both over refusing to provide a reference or for firing an employee after she requested leave); and respecting the autonomy of managers and employees to make decisions. Finally, given that the supervisor was scheduled to take leave for the birth of her child, Micah felt a mechanical application of the law failed to consider the implications firing her had for the employee – she would be without a job or healthcare shortly before giving birth. When Micah framed the issue in terms of a loyalty to all employees – including departing employees – and the long-term interests of the company the General Counsel agreed with the advice. Rather than fire the supervisor, he worked to improve work conditions, develop a uniform policy on references, and implement annual feedback from all employees to surface concerns and improve retention.

Scenario IV: You Want To Do What!
GVV Rationalization: Materiality/Legality
GVV Strategy: Listening

A partner named Ashley Gershmen works in the West Coast office of an international law firm. Several years ago, the firm's managing partner asked her to work on a high profile case for a client. Software Inc. (Client) had been hired by an automotive company to manufacture software that regulated emissions similar to the now infamous defeat devices that Volkswagen produced to avoid detection on car exhaust emission tests.[13] The Client told Ashley that the device would only change the emissions readings by an incremental amount. It wanted assurance that this minor adjustment was legal so it could accept the lucrative project. The Client also informed her that its own in-house legal department concluded the device was legal because European law allowed automakers to use such software if it was necessary to improve durability or protect the engine from harm. The Client wanted to exploit this area of the law and it wanted a second opinion from Ashley regarding its legality. Interestingly, Ashley learned some time after she represented the Client that this was the same argument Volkswagen initially used to justify its practice.[14]

Clients often employ this type of reasoning when seeking advice. It was a variation on what GVV refers to as materiality. Materiality refers to the argument that an action is insubstantial, does not hurt anyone, or does not make a difference to the long-term outcome. Framing the question in terms of materiality shifts the focus from the action to some external method of measurement. In this instance, the Client was trying to use a materiality argument – it adjusted the emissions reading an incremental amount – to justify engine improvements so it could accept the contract. It also tried to argue that because it was legal it was acceptable.

Ashley felt confident she could construct a nuanced legal argument to justify the Client's position. Although she knew this is what her Client wanted, it did not sit well with her. The question that remained was how to voice her values without alienating her Client. Due to confidentiality concerns, Ashley did not have an option to build coalitions with outside groups. Similarly, bridging the gap did not appear to be a strategy because the Client already communicated it wanted to accept the work. While reframing might be an option, she worried the Client would feel she was imposing her values on its business decision. She finally decided to ask additional questions, a strategy that proved effective with other clients. Ashley was confident that by positing questions to clarify, probe, summarize, and reflect on the Client's strategy she could expose the unethical and troubling nature of the approach. This would allow the Client to reconsider the strategy and work with her to arrive at a mutually acceptable solution.

Ashley asked whether the company had conducted a stakeholder analysis to determine the potential consequences the decision may have on others. She inquired about the company's tolerance for risk. A high-risk tolerance might justify actions that could result in harm to brand, decrease in stock value, negative publicity, and legal fees while a low risk tolerance would not.

Finally, she explored the reaction of the team tasked with completing the work. An interesting byproduct of these questions was that it prompted the executives to reconsider their initial position. The act of answering questions and reflecting on the responses – even within the safe confines of a private, attorney-client discussion – made the Client so uncomfortable he realized it would be impossible to take this position publicly under intense media scrutiny. The company declined the project. Years later, after the VW scandal broke, the Client recalled the session with Ashley and thanked her for helping it arrive at the best decision. The company remains a client of her firm to this day.

Examples: addressing internal matters within law firms

There are myriad examples of sexual harassment, pay disparity, and discrimination within law firms. One of the most recent involves allegations by three female attorneys detailing instances of sexual assault, harassment, and retaliation at DLA Piper – one of the world's largest law firms with lawyers in over 40 countries – by former male partner Louis Lehot.[15] Rather than recite similar situations, the scenarios that follow focus on more subtle forms of misconduct that are often overlooked or minimized. While these examples do not garner attention-grabbing headlines or result in litigation, the behavior nonetheless is problematic because it can signal a toxic culture, foster tolerance for mistreatment, or embolden more egregious conduct.

Scenario V: Giving Credit Where Credit Is Due
GVV Rationalization: Status Quo/Inherent Law Firm Structure
GVV Strategies: Research and Building Coalitions

Luciana Fernandez was a new litigation associate at the firm Mackenzie & Cook (Firm). She quickly obtained a reputation as one of the top first year associates in her class. Partners asked her to work on their cases because of her superior research skills, excellent reasoning, and insightful perspectives. One partner, Simon Davidson, represented the law firm Knight & Smith (Client) in a gender discrimination case.

Simon asked Luciana to prepare a motion for summary judgment (Motion). He explained that the case was a high profile one that would set a precedent for other cases involving the same firm. Over the next month, Luciana spent 60 hours researching and drafting the motion. Simon spent 30 minutes reviewing the Motion and making some minor editorial changes and then filed it with the court. He commended

Luciana's work and stated that he hoped they would be able to strike out a few of the claims.

The week of the oral argument, Luciana spent ten hours preparing materials for Simon's oral argument. She then met with him for 30 minutes to highlight the relevant cases, discuss the main points, and conduct a dry run of the argument.

Ultimately, the judge granted the Client's Motion on all ten claims, citing the compelling arguments and substantial precedent cited in the brief. The Client was ecstatic.

After the judge announced her ruling, Simon, Luciana, and the Client celebrated over lunch. The Client complimented the extensive research and creative arguments. Simon thanked the Client, but made no reference to the work Luciana did. Indeed, when the Client implied that Luciana's role was limited to finding the appropriate documents requested in the courtroom, Simon did not disabuse the Client of the notion.

The next week Luciana had her first-year evaluation. She received great feedback from everyone, including Simon, but she noticed that Simon had not commented on her extensive work on the discrimination case that resulted in an unprecedented victory. She also learned after reviewing the monthly client bills that Simon had written off most of her time on the case – the bill now stated that she did only ten hours of work rather than 70 hours. Most surprisingly, the bill now recorded Simon as doing 30 hours of work rather than one hour.

Luciana was discouraged that the Client was unaware of her work and Simon took credit for her work – both of which could negatively impact her career advancement, compensation, additional opportunities, and professional reputation.

Luciana knew she needed to speak up, both to address her own sense of fairness and to ensure her work was recognized for purposes of compensation and advancement. Simon was an influential and well-respected rainmaker at the Firm. Therefore, before discussing the matter with him, she decided to conduct research on the Firm's policies and practices. She learned from both the human resources department and a senior associate that partners sometimes write off hours by junior associates if they feel the time spent was longer than necessary or is a training cost the Firm should absorb rather than a client (e.g., having an attorney sit in on a deposition to observe what happens). However, partners are never permitted to add time to a case if they did not actually work those hours. Luciana also consulted with her mentor at the Firm – another partner. Her mentor supported Luciana raising the issue and even offered to advocate on her behalf at the partners' meeting. The two of them then practiced role-playing Luciana's conversation with Simon.

Luciana arranged to meet with Simon in his office. She knew the best approach with Simon was to be direct, so she presented the points she had rehearsed with her mentor. Simon justified his actions based on the Firm's hierarchical structure – the associates did work for the partners and the partners were the face of the Firm. He claimed it was common for partners to write off associate hours, handle the oral arguments, and take the lead with clients. Luciana explained that while she agreed with those points, increasing his time on the timesheets was not a practice sanctioned by the Firm. She also explained that allowing the Client to believe Simon did all the work and not acknowledging her role on her evaluation could harm her reputation, or at least not help her. He responded that the timesheets changes did not result in additional charges to the client because 60 hours of her time cost the same as 30 hours of his time. Luciana reiterated that the Firm does not condone adding time regardless of whether the overall cost is the same. In addition, it diminished her role. Further, it could leave partners with the impression she was inefficient (they see the write offs each month) or had time to work on their projects despite her claims she was busy.

Although Simon was not particularly receptive to her feedback, Luciana accomplished various important changes by voicing her values. By conducting research, building coalitions, and practicing her script, Luciana ensured Simon did not engage in the conduct again; she received the recognition she deserved at the partners' meeting (albeit the Client remained unaware); she paved the way for others to speak up regarding workplace inequities; she protected the firm from unauthorized billing practices; and she gained experience about advocating for herself. While the work environment was somewhat tense for several months after this encounter, it eventually resulted in a better working relationship between Luciana, Simon, and the other attorneys. Simon acknowledged that he respected the professional way Luciana had handled the situation, learned to see his actions from another's perspective, and developed better case management skills for all matters going forward.

Scenario VI: Doing What It Takes to Win
GVV Rationalization: It Is for the Greater Good
GVV Strategy: Listening

Jennifer Ambrose was a senior associate in the labor and employment department of Scheel & Post (Firm). Jennifer would be going up for partner the following year. She was well regarded, and most felt her candidacy would sail through the approval process. Jennifer just announced to the firm that she was three months pregnant with her third child. Assuming everything went well with her pregnancy, she expected to work until her due date that May.

One of the partners, Ellen Borkowski, was defending her client in a pregnancy discrimination case. The client was a transnational corporation (Client). The parties were unable to settle the matter, and the trial was set for February.

Ellen and Jennifer had never worked together. Ellen had a group of five attorneys with whom she preferred to work. Nonetheless, Ellen asked Jennifer to be second chair on the upcoming pregnancy discrimination trial. Jennifer thought this was odd because the attorneys Ellen typically worked with were all available. She could not help but wonder if Ellen asked her because she would be six months pregnant at the time of the trial. She decided to ask. Ellen smiled and said, "Well it had crossed my mind that we would seem more sympathetic to the jury if one of the attorneys defending the Client was a pregnant woman." Jennifer's face registered disappointment. Ellen quickly added, "I also think it would be good for us to work together before you are up for partner."

Jennifer left Ellen's office quite discouraged. She had seen the Firm employ this tactic before, trotting out attorneys based on their race, gender, sexual orientation, religion, or ethnicity when it was convenient to help a client's case or the Firm's brand. She did not want to be part of it. Yet, she worried if she did not, it would hurt her chances of becoming partner. Also, it was a great opportunity to get trial experience.

Jennifer decided she would decline the assignment, but she needed to proceed with caution, especially given her partnership candidacy.

Although she could claim it was due to her workload, she knew that reason was disingenuous and easily remedied. She decided to be direct and candid – she was uncomfortable working on the case because she was being asked to do so based on her pregnancy. She set about writing out a script anticipating justifications and outlining possible actions.

Ellen would most likely claim Jennifer was not being a team player. Jennifer could counter that the jury might view Jennifer's presence as a thinly veiled attempt to garner sympathy. This could offend the jury and backfire on the Client. If she was needed on the case, she could assist behind the scenes by preparing motions, conducting research, and preparing witnesses.

In addition to anticipating responses, Jennifer could gather data to support her position. Most large firms work with jury consultants on high profile cases. Jennifer could enlist the help of a jury consultant the Firm used in the past. She could also draw on examples from the media or past cases to see if there were repercussions for similar approaches.

Finally, Jennifer could ask Ellen probing questions. For example, how would she respond to a question from a reporter about why Jennifer was on the case? Would she feel comfortable employing this tactic when it involved race, religion, or ethnicity? How would Ellen feel if she or her daughter were asked to work on a project solely because of their gender? Is the Firm willing to risk potential backlash? Would the decision hinder the Firm's diversity efforts? Could she obtain input from the Firm's affinity groups? Would having Jennifer on the case make the Client look desperate – as if the Client cannot win on the merits? These types of questions could uncover weaknesses in Ellen's original idea and lead her to the same conclusion.

Now that she had her script containing responses to possible justifications, data to support her decision, and a list of questions to prompt further reflection, Jennifer was ready to meet with Ellen. Jennifer began the meeting by agreeing that it would be great for the two of them to work together. Next, she discussed the data she collected from the Firm's jury consultants and cited several examples of similar tactics backfiring with the media. She used these data to solicit Ellen's thoughts about whether having Jennifer at counsel's table could have the opposite effect on the jury. Ellen seemed receptive to the data and examples Jennifer presented so Jennifer continued with additional questions to encourage Ellen to reconsider her position. Jennifer concluded the discussion by stating that she assumed Ellen would want time to consider the new information before deciding.

Jennifer knew she needed to provide a way for Ellen to "save face." Jennifer did this by giving Ellen time to reflect on the information rather than demanding an immediate response. Her approach also allowed Ellen to feel in control of the decision (even though Jennifer knew she was going to refuse to be second chair). Finally, Jennifer intentionally used the "new information" to provide Ellen with a way to reconsider her initial position without having to admit to herself or others that her initial decision was flawed. Ellen announced several days later that – based on new information from the Firm's jury consultants – she decided to have another attorney second chair the trial. She asked Jennifer to oversee the trial preparation. When Jennifer went up for partner the following year, Ellen was one of her staunchest allies.

Key insights

These real-life examples reveal several key takeaways. First, GVV is an accessible framework. Individuals, departments, or organizations can utilize it to develop and to practice how to introduce values-based discussions into their decisions by considering one's audience, determining the appropriate communication style, gathering data, charting steps, and acknowledging potential risks. Second, the conversation does not end when someone offers resistance or counters with a justification. People often default to existing policies (i.e., status quo), minimize consequences (i.e., materiality), point to someone in the chain of command (i.e., locus of responsibility), or question one's loyalty (i.e., locus of loyalty). Advance preparation on how to respond to these common rationalizations can bolster confidence and improve success. Third, you do not have to "go it alone." One of the most important GVV strategies is finding allies (i.e., building coalitions). This can occur within an organization or outside an organization. It is more difficult for others to dismiss an idea or single out someone for ridicule or retaliation when the response comes from a group. Individuals or groups also can consider the problem from multiple perspectives (i.e., reframing), connect the decision to the organization's values or mission (i.e., bridging the gap), or pose questions and reflect ideas that highlight inconsistences (i.e., listening). These strategies defuse the situation and move away from moral preaching that can shut down conversations. A crucial aspect of using these strategies effectively is rehearsal. Practice helps build moral muscle memory, which makes it easier to speak up by normalizing acting on one's values. Finally, speaking up can have many positive results: making better decisions; influencing others to speak up; bringing awareness to a topic; helping change an organization's culture; putting a mechanism in place for raising questions; changing future conduct; increasing transparency; and providing practice. By looking at the value of speaking up in the broader context of what it means to do so successfully, it becomes easier to do.

Conclusion

The GVV framework represents an innovative approach to values conflicts in the workplace. Given the moral imperative to bring ethical considerations into the decision-making process, the rise of CSR, the financial consequences of failing to consider ethical issues, and client demands, the time is ripe for lawyers to incorporate values discussions when consulting with clients and managing internal workforce challenges. GVV provides an accessible way for lawyers to do this. By anticipating common reasons and rationalizations, devising strategies for responding to such reasons, and practicing prepared scripts, lawyers can better serve their clients and their firms. Perhaps most importantly, the public continues to be skeptical of the legal system and lawyers. Incorporating a GVV approach into legal analyses could provide a new way forward for the legal industry and bolster credibility and trust.

Notes

1 Gentile, M. (2010). *Giving voice to values: How to speak your mind when you know what's right.* Ann Arbor, MI: Yale University Press.
2 Plump, C. (2018). *Giving voice to values: Effective advocacy with integrity.* New York: Routledge.

3 Gentile, M. (2010). *Giving voice to values: How to speak your mind when you know what's right.* Ann Arbor, MI: Yale University Press.

4 Wells, P. (2018, February 22). Ogletree hit with sexual harassment lawsuit. *Bloomberg Law.* Retrieved from https://news.bloomberglaw.com/daily-labor-report/ogletree-hit-with-sexual-harassment-lawsuit

5 Wells, P. (2019, April 3). Jones Day accused by female lawyers of sex bias, unequal pay. *Bloomberg Law.* Retrieved from https://news.bloomberglaw.com/daily-labor-report/jones-day-accused-by-female-lawyers-of-sex-bias-unequal-pay-1

6 Weiss, D. (2018, August 13). Proskauer partner resolves her gender bias suit against the firm. *ABA Journal.* Retrieved from www.abajournal.com/news/article/proskauer_partner_resolves_her_gender_bias_suit_against_the_firm

7 All names have been changed to protect the identity of the people, companies, and law firms involved in these real-life scenarios. In some instances, facts from several companies have been compiled into a single scenario to further protect individual identification.

8 Tan, Y. (2019, April 3). Brunei implements stoning to death under anti-LGBT laws. *BBC News.* Retrieved from www.bbc.com/news/world-asia-47769964

9 Specia, M. (2019, April 12). Facing uproar, Brunei says stoning law is meant to "educate and nurture". *The New York Times.* Retrieved from www.nytimes.com/2019/04/12/world/asia/brunei-stoning-law-defense.html; Waterson, J. (2019, April 5). Companies abandon Brunei's Dorchester hotel over gay sex law. *The Guardian.* Retrieved from www.theguardian.com/world/2019/apr/05/brunei-dorchester-hotel-london-companies-cancel-events-gay-sex-law

10 Chappell, B. (2019, May 6). Brunei won't enforce death-by-stoning law for gay sex, Sultan say. *NPR.* Retrieved from www.npr.org/2019/05/06/720598000/brunei-wont-enforce-death-by-stoning-law-for-gay-sex-sultan-says

11 Emont, J. (2019, May 6). Brunei backs away from death penalty for gay sex. *The Wall Street Journal.* Retrieved from www.wsj.com/articles/brunei-extends-moratorium-on-capital-punishment-to-adultery-gay-sex-11557111546

12 Long, C. (2017, May 7). *Godfather quotes that prove you should never take sides against the family.* Retrieved from https://uproxx.com/movies/godfather-family-quotes/3/

13 Hotten, R. (2015, December 2015). Volkswagen: The scandal explained. *BBC News.* Retrieved from www.bbc.com/news/business-34324772

14 Cremer, A. (2016, November 3). VW says defeat device in conformity with European law. *Reuters.* Retrieved from www.reuters.com/article/us-volkswagen-

emissions-lawsuit/vw-says-defeat-device-in-conformity-with-european-law-idUSKBN12Y2VJ

15 Rubino, K. (2019, October 23). Third woman with allegations against former DLA Piper partner says he's a bully who called her a "dumb b*tch". *Above the Law*. Retrieved from https://abovethelaw.com/2019/10/third-woman-with-allegations-against-former-dla-piper-partner-says-hes-a-bully-who-called-her-a-dumb-btch/

9

IMPLEMENTING GIVING VOICE TO VALUES INTO THE WORKPLACE

Insights from the experience of four organizations

Jerry Goodstein

One of the most significant developments in ethics education within the past decade has been the emergence and growth of Giving Voice to Values (GVV). GVV has been introduced as an integral component of ethics education and training in over 1,200 educational settings and public, private, and non-profit organizations around the world. Of particular importance has been its expansion out of classrooms and into corporate settings.

Writing about the evolution of GVV into the workplace Gentile (2014, p. 182) noted,

> Although originally developed for use in management education settings, increasingly individual managers as well as companies have been attracted to the pragmatic and intuitive approach GVV offers for ethics training. GVV is distinguished by its emphasis on action and its plain-spoken acknowledgement that often the challenge is not a matter of employees' lack of knowledge concerning the relevant laws or ethical obligations, or of employees who want to be

unethical, but rather a matter of inconsistent organizational messages and employees' lack of skill and confidence in dealing with them. GVV is all about addressing this concern and helping individuals as well as organizations learn and practice how to voice their values when they know what's right.

This chapter focuses on the experiences of four organizations operating in diverse industries: Lockheed Martin (aerospace and defense), ProcessTech (name and industry intentionally disguised by request), the CFA Institute (professional training for investment professionals), and Prudential Insurance (insurance and other financial investment products). Their experience with GVV ranges from Lockheed Martin which was one of the first corporations to introduce GVV in 2011, to the CFA Institute, which more recently introduced GVV in 2017. Each of these organizations learned about GVV and worked closely with Mary C. Gentile to implement GVV, adopting a range of approaches that best fit the needs of their employees/members.

I spoke with representatives of these organizations, each of whom had been directly involved with leading the implementation of GVV into these organizations. John Heiser is currently CEO of LabVantage Inc. and held the position of CEO of ProcessTech when GVV was implemented in 2016. David Gebler and Blair Marks serve respectively as Senior Manager, Ethics Engagement and Integrated Education and Vice President, Ethics and Business Conduct for Lockheed Martin. Tony Tam is Director of Ethics Training for the CFA Institute. Royanne Roi served as Corporate Chief Ethics Officer for Prudential and was responsible for leading the effort to implement GVV worldwide within the organization. We spoke on average between 45 and 60 minutes, covering a series of questions included in the Appendix to this chapter. We explored a variety of broad topic areas, summarized next. Where possible I include quotes that reflect more directly the richness of the experience and insights of these leaders.

Why select GVV for ethics training?

An initial area of focus for the interviews was on the motivations for implementing GVV and the ways GVV was introduced into these organizations. A common thread connecting each of these four organizations was learning about GVV through their direct and indirect interaction with Mary. This happened in a variety of ways. John Heiser met Mary in 2015 while attending an executive PhD program at the Center for Values Driven Leadership at Benedictine University in Illinois. Mary was doing a presentation on GVV. As John listened to Mary he reflected on the early part of his career when he worked in the legal department and ethics was framed in terms of legal compliance. "I'm sitting here listening to Mary say 'Let's stop talking about is this right or wrong? – we know that for the most part. How do we allow ourselves to have a productive conversation when a values conflict comes up?' That's usually the problem." Following the presentation John caught up with Mary and told her, "You know Mary, you really touched me with your talk. I'd love to keep in contact with you. . . . We did."

What ultimately prompted John to follow up with Mary were some revealing discussions he had with employees at ProcessTech. After being named President, John traveled throughout the company conducting "skip level meetings" where John would "skip" front line managers and meet directly with employees. A number of employees raised concerns with John related to process improvement and pressures to move the product in ways that might compromise the quality of the manufacturing process. John was learning about these values conflicts coming up across the organization. "I said, you know what? Let me call Mary, because this to me is a true giving voice to values opportunity."

The inspiration for introducing GVV into Lockheed Martin came in 2010 when the then Vice President of Ethics learned about GVV and wanted to consider its potential for Lockheed Martin. The team reached out directly to Mary. While ethics training was already an integral component of employee training and development since the merger of the Lockheed Corporation and the Martin Marietta Corporation, Blair recalls, "What was new was adapting the GVV techniques into a framework for Lockheed Martin." The intent was to shift the emphasis in ethics training at Lockheed Martin from "what's wrong" to "focusing on what can you as an individual do about it if you see something happening and you know it's wrong . . . how do you speak up?" Blair and David recalled,

> The big shift that we were making was to really equip our workforce with the toolset so that they knew not just that's wrong and it

shouldn't happen, but here's what I can do about it to prevent that from becoming a problem.

Lockheed Martin renamed the initiative, "Voicing Our Values."

Tony Tam learned about GVV a number of years ago after reading *Giving Voice to Values* (Gentile, 2010). "I was intrigued by her approach to dealing with ethical dilemmas, which was focused really on doing things, rather than thinking about doing things." In 2017 Tony said he:

> was given the mandate to develop our ethics educational products for CFA Institute members globally. . . . I straight away thought of Mary's book and whether we could use her ideas and pedagogy as a way to provide education to our members relating to how to take action.

Tony indicated that CFA ethics training was focused on determining, "What is the right thing to do?" and he felt that many people "never get to the next stage of actually doing the right thing." Tony contacted Mary directly to learn more about GVV and was impressed with the broad adoption of GVV in so many corporations around the world.

Royanne met Mary the first year she became the Global Ethics Officer for Prudential Insurance. Mary was an invited speaker for an annual ethics day global leadership conference hosted at Prudential for senior leadership. Mary spoke to the Prudential leadership about GVV and impressed Royanne with its practical focus and its potential to be adapted at Prudential's worldwide locations. "I was so enamored with her Giving Voice to Values program that I decided I would try to have every Prudential employee, all 43,000 employees, take the course in some form."

In each of these organizations what seemed to be a primary motivation – what seemed to inspire these leaders – was the emphasis at the heart of GVV from thinking about the "right thing to do" to acting on one's values. It is also clear that learning about GVV from Mary and the personal connection with her made an important difference in deciding to implement GVV in these organizations.

Implementing GVV: strategies, enablers, and challenges

I was interested in learning more about how each organization implemented GVV in ways that fit with their unique goals and organizational structures and processes. I asked each representative to share with me how they approached implementing GVV into their organizations, as well as key enablers and challenges to implementation efforts. What emerged from these conversations were four distinct approaches.

John was looking for a way to implement GVV that would work with his global workforce which consisted of around 40–50 managers and 800 employees. He spoke with Mary about the potential of partnering with Nomadic, an organization that had worked with Mary to develop online GVV training materials for other corporations. John adopted "a three pronged approach" for ProcessTech where he was directly involved with each stage of implementation. The first step involved Mary introducing GVV to the senior leadership team and then meeting directly with these senior leaders. John then worked with Nomadic to develop an online "cohort based program" that could be delivered around the world. John noted, "We had the management team go through it, and then we did a live session with the management team, which I facilitated." The last stage of implementation involved live training sessions at all worldwide factory locations led by John,

> where we actually took the GVV learnings from the Nomadic plat-
> form, and made it specific to our company . . . I actually facilitated
> every single workshop that we did, which I think ultimately was
> about 10, because I had to do shifts at the factories.

Lockheed Martin utilized an in-person approach to implementing GVV into its existing ethics awareness training. Blair noted, "So ethics awareness training has always been one hour, once a year, for 100% of every of the employees, leader led." The in-person training was critical to Lockheed Martin. "Having the discussion with your supervisor and your peers is very powerful as opposed to an online course which can be very effective for knowledge transfer. But this goes deeper than knowledge transfer. It's really culture-based."

Lockheed Martin worked closely with Mary to develop online case studies and a "Voicing Our Values" process based on GVV principles and practices consisting of four key components: ask questions, obtain data, talk to others, and reframe the issue. If individuals are not able to resolve a particular conflict or if there is a serious compliance breach, then it is critical to take a fifth step and report violations (www.lockheedmartin.com/en-us/who-we-are/ethics/ethics-awareness-training.html).

Blair and David described the structure of the training:

> There are multiple cases every year. The leader of the room chooses the cases that are relevant for the group. You watch a first video that lays out a scenario, you stop for a discussion and we give you discussion questions, and then you come back with a closing video that typically is going to show, okay, what happened?

Blair and David emphasized the importance in these training sessions of having employees "talk about what did you see, how could this happen and how can we either prevent it or what do we do if that happens in our workspace?" Within these training sessions employees have an opportunity to talk about the issues raised in the videos and to generate and discuss different approaches to scripting, re-framing, and adopting different responses to conflicts shown in the videos.

Tony found himself with the challenge of implementing GVV into a widely dispersed professional association composed of 160 societies with about 160,000 members. Tony noted that the CFA does not have a mandatory ethics requirement for their continuing professional development program. He decided to introduce GVV to the membership by creating a customized Nomadic online training program called "GVV for Investment Professionals." He made the training publicly available to all CFA members on the member website and through a specific member app. Implementing GVV in this way, according to Tony, offered members another avenue to pursue in meeting their voluntary continuing professional development requirements,

> So those are probably the three approaches that we are using right now. One, is a general blast to members. Two, is working with regulatory bodies in certain parts of the world to get our product accredited and three, is to target the members who are active in doing voluntary CPD to get them to say this is another way to actually get your CPD credits (Continuing Professional Development).

Royanne highlighted a multi-stage process employed to introduce GVV (renamed "Voicing Our Values") into Prudential from 2014–2016.

> First of all, we had Mary at our annual ethics leadership conference, in order to ensure that our top leadership got to experience VOV training as individuals. We wanted to make sure that top management would be ready to receive 'voices' before we trained lower levels of the organization.

Following the introduction of VOV to Prudential's leadership, Royanne and her team began in-person training employees (groups of 35–150 employees) within the United States and in Japan, where more than half of Prudential's workforce was located. She worked with Prudential leaders in Japan and together they created 11 different customized case studies – specific to Japan business and culture. Early support from senior leaders was critical, including keynote speeches at the VOV training and participation in some of the VOV trainings from beginning to end. Support from employees was also strong. Royanne noted that evaluations of Prudential training in the US and overseas were quite positive with many employees giving 5-star YELP-like reviews and ratings of 96/100.

Royanne also traveled to South America and the European Union to provide in-person training to senior managers in various business lines (including asset management real estate investment). These leaders invited Royanne to all-day conferences and dedicated 1.5–2 hours during the conferences to provide VOV ethics training – further advancing ethics as an integral part of Prudential's business strategy.

In addition to face-to-face VOV training, Royanne designed and implemented a hybrid version of VOV within the largest subsidiary in Japan and in other regions of Prudential. This hybrid version included an independent video and worksheet component, with trainers facilitating complementary in-person discussions with employees. After three intensive years, Royanne eventually packaged the VOV hybrid training into an as-needed training course by creating a manager's toolkit for future use. This was designed to be "training-in-a-box" – any manager at any level could conduct VOV training with a prepared script, DVD, curated questions, and a worksheet. Outside organizations started to invite Royanne to present GVV, which she did at no charge. She also starting teaching

GVV to high school students in the US and Japan, and college students at four international universities.

There were some common enablers to the implementation of GVV that emerged in these conversations. Senior leadership buy-in and support was critical to the implementation of GVV at each organization. As highlighted earlier John, in his role as President of ProcessTech, was a significant supporter of GVV and was personally involved with the introduction of GVV into the company. John noted, "People understood I took this seriously. When the President is coming out saying, 'We're going to do this, and this is why it's important, and you all should be engaged in this, they got it.'" Tony's executive leadership role in ethics training and development at the CFA Institute also was critical in his ability to integrate GVV into existing ethics training at the CFA. Royanne underscored having benefitted from "having extremely powerful sponsors," including senior leaders.

At Lockheed Martin in addition to leader involvement and support in annual ethics training, the implementation of GVV is further facilitated by a broader cultural commitment to ethics. David spoke in particular about an initiative called "Integrity Minute." "We have a program called Integrity Minute which comes up three to four times a year, which is a really popular non-mandatory kind of ethics soap opera that we release two, three minutes segments in a three week pattern." David noted the importance of "Integrity Minute" in reinforcing the ethical culture at Lockheed Martin and more specifically their Voicing Our Values initiative.

David and Blair also spoke of the importance of direct interaction and working closely and regionally with ethics officers in each of the business areas within Lockheed Martin.

> Each of the ethics directors as well as their ethics officers are involved in local messaging, everything from their own podcasts and cartoons to events in person. So we try to make sure that ethics is not only a once a year event and is more than just what comes out of our office. It's really something that permeates the culture.

Along with benefits of introducing GVV into these organizations, these leaders also discussed important challenges they faced in introducing GVV into their organizations.

While senior leadership can be an important enabler for GVV in the workplace, John expressed concerns with the difficult position mid-level managers might be in as more individuals feel empowered to raise ethical/values-based concerns in the organization. He spoke of the "risk" mid-level managers might be concerned about when raising issues with more senior leaders and the "fear" of being seen as lacking competence and not doing one's job effectively.

> Yeah, because if you think about it, if I'm a supervisor and all of a sudden people are having problems in my department, and I'm now raising those conflicts up, I think in some organizations there's this sense of, God bless, why can't you just manage this? What are we paying you for?

John attempted to respond in a positive way to these risks and fears by emphasizing that middle managers' efforts to elevate values-based concerns raised by employees should be seen as a strength and a sign of competence that in the long run would benefit the organization by allowing leaders to address these concerns in a "productive, positive manner at the time, with the right parties involved." John went on to argue that GVV can in fact reduce values conflicts over time,

> if you have a values culture, particularly one that deals with giving voice to values . . . people are solving it [ethics issues] at the level they should be. Actually your reported instances actually go down, because again, they get addressed in a productive, positive manner at the time, with the right parties involved.

A challenge that a few interviews surfaced is adapting GVV to a global context. Tony is looking to increase CFA member involvement with GVV training for his 160,000 worldwide members. While GVV is currently not a mandated requirement for ethics education, Tony discussed the importance of making GVV a more integral component of meeting professional ethics standards in the industry. He was optimistic about the potential of working with local regulatory bodies around the world to have GVV over time accredited "as a recognized component of financial industry continuing professional development."

David and Blair framed their challenge in terms of adapting GVV materials for its global employee base.

> GVV is used all over the world, quite literally. How do we make sure that as we create material, share material, that we're doing it in a way that is relevant not just to our United States based population but to our employees in the rest of the world?

They noted that one way Lockheed Martin is attempting to meet this challenge is to work with both translators and also ethics officers based outside of the United States.

Evaluating the impact of GVV in the workplace

I asked each of these leaders about different ways they were able to evaluate the impact of GVV in their organizations and different ways employees were putting into practice their GVV training and education. John, as well as David and Blair, had been able to work with GVV in their respective organizations over a period of years and were in a particularly good position to be able to speak to how GVV was making a difference in their organizations.

John discussed his perceptions of GVV's impact in a variety of ways.

> We did an employee engagement survey all the time, and I probably can't get this for you, but we actually did start to see engagement scores go up a bit. I think people started to realize that they could voice values, and that they would be acted upon.

There were a number of examples and stories John offered to highlight how GVV was making a difference particularly at the front line levels of the organization.

> We had instances where people felt they used the framework, they looked for allies, they looked for other avenues, to get their message across. They thought through it before they went to their boss and their supervisor. We started to see it being implemented at a grassroots level.

One story in particular seemed to capture how some employees had truly taken GVV to heart. John spoke at length about Rose, a long-time (25–30 years) member of the administrative staff who supported the sales organization. "One of her jobs was when we had reseller agreements, distributor agreements that needed to be updated, they would come to her and she'd process it, get it updated, and send it out for a signature." In one instance,

Rose got one of these contracts,
and she did not agree with the
changes that were being made.
This is an administrator.
You've got the sales folks saying,

'Do it.' She gets the contract, and she goes, 'This just doesn't look right to me,' so she called the sales manager . . . Giving Voice to Values . . . and said, 'Look, I just don't think this is right. It's different than what we've done, I don't think it's right.'

Rose continued up the chain of command with each person telling her it's not something she should be worried about and asking her to just send out the contract. Eventually Rose reached John and shared with him her concerns. John told Rose he'd take a look and get back to her.

About a week and a half goes by, and I'm busy, I haven't gotten to it. She says to me, 'Hey John, have you had a chance to look at the agreement yet?' No, I'm sorry Rose, I haven't had a chance, but I will. I'll look at it this week. Another week goes by, I still haven't looked at it. This is where Giving Voice to Values came in. She knew how busy I was, so what she did was rather than have me read the entire agreement, because she knew that's what was taking the time, she highlighted for me side by side what the revision was and what was in the original language, and then gave that to me. I will tell you as soon as I read it, I said, 'Rose, you are absolutely right. We cannot accept this change.' I said, 'Thank you so much for your perseverance in bringing that up to me.' You know what she said to me? 'Just giving voice to values, John.'

John also identified some areas where GVV had not made the desired level of impact, specifically within the leadership team.

Here's some data that I got, Jerry, that I thought was important. When I looked across, remember, we did the management team first and then we did the employee base. The management team had the least amount of participation scores, and the least amount of time spent on it overall, compared to all of the groups. I talked to the management about that in a management meeting. I said, 'You know, here we rolled this thing out. Our employees paid really strong attention to this, but yet when I look at the data, where we seem to be light was in the management group. That does not send the right signal.' We talked about that, and in fact, when I left, I was working with Mary about actually doing some additional management training around how as a manager, when you receive a values conflict under the framework, how do you respond appropriately.

David and Blair focused their comments assessing the impact of GVV on Lockheed Martin's ongoing evaluation of their ethics initiatives. Lockheed Martin annually surveys employees about their awareness of and response to ethical incidents in the workplace. While not able to share specific results, David and Blair shared some recent changes Lockheed Martin had made in their annual ethics survey to get a clearer sense of how employees respond to violations of ethical conduct.

We asked, 'Did you observe this conduct? Yes or no?' If the answer to that is yes, then we don't just ask 'Did you report it?' We ask 'What did you do about it?' And we then give them the option to tell us, 'I took care of it myself, and here's how I did that. I talked to someone else, I went . . .' So we embedded some questions related to GVV.

In a number of important respects including this question about how individuals responded to violations of ethical conduct signals the importance of voicing values and the role of GVV within Lockheed Martin. Blair indicated that Lockheed Martin intends to include the GVV question set regularly in their all-employee surveys.

David and Blair also discussed an indicator of GVV's potential impact on ethical behavior at Lockheed Martin – contacts to the Ethics office, including Helpline calls. They noted a readiness and willingness within the organization for individuals to contact Ethics and leave their names, rather than report incidents anonymously. David and Blair reported that currently less than 10% of all contacts are anonymous, an exceptionally low rate when compared with other organizations, and one that has declined by over 30% since the implementation of GVV within Lockheed Martin.

While Royanne was only able to work with GVV over the three year-long period of implementation at Prudential, she offered some valuable insights on the topic of assessment. She specifically focused on the role of post-training GVV experiences and stories as opportunities for evaluating the effectiveness and measurable impact of the training, "I would really, really like, for her [Mary] to call out and ask for stories from people after they've received their Voicing Our Values Training and find out how did it go? We always want to know the epilogue." Royanne thought a potentially fruitful follow-on could be for organizations implementing GVV to collect these stories "a month later, six months later, a year later" and to share some of these post-training GVV stories on the various company websites, as well as integrating some of the stories into GVV training at these organizations.

New directions for GVV and ethics education in workplace

An important focus for our conversations was on ways of developing GVV for the future. Each of these leaders recognized opportunities for extending and expanding GVV in the workplace. John spoke in depth about the importance and challenge of developing leadership skills, particularly for mid-level managers implementing GVV. John noted,

> We were in the process of really doing more management development around Giving Voice to Values when I left ProcessTech [his prior organization before becoming CEO of LabVantage], so that's kind of where we left it. But for me, bar none, Jerry, I think that's critical for your mid-level managers. They've got to understand it [values conflicts being raised by employees], and understand how to receive it, and process it, and do something in a GVV context.

John also highlighted the potential of GVV to be integrated into the board of directors level. "I mean you're seeing this in the news all the time now, the issues we're having with boards in terms of their governance, and how they handle value conflict. . . . I think that's an area, Jerry, that needs help." John pointed to his involvement with the Center for Higher Ambition Leadership at Harvard University and conversations he is having with other senior executives regarding the importance of addressing values conflicts at the board level and the potential role GVV can play in addressing these values conflicts. There are others who have recognized this opportunity to explore the role of GVV within the board of directors, and Cynthia Clark has a published GVV book series contribution on *Giving Voice to Values in the Boardroom* released by Routledge in early 2021.

The topic of organizational culture emerged in these conversations as an important area of future development. Gentile (2014) recognized the potential for GVV to have a broad influence in organizations. She noted that the kinds of questions and skills developed through GVV training "can become familiar and . . . easily referenced in other training programs and managerial conversations, whether or not the topic is ethics-related" (Gentile, 2013, p. 175).

David and Blair reinforced this perspective in discussing how Lockheed Martin's Voicing Our Values initiative has been instrumental in supporting a "speak up culture" that has implications beyond the domain of ethics. David noted,

> I feel that boosting our values is far more than just the theme of our ethics awareness training. So for example, one area is best practices in innovation. There's been talk for the past few years about the need for companies that really want to excel in innovation to actually focus on making sure that you can speak up.

David felt that Voicing Our Values supported this effort and was critical, along with leadership development efforts, to encouraging the kind of honesty and directness necessary for having "tough conversations" whether with respect to ethical compliance or other key outcomes such as innovation, quality, and efficiency.

John similarly viewed GVV as part of a broader organizational culture where values conflicts are normalized and can become a foundation for growth and learning. He specifically saw a key role GVV could play in enhancing process improvement,

> Again, when you think about continuous improvement, it's a similar kind of story that gets told. I've got an opportunity to make a difference here, and change this process for the better . . . conflicts are going to arise, and values are going to come into that conflict. It's an opportunity to use GVV in that setting as well.

Royanne echoed the potential role GVV can play in developing a "speak up" culture and specifically one where managers are in a better position to accept "bad news." She framed this opportunity as a kind of challenge for organizations,

> It's how as a manager, what behaviors specifically are necessary in order to accept bad news . . . to create a speak-up culture? Don't create a culture of silence where somebody comes to you to bring you some bad news and you scream at them. And then you wonder why it takes them three hours to bring you a problem . . . why nobody wants to tell you stuff.

In "Three Leadership Challenges for Giving Voice to Values" Mary C. Gentile shared her experience working senior and middle managers who met to discuss this challenge.[1] Mary asked senior leaders to meet as a group and discuss the question, "How can managers raise issues with me in a way that makes it easier for me to respond effectively?" The middle managers worked on a different question, "How can I raise issues effectively with my seniors in the organization – and what would I hope for from them in response?" When the two groups debriefed their conversations, senior leaders offered insights on how middle managers could best communicate their issues and concerns. The focus was not so much on the content of these issues/concerns, but rather on how the issues were communicated.

Senior leaders recommended that middle managers for example recognize the time pressures these leaders confront and rather than just catching them in the hall, to actually schedule a meeting where they present information more "clearly and concisely," with data when possible. These leaders also encouraged the middle managers to "avoid accusations" and to present when possible any background analyses that would enhance understanding of the issues, as well as potential recommendations. On the other hand, middle managers asked that they be thanked for bringing difficult matters up; that they be kept informed, to the extent possible, of what steps were being taken; and they not be punished for raising the issues. Both groups of managers proceeded to create a "GVV Deal" where senior leaders and middle managers committed to these approaches for voicing values.

A final area of focus for future development related to understanding more about the personal characteristics and competencies that support GVV in the workplace. John thought about this topic specifically in regard to identifying employees with management potential. He asked,

> As you're recruiting into your management level, can you assess sort of competencies or capacity around GVV? Can you look for things like empathy, humility, and how do you assess that? If you think about it, there's a lot in terms of empathy, humility, compassion, that come into play if you're going to really do it in a good way.

Tony envisioned directing greater attention to the role that self-understanding plays with regard to GVV in the workplace. He noted that the CFA Institute is in the process of developing an in-house ethics workshop emphasizing self-awareness and self-understanding. Tony explained how this kind of self-understanding might influence the communication style one might feel most comfortable with in voicing one's values.

> Once you understand yourself, then I think you can find the tools that fit more with you. So, for example if you are an introvert and data-driven kind of person, trying to train you to be a debater and verbalizing your concern will likely fail. It's probably easier for you as a person to find evidence and produce a memo to document your thinking with regard to the problem and surface your concerns that way, as opposed to trying to talk it through with someone else. Because I think it will be less effective trying to persuade someone if you don't have the eloquence to make your case in a way that is compelling to that person.

Moving in this direction would align the CFA Institute's efforts with the fifth pillar of GVV which is about self-awareness and "playing to one's strengths" when responding to values conflicts.

Conclusion

Stepping back from these conversations, I was struck by the passion and commitment these leaders expressed for GVV and its importance in the workplace. Each leader underscored the value of the unique approach of GVV in developing skills to better enable employees to take action in workplace situations where they perceive conflicts with their values. These conversations also highlighted the flexibility and versatility of implementing GVV in different organizations operating in different sectors. Whether through the use of online modules, in- person training, or combinations of both approaches, each organization was able to utilize GVV in ways that made sense for each organization and its particular needs. These leaders also were committed to implementing GVV throughout the organization – at all levels and in all locations – and sustaining this commitment over time. At the same time, they recognized some of the unforeseen challenges in sustaining this kind of commitment, for example changes in senior leadership that might weaken support for GVV, or decisions made to adopt a different strategy for ethics education and training. Finally, there was real optimism about the future of GVV within these organizations and beyond and an openness to exploring new possibilities for extending GVV in new directions.

In listening to these leaders discuss the implementation of GVV within these organizations, I learned a great deal that I was not aware of, despite my active involvement with GVV for over a decade. I wondered how much we know about how other organizations are integrating GVV into their ethics education and training efforts. In addition to the insights offered by the leaders I spoke with, what might we learn from the implementation of GVV in other workplaces? Would it be possible to identify "best practices" drawn from the experience of numerous organizations that could guide future implementation efforts? I believe that there could be real opportunities for business school faculty and corporations, for example, to collaborate and develop cases, academic and practitioner articles, and books that focus specifically on how GVV is being extended outside the classroom and introduced and integrated into workplaces around the world.

I also was inspired by these conversations to think about how the workplace provides some unique opportunities for "follow-up" innovations beyond initial GVV training efforts. Working with leadership, in some of the ways highlighted earlier, is one example.

However, there are other possibilities to consider. Organizations could develop peer coaching skills workshops to support the development of peer coaching networks within these organizations (Gentile, 2013). In addition to the fundamental GVV skills training employees receive (e.g., scripting, peer coaching), there might be opportunities to follow-up with skills training, such as listening skills, that can be applied directly to GVV contexts. Finally, organizations can take steps (e.g., surveys, small group meetings) to follow employees over time who participated in GVV training. This would provide an opportunity for organizations to learn from employees about their experiences putting GVV into practice, and to identify strategies to enhance the effectiveness of GVV education and training.

Finally, I was moved in each of these interviews by the deep respect and genuine regard these leaders expressed for Mary and what GVV meant to these leaders and their organizations. At the conclusion of my conversation with Blair and David, for example, Blair told me,

> We think absolutely the world of her [Mary], and it's just been a phenomenal working relationship for all these years. But I laugh – we're the company that put her on all seven continents. Maybe you don't know that story, but we had people working in Antarctica. She was making a presentation somewhere and was talking about GVV being represented on six continents and I said, 'No, Mary, you're on seven continents!'

It seems clear from these interviews that GVV has a bright future in ethics training in the workplace . . . *everywhere* around the world!

Note

1 This article is unpublished and available upon request from Mary Gentile.

References

Gentile, M. C. (2010). *Giving voice to values.* New Haven, CT: Yale University Press.

Gentile, M. C. (2014). Giving voice to values in the workplace. In L. E. Sekerka (Ed.), *Ethics training in action* (pp. 167–182). Charlotte, NC: Info Age Publishing.

APPENDIX: QUESTIONS FOR GVV INTERVIEWS

1. When did you/(name of organization) initially contact Mary about GVV? What motivated your interest in GV?

2. How has (name of organization) introduced and integrated GVV into the organization (e.g., specific training initiatives, areas of the organization where introduced, etc.)?

3. What have been the benefits to (name of organization) from the introduction and integration of GVV into the organization? What considerations (e.g., management support, employee interest) have been most critical in realizing these benefits?

4. What challenges did (name of organization) face over time in this process of implementing GVV? How has (name of organization) attempted to address these challenges?

5. Are there particular issues/challenges (name of organization) is facing now and likely into the future where you believe GVV may be helpful? In what ways can GVV be of value in responding to these issues and challenges?

6   Do you see particular areas in the GVV curriculum (e.g., developing scripts, peer coaching, leadership training) that represent areas for innovation and opportunity for Mary and GVV?

7   Is there anything "missing" in GVV that you believe could represent areas of innovation and opportunity for Mary and GVV?

8   Is there anything you would like to discuss that we have not touched upon in the other question?

10

GIVING VOICE TO VALUES

Implementing values-driven leadership development in the Chinese context

Liang Yu

Giving Voice to Values (GVV) is an innovative approach to values-driven leadership development that has shifted the focus of teaching ethics from ethical reasoning to ethical implementation. The GVV pedagogy focuses on building student competence, and therefore, confidence, to enact their values effectively.[1] It has been piloted in more than 1,170 schools, companies, and other organizations on all seven continents. This chapter explores how GVV is implemented in the Chinese cultural context.

Chinese cultural context: what is different?

Although Chinese culture is often automatically associated with Confucian traditions, this idea is rather simplified as it disregards the multiple traditions that have exerted their influence on the respective cultural context.[2] The origins of the core Chinese values are embedded in the philosophical schools referred to as Hundreds of Schools of Thought, which thrived during the Spring and Autumn Period more than 2,500 years ago. It is generally acknowledged that, from then onwards, Chinese thought has been mainly shaped by three forces, namely, Confucianism, which strongly emphasizes the respect for the system of social hierarchy; Taoism, which deals with the human relationship with nature and projects the dialectic philosophy; and Buddhism, which highlights human relationship with the Buddha and conceptualizes human life as one filled with suffering that could be overcome through spiritual emancipation. Confucianism, in particular, has had a profound impact on the cultural, political, educational, ethical, and social life of the Chinese people. This chapter will introduce some examples of Confucian ideas to reflect their significant impact on the implementation of GVV in the Chinese cultural context.

Confucian virtue ethics emphasizes self-reflection and cultivation, continuous learning, emulation of moral exemplars, and the attainment of skilled judgment rather than the knowledge of rules on the path of becoming a sage. There are three virtues that Confucius advocates, namely, *humaneness/benevolence* (*Ren*, "仁"), *righteousness* (*Yi*, "義"), and *ritual* (*Li*, "禮"). Table 10.1 summarizes the three virtues and their implications accompanied by the examples from the *Analects*, the ancient Chinese collection of sayings and ideas attributed to Confucius and his contemporaries. Late Confucian philosophers, such as Mencius (372–289 BC) and Dong Zhongshu (179–104 BC), further extended the list to include five instead of the original three Confucian virtues by adding *wisdom* (*Zhi*, "智") and *trustworthiness* (*Xin*, "信"). These five virtues have influenced the lives of Chinese people for thousands of years and highlighted what is fundamentally a Confucian virtue-based hierarchical model of relations. As reflected in the *Analects*, "The relation between superiors and inferiors, is like that between the wind and the grass. The grass must bend, when the wind blows across it."[3]

In 136 BCE, around 350 years following the death of Confucius, Dong Zhongshu (179–104 BCE), a Confucian scholar, established Confucianism both as the state ideology of China and as the basis of the official political philosophy, which is a position it held for 2,000 years.[12] He advocated the idea that those occupying superior social positions (ruler, father, and husband) always guide the ones occupying inferior positions (subject, son, and wife). The Three Cardinal Guides, which were adopted by the ruling class afterward, imposed shackles on minds and personalities, and made China one of the world's most hierarchical and status-conscious countries.

Table 10.1 Main Confucian virtues and their implications

Confucian virtues	Meaning and implications	Examples from the Analects
Humaneness/ Benevolence (Ren, "仁")	Ren is the virtue of perfectly fulfilling one's responsibilities, duties, and rituals for the benefit of others.[4]	Confucius said, "Now the man of perfect virtue, wishing to be established himself, seeks also to establish others; wishing to be enlarged himself, he seeks also to enlarge others."[5] Yen Yuan asked about perfect virtue. The Master said, "To subdue ones-self and return to propriety (Li), is perfect virtue."[6]
Righteousness (Yi, "義")	Yi contrasts with action done out of self-interest. While pursuing one's self-interest is not necessarily bad, a better, more righteous person is the one whose life is based on following a path towards enhancing the greater good. Thus, an outcome of Yi is doing the right thing for the right reason.[7]	The Master said, "The mind of the superior man is conversant with righteousness; the mind of the mean man is conversant with gain."[8]
Ritual (Li, "禮")	Li means doing the appropriate thing at the appropriate time, highlighting maintaining the existing norms such as the etiquette of daily behavior, a ceremony, and social and political institutions. It also advocates that sages sometimes violate the existing norms in order to attain the moral good. Training of the Li of past sages cultivates in people virtues that include ethical judgment about when Li must be adapted in light of situational contexts.[9]	The Duke Ching, of Ch'i, asked Confucius about government. Confucius replied, "There is government, when the prince is a prince, and the minister is a minister; when the father is a father, and the son is a son."[10] Confucius said, "In festive ceremonies, it is better to be sparing than extravagant. In the ceremonies of mourning, it is better that there be deep sorrow than in minute attention to observances."[11]

Confucian virtues place considerable importance on the interpersonal relationships, which ensues from the unique system of state governance. According to Fei Xiaotong (1910–2005), one of the most influential Chinese sociologists, Western views suggest a dichotomy of social order between "rule by men" versus "rule by law," whereas the Chinese case suggests a third alternative, namely, "rule by ritual." According to Francis Fukuyama:

> because of the dominance of Confucianism for over the last two and a half millennia, the Chinese society in tradition is not regulated by a constitution or system of laws flowing from it but by internalization of Confucian ethical principles on the part of each individual as the result of a process of socialization.[13]

Chinese social structure differs considerably from that of Western societies: according to Fei, Western individualism treats an individual as an abstract member of groups defined by categories (the so-called *organizational mode of association*, "团体格局"), whereas Chinese society defines every individual according to positions in different egocentric networks (the so-called *differential mode of association*, "差序格局"). One important implication is that in Western societies, the entire set of social relations is seen as embedded in an encompassing order defined on the level of the categorical group (for example, individuals as citizens of a nation-state), whereas in Chinese society social order consists of a set of individualized, "egocentric," and overlapping social circles.[14] Such a social circle forms the basis of *guanxi*, a Chinese concept denoting interpersonal connections that enables a bilateral flow of personal or social transactions. In order to maintain a good *guanxi*, each party of a connection is expected to provide benefits to the other individual according to the obligations of a certain mode of association. Different from the network patterns in the West where personal and familial ties may be perceived as a form of nepotism, the Chinese people maintain and reinforce *guanxi* through long-term interactions and perceive *guanxi* as an obligation to others.

The impact of traditional values in the workplace

Influenced by the traditional values, the modern workplace culture in China is characterized by firm, patriarchal, hierarchical orders, and sophisticated social networks. As mentioned, governance by ethics (*Li Zhi*, "禮治") is preferred over governance by law (*Fa Zhi*, "法治"). The disregard for institutional law means that those who occupy positions of authority (*Ren Zhi*, "人治") have the power of influence. Emphasis on personal power promotes the practice of authority since an individual, rather than institutional authority, defines what is permissible in a given context at a particular time. A "voice," in Chinese organizations, is then viewed as the mark for superiority, seniority, and expertise. Junior employees are expected to keep opinions to themselves, and thus minimize risks and adopt a subordinate role,[15] unless specifically and directly asked to voice them. Leaders, on the other hand, are expected to behave ethically and demonstrate paternalistic leadership, which is defined in East Asia as "a style that combines strong discipline and authority with fatherly benevolence"[16] with three distinct dimensions: authoritarianism, benevolence, and morality.[17] According to a recent leadership study titled *Paternalistic Leadership and Employee Voice in China*, benevolence is more influential than authoritarianism and morality in enhancing the subordinates' status-based self-concepts and the quality of social relationships.[18] According to the same study, employees may voice their opinions more freely if they feel that they enjoy within-group status, which, in general, is in line with the Confucian principle of benevolence even in modern times.

The work culture in Chinese organizations is also relational. In the business context, *guanxi* is often seen as an instrumental concept practiced to maximize one's access to critical advantages in favor of resources, information, or networks.[19] Instrumentality, however, is only one facet of *guanxi* and as such always favors accumulate reciprocal responsibilities.[20] Experienced business people are devoted to developing and cultivating *guanxi* in order to maximize their chances of success in their professional contexts; the exercise of *guanxi* is the one of key factors for business success in China.[21] "Who you know," in Chinese society, is much more important than "what you know." In reality, the exercise of *guanxi* can occasionally lead to ethical challenges: employment may be offered to individuals with good *guanxi*, and business deals and contracts may be established based on social connections rather than on objective evaluation of individuals' abilities.

Giving voice to values in the workplace in China

The implementation of GVV in the Chinese cultural context appears to be unique. To rephrase, arguably most of the ethical dilemmas that working professionals could encounter in their daily lives in China have unique cultural characteristics: the boundaries between ethical business and the appropriate use of authority and *guanxi* are often blurred. The typical ethical dilemma would involve obeying unethical instructions from an authority figure or deciding on paying off a customer because of the importance attributed to *guanxi*. People often mistakenly attribute these ethical dilemmas to Chinese traditional values, and the inappropriate use of *guanxi* or one's authority contradicts the commonly shared Confucian virtues. For example, although authorities are respected within the Chinese cultural context, if positions of authority are used to jeopardize the public for the benefit of the individual interests, direct conflict ensues with the Confucian virtue of ritual. Moreover, Confucius also preaches the importance of ethical conduct for people in positions of authority as exemplified in the following: *"If a minister make his own conduct correct, what difficulty will he have in assisting in government? If he cannot rectify himself, what has he to do with rectifying others?"*[22] Whereas this ethical dilemma seems to be specific to China, unethical actions of this kind are viewed as problematic all the same and challenged by many. Therefore, perhaps contrary to expectations, the implementation of GVV in China does not significantly differ from its implementation elsewhere.

It is worth noting, however, that the hierarchical and emotional pressure towards not voicing one's values is much higher in China when compared to countries such as the US or Germany. Since early childhood, people are taught to respect those in positions of authority and the society as a whole works with deeply connected *guanxi*. Chinese business leaders find it difficult to balance the emotional challenges of value conflict regarding *guanxi* and *respect for authority*, and it would seem to be most important, within such a cultural context, for leaders to practice responding to ethical challenges and straining the "muscles" for voicing their values in a way that is more consistent with Chinese culture norms.

The traditional values also impact the way people voice their opinions. In general, the Chinese communication style is characterized as indirect and implicit, facilitating healthy and harmonious personal relationships.

This communication style may be viewed as submissive or obedient, but it does not suggest that Chinese people will always follow the instructions from those in power. Wise and persistent individuals are able to find ways of voicing their opinions. Lao Tzu (601–531 BC), an ancient Chinese philosopher and a senior contemporary of Confucius, for example, expressed his thoughts through a water analogy: *"there is nothing in the world more soft and weak than water, and yet for attacking things that are firm and strong, there is nothing that can take precedence of it; – for there is nothing (so effectual) for which it can be changed."* In this regard, the adherence to traditional virtues facilitated the development of peoples' agility and creativity in implementing and voicing their values depending on the different people, contexts, and timing. Experienced communicators are very flexible in adjusting their message, catering to their audience, timing their delivery, choosing the appropriate influence tactics, while paying respect and saving face according to specific context. It is thus no wonder that Fox Butterfield (1939–), a well-known journalist of the *New York Times*, thus concluded in his book *China: Alive in the Bitter Sea* that "Chinese people have turned the art of personal relations into carefully calculated science."[23]

In order to illustrate in more detail how GVV can be implemented in the Chinese workplace, I turn to the case study on Ma Jun and his efforts to voice his values in China conducted by Xiaojun Qian and Peng Jiang. Their analysis provides an excellent example of values-based leadership practices in contemporary China.

A case study on Giving Voice to Values: Ma Jun and the Institution of Public and Environmental Affairs (IPE)[24]

Due to his concern for the severe environmental deterioration in the country, Ma Jun undertook a mission to bring back blue skies and clear water in China by setting up an environmental non-governmental organization (NGO). The case study focuses on the contribution of Ma Jun, as an individual with limited power, to solving this seemingly impossible task in the sophisticated context of Chinese society.

Ma Jun spent the first ten years of his career in the *Southern China Media Post*, one of the highest circulating Hong Kong newspapers, where he became aware of the country's impending ecological catastrophe brought about by the rapid economic growth. He then proceeded to work for an environmental consulting firm where, in spite of gaining considerable environmental advisory skills, he realized that the consulting firm was not able to solve the systemic environmental problem. Ma Jun was admitted into Yale's World Scholar program in 2004, where he concluded that the key reasons for China's environment deterioration are the absence of "public participation." Whereas most NGOs primarily focused on environmental protection education or policy advocacy, Ma Jun decided to set up an NGO promoting environmental information disclosure and advancing multi-party, government, business, and public participation.

In order to understand Ma Jun's unique approach in voicing his values in China, the contemporary political, social, and cultural context needs to be examined. China's one-party hierarchical government always tries to maintain a delicate balance between controls (to ensure that political order is not threatened) and democratization (to ensure innovation and economic growth). Perhaps because of its recent turbulent past including mass campaigns and longer periods of political upheaval, the Chinese government seems intent on avoiding revolutions and sudden political and social changes.[25] Hence, social movements whose aim was to mobilize radically the Chinese populace have met a similar fate: suppression and de-legitimization.[26] In such circumstances, the social and political changes in China assume a unique form, namely, what we are witnessing is a gradual shift towards a polity adapted to an increasingly complex and pluralist society.[27] In the environmental realm, social activism is no exception and it follows the same path.

When Ma Jun decided to establish an NGO in early 2000, China's local government managed the local environment protection bureau's performance and budget, in spite of the country's top-down management system for environmental protection. The local government, however, prioritized economic development over environmental protection. In spite of the large number of laws and regulations for environmental protection, their implementation is rather weak. Ma Jun faced a number of challenges within this context. He aimed to (1) voice his values and promote environmental activism in a restrictive political environment with rapid socio-economic changes; (2) re-shape the system with multiple stakeholders with misaligned and sometimes conflicting interests;

and (3) voice his values in ways that aligned with the broader Confucian virtues in contemporary China. The challenges arising in this context provide a fertile ground for understanding the nature of GVV implementation in China.

Ma Jun clearly understood the unique Confucianism and semi-authoritarian context in which he established his NGO. Rather than starting a widely supported environmental movement, he successfully embedded his activism in a non-confrontational, low profile, benign, and incremental fashion. Instead of opposing governmental authorities (governments' priority for GDP, multinational corporate's reliance for business performance), Ma Jun sought all opportunities to establish bonds based on trust with other authorities (central and local environmental departments, headquarters for multinational corporations). Throughout his interaction with key stakeholders, such as the government and multinational corporations, he presented the role of his NGO as that of a partner rather than an opponent.

Ma Jun also adopted a benevolent attitude and had a sage approach in handling requests for favors from *guanxi*. After the IPE gained complete public trust, many companies with violation records started to approach Ma Jun, through different *guanxi*, in an attempt to remove their records from the IPE's "blacklist." Ma Jun and his team thus experienced considerable pressure as well as temptation. Ma Jun decided to assume a benevolent attitude, which is a core Confucian virtue: IPE as an NGO gained much power by gathering data and establishing public trust, which was best used for the benefit, and not harm, of the key stakeholders. For those companies that made great strides to improve their environmental practices, which yielded results, an option of record removal was to be offered to incentivize further efforts. Ma Jun also renounced IPE's power to remove the enterprise violation record to Green Choice Alliance, a corporative network established by approximately 20 NGOs. If a company requested removal from the list, (all) member institutions of the Green Choice Alliance need to give their consent. In this way, Ma Jun avoided conflicts arising from requests for favors within his *guanxi* as they could lead to blurring of boundaries between professional judgment and favoritism. Such restraint, embeddedness, benevolence, and wisdom in human relationships have not hampered his green activism at all but it strengthened instead. Details of this case are provided by Darden Business

Publishing and the way Ma Jun practiced GVV is summarized in Table 10.2, which includes the information on the critical stakeholders and Ma Jun's actions that embodied his values.[28]

By voicing his values as described earlier, Ma Jun clearly demonstrated an understanding and respect of the Chinese cultural context: he showed respect for authorities instead of openly defying them, skillfully handled *guanxi* instead of being constrained by it, and based all his decisions on his core values. He also effectively used almost all of the GVV principles: anticipating typical reasons and rationalizations, identifying levers for different stakeholders, and developing structure and incentives for addressing the challenges. In a sense, voicing and enacting values within the Chinese culture is common albeit indirect practices.

With his effort, Ma Jun was included in the TIME's 100 most influential people of 2006, and, in 2008, he was included in *The Guardian*'s one of "*the 50 people that can save the planet.*" In 2012, he was nominated by an international environmental organization for the Goldman Environmental Prize known as the Green Nobel Prize, which he eventually won. In 2018, ecological civilization became part of China's constitution as the ideological framework for the country's environmental policies, laws, and education. Ma Jun's IPE is currently making more significant progress in re-shaping the country's environmental practice as a result.

What is the future for GVV in China? I close this chapter by considering some of the important societal changes likely to influence the development of GVV and the teaching of business ethics within China.

Changing institutional and sociocultural context in China for GVV

Francis Fukuyama defines the Chinese society as a "low trust" society in which trust is high within the family/kinship borders but low outside them.[29] However, the past four decades (1978–2018) in the People's Republic of China have seen dramatic changes, which considerably boosted the trust in society as a whole in a four-fold way. (1) Technologically, the advancement of e-commerce and social media provided information transparency, democratized market transactions, and leveled the playing field. (2) Socially, the social security system has made vital signs of

Table 10.2 Ma Jun's enactment of his values

Stakeholder	Context	Levers	Structure	Incentive
Environmental Protection Department	Local environmental departments are directly supervised by the local governments, which prioritize GDP over environmental protection. The local environmental departments saved many environmental data, which were, however, fragmented and scattered due to the lack of local inter-departmental cooperation.	• Environmental officials aim to increase the public availability of the environmental data. • Ministry of Environmental Protection mandates that all authorities should disclose environmental related data.	Make the environmental data accessible online to the public by cleaning and integrating data from local environmental departments.	Empower local environmental departments and ministry to do something that they cannot accomplish independently.
Multinational Corporations	The local branch of a particular multinational company violated the environmental regulations. The violation was unnoticed by the headquarters until IPE published the violation.	• Headquarters' commitment to environmental protection. • Multinational corporations' supply chain policy.	• Establish a violation disclosure system. • Establish the Green Supply Chain index and persuade multinational corporations to improve their practice.	Establish a system that can allow companies to remove their violation records through the Green Choice Alliance.
The Public	The public initially have no platform to monitor the environmental data in their city/community, and they have no access to the environment protection courses.	• Public concern for community environment and willingness to participate in environmental activities.	• Initiate "Picture taking" activities for the public where the public could post the environment pollution pictures online and urge companies to change their practices.	Public concern can garner the attention from the government and corporations alike.

progress, so that people do not necessarily have to rely on families and kinship for pension and healthcare. (3) Legally, China's fifth-generation leadership have given the rule of law much greater prominence in official rhetoric than their predecessors. (4) Demographically, 400 million people were born in China between 1982 and 1998, which is five times as many people as those born in the United States.[30] Having grown up with a more open view on the outside world, the generation of Chinese millennials are generally open-minded.

According to the research from the World Value Survey, a global project that explores people's values and beliefs, economic development has systematic and, to some extent, predictable cultural and political consequences. Post-industrialization promotes a shift towards the values of self-expression: more trust, tolerance, and greater emphasis on well-being. Such economic development tends to stir societies in a common direction, but, rather than converging, they seem to move along paths shaped by their culture heritages[31] and "distinctive culture traits endure long periods of time and continues to shape a society's political and economic performance."[32]

With the increasing level of trust in the society, it can be safely assumed that "giving voice to values" will become easier in contemporary China. Moreover, the traditional Chinese values will arguably endure, especially in government and state-owned enterprises. For all that, in order to establish effective practices that enable enacting values, a certain level of understanding of the Chinese cultural context is required.

The future of GVV in China

The question that still requires an answer is: what are the implications of these institutional and sociocultural changes in China for business ethics education and for teaching GVV in particular? Although China's traditional ethics education dates back to Confucius's times, business ethics education in China is a recent phenomenon. China's first MBA programs were established in 1991, with the number of hosting institutions on the rise ever since, reaching 126 in 2007. However, until 2008, only 37 programs included business ethics in their curricula, and in less than half of them it was a compulsory course.[33]

Overall, the business ethics education in China is still primarily focused on "awareness and analysis" and less so on actions. According to a 2008 report by Zucheng Zhou, the primary goal of business ethics education in China is cultivating students' ethical sense, awareness, and analysis for ethical dilemmas.[34] According to limited research, action-orientated pedagogy such as GVV is only practiced by a limited number of faculty members at Tsinghua University, CEIBS, and the Duke Kunshan University. It is time for business ethics education to move into a new era where more emphasis is placed on moral competence.

To effectively teach moral competence, a different instructional method would need to be used in business school classrooms. As mentioned earlier, the Chinese students will have a higher emotional barrier to value conflicts than their Western peers will, and it is essential for any educators to break down the emotional barrier before students learn how to respond to ethical challenges. One way that can help achieve this is to use the Chinese specific case studies, which could help to acknowledge the reality of the Chinese cultural context. Another way to break down the emotional barrier is to create emotional distance from the issue by asking what the protagonist in the case would do instead of asking, "what would you do?"[35] Besides breaking down the emotional barriers, the educators would need to move away from the traditional theoretical or philosophical way of teaching on ethical reasoning; instead, they need to engage students in action-orientated discussions. Appropriate GVV framework such as identify the key stakeholders and their risk involved, anticipate the common reasons and rationalizations, prescribe the response, setup structure/incentives etc., could be introduced so that students will learn how to put an ethical decision to work.

In order to further expand the influence of GVV in China, it is critical to establish a network of GVV educators from different business schools who understand GVV and would be able to teach effectively. The National Symposium on MBA Business Ethics Education, the annual conference organized by the Department of Degree Management and Postgraduate Education in Ministry of Education, would comprise an ideal platform for discussing GVV adoption in China. The symposium is attended by hundreds of business ethics professors each year and is led by the leading Chinese ethics scholars. Teacher training should be offered, and Chinese based case development should be encouraged. In order to ensure better promotion of GVV in China, it would be essential to leverage the existing faculty network and program reputation (including, for example,

Tsinghua, Duke Kunshan, and CEIBS) to promote the pedagogy further, and integrate research and faculty training into GVV's global plan to ensure its sustainability.

Notes

1 Gentile, M. C., Lawrence, A. T., & Melnyk, J. (2015, Spring). What is a giving voice to values case? *Case Research Journal, 35*(2), 1–10. Retrieved from www.nacra.net/case-research-journal/

2 Abrami, R. M., Kirby, W. C., & Warren McFarlan, F. (2014). *Can China lead: Reaching the limits of power and growth* (p. 11). Cambridge, MA: Harvard Business Review Press.

3 Confucius. (2016). *Confucian analects: The Chinese classic translated* (James Legge, Trans., p. 424). Beijing: Liaoning People's Publishing House.

4 Wikipedia. *Confucius*. Retrieved September 6, 2020, from https://en.wikipedia.org/?title=Confucius

5 Confucius. (2016). *Confucian analects: The Chinese classic translated* (James Legge, Trans., p. 395). Beijing: Liaoning People's Publishing House.

6 Confucius. (2016). *Confucian analects: The Chinese classic translated* (James Legge, Trans., p. 395). Beijing: Liaoning People's Publishing House.

7 Wikipedia. *Confucius*. Retrieved September 6, 2020, from https://en.wikipedia.org/?title=Confucius

8 Confucius. (2016). *Confucian analects: The Chinese classic translated* (James Legge, Trans., p. 122). Beijing: Liaoning People's Publishing House.

9 Wikipedia. *Confucius*. Retrieved September 6, 2020, from https://en.wikipedia.org/?title=Confucius

10 Confucius. (2016). *Confucian analects: The Chinese classic translated* (James Legge, Trans., p. 416). Beijing: Liaoning People's Publishing House.

11 Confucius. (2016). *Confucian analects: The Chinese classic translated* (James Legge, Trans., p. 75). Beijing: Liaoning People's Publishing House.

12 Encyclopædia Britannica. *Dong Zhongshu*. Retrieved September 16, 2019, from www.britannica.com/biography/Dong-Zhongshu

13 Fukuyama, F. (2018). *Trust: The social virtues and the creation of prosperity* (p. 85). Guilin: Guangxi Normal University Press.

14 Herrmann-Pillath, C. (2016). Fei Xiaotong's comparative theory of Chinese culture: It's relevance for contemporary cross-disciplinary research on Chinese

"collectivism". *The Copenhagen Journal of Asian Studies*, *34*(1), 29. https://doi.org/10.22439/cjas.v34i1.5187

15 Chatterjee, S. R. (2001). Relevance of traditional value frameworks in contemporary Chinese work organizations: Implications for managerial transition. *Journal of Human Values*, *7*(1), 21–32. https://doi.org/10.1177/097168580100700103

16 Farh, J.-L., & Cheng, B.-S. (2000). Cultural analysis of paternalistic leadership in Chinese organizations. In J. T. Li, A. S. Tsui, & E. Weldon (Eds.), *Management and organization in the Chinese context* (pp. 84–127). London: Palgrave Macmillan.

17 Farh, J.-L., Cheng, B. S., Chou, L.-F., & Chu, X. P. (2006). Authority and benevolence: Employees' responses to paternalistic leadership in China. In A. S. Tsui, Y. Bian, & L. Cheng (Eds.), *China's domestic private firms: Multidisciplinary perspectives on management and performance* (pp. 230–260). Beijing: Routledge.

18 Zhang, Y., Huai, M.-Y., & Xie, Y.-H. (2015). Paternalistic leadership and employee voice in China: A dual process model. *The Leadership Quarterly*, *26*, 25–36. https://doi.org/10.1016/j.leaqua.2014.01.002

19 Chatterjee, S. R. (2001). Relevance of traditional value frameworks in contemporary Chinese work organizations: Implications for managerial transition. *Journal of Human Values*, *7*(1), 21–32. https://doi.org/10.1177/097168580100700103

20 Yeung, I. Y. M., & Tung, R. L. (1996, Autumn). Achieving business success in Confucian societies: The importance of Guanxi (connections). *Organizational Dynamics*, *25*(2), 55–65. https://doi.org/10.1016/S0090-2616(96)90025-X

21 Yeung, I. Y. M., & Tung, R. L. (1996, Autumn). Achieving business success in Confucian societies: The importance of Guanxi (connections). *Organizational Dynamics*, *25*(2), 55–65. https://doi.org/10.1016/S0090-2616(96)90025-X

22 Confucius. (2016). *Confucian analects: The Chinese classic translated* (James Legge, Trans., p. 416). Beijing: Liaoning People's Publishing House.

23 Butterfield, F. (1982). *China: Alive in the bitter sea* (p. 32). New York: Times Books.

24 Qian, X., & Jiang, P. (2020). *Ma Jun and the Institute of Public and Environmental Affairs*. Darden Business Publishing, Case Study. Retrieved from http://store.darden.virginia.edu/ma-jun-and-the-institute-of-public-and-environmental-affairs-a

25 Ho, P., & Emmonds, R. (Eds.). (2008). *Embedded activism and political change in a semi-authoritarian context, China's embedded activism – Opportunities and constraints of a social movement* (p. 2). New York: Routledge.

26 Ho, P., & Emmonds, R. (Eds.). (2008). *Embedded activism and political change in a semi-authoritarian context, China's embedded activism – Opportunities and constraints of a social movement* (p. 1). New York: Routledge.

27 Ho, P., & Emmonds, R. (Eds.). (2008). *Embedded activism and political change in a semi-authoritarian context, China's embedded activism – Opportunities and constraints of a social movement* (p. 2). New York: Routledge.

28 Qian, X., & Jiang, P. (2020). *Ma Jun and the Institute of Public and Environmental Affairs.* Darden Business Publishing, Case Study. Retrieved from http://store.darden.virginia.edu/ma-jun-and-the-institute-of-public-and-environmental-affairs-a

29 Fukuyama, F. (2018). *Trust: The social virtues and the creation of prosperity* (p. 62). Guilin: Guangxi Normal University Press.

30 Dychtwald, Z. (2018, February 17). Chinese millennials are about to kick US millennials' butts. *New York Post.* Retrieved from https://nypost.com/2018/02/17/chinese-millennials-are-about-to-kick-us-millennials-butts/

31 Inglehart, R. (2001, March–April). Modernization's challenge to traditional values: Who's afraid of Ronald McDonald? *The Futurist, 35*(1), 16–21. Retrieved from www.questia.com/library/p5095/the-futurist/i2570301/vol-35-no-2-march

32 Inglehart, R. (2001, March–April). Modernization's challenge to traditional values: Who's afraid of Ronald McDonald? *The Futurist, 35*(1), 16–21. Retrieved from www.questia.com/library/p5095/the-futurist/i2570301/vol-35-no-2-march

33 Zucheng, Z. (2008). Business ethics education in China's MBA curriculum. *Journal of Business Ethics Education, 5*, 261–288. https://doi.org/10.5840/jbee2008512

34 Zucheng, Z. (2008). Business ethics education in China's MBA curriculum. *Journal of Business Ethics Education, 5*, 261–288. https://doi.org/10.5840/jbee2008512

35 Gentile, M. C. (2016, December 23). Talking about ethics across cultures. *Harvard Business Review.* Retrieved from https://hbr.org/2016/12/talking-about-ethics-across-cultures

11

THE PROMISE OF GIVING VOICE TO VALUES FOR COACHING LEADERS

Rachel Schaming

My introduction to Giving Voice to Values

In the preface of *Giving Voice to Values*, Mary C. Gentile states:

> The main idea behind Giving Voice to Values (GVV) is the observation that a focus on *awareness* of what the right thing to do may be insufficient. Precious little time is spent on *action* – that is, developing the 'scripts' and implementation plans for responding to the commonly heard 'reasons and rationalizations' for questionable practices, and actually practicing the delivery of those scripts.[1]

As leaders and managers, no one needs to remind us that we live in a global economy that constantly bombards us with change and complexity. Every year, new technologies, markets, and competitors emerge at an ever-increasing pace. As change accelerates, so does uncertainty. Future threats and opportunities become harder to predict. We also live in an increasingly complex, interconnected world, where quality attention to internal and external customers, strategic allies, and other stakeholders is essential for success. Knowing and honoring our values is more important than ever.

Giving Voice to Values (GVV) spoke to me in such a deep way when I was given a copy of Mary's book. Why was this? The thread that stood out for me with Mary's work was not in developing skills for distinguishing right from wrong but HOW to act on values despite opposing forces.[2] Over a 30-year career, I have encountered hundreds of these crossroad moments where leaders struggled with civility and ethics concerns. I began to see a pattern. Extremely bright and intelligent leaders when under stress frequently behaved in an abrasive or bullying manner. At times, ethical missteps were occurring. Often, they were in peril of losing their jobs. They had lost ownership of their personal values and, at times, described shaky ethical conduct. These leaders had mastered rationalizations for their conduct and slippage in honoring their values. Rationalizations[3] such as "I don't know how to say no." Or, "Everyone else is doing it." Or, "My hands are tied." The rationalizations imprisoned these leaders from taking action.

During the early years of my career, there were no human resource or coaching programs addressing the competencies in GVV. As a senior human resource leader in multiple industries, my role was to support leaders as an executive coach and human resources advisor. Some leaders were early in their careers – others were senior executives faced with ethical challenges. As I worked one-to-one with these leaders, I frequently saw they had lost their moral compass. Surprisingly, the leaders often recognized the slippage. Often, they knew the right thing to do; however, moving to action was at times an exceptionally difficult challenge. Action was particularly difficult when pressured by a boss, peers, or others to do the opposite or look the other way.

As I read Mary's words in *GVV*, it felt like manna from heaven. Within the pages of *GVV*, I found the guidance I was searching for in supporting others to pause, reflect, and find their authentic voice and values. I observed that in some situations, it was easier to be true to personal values than in others. The leaders I worked with gave specific examples of challenging situations – often involving a superior or a situation where there was conflict. As I incorporated the principles of GVV in my work as a coach, executive leader and human resources/organizational consultant, I was amazed at how quickly these leaders grasped the idea of practicing and scripting. Traditional HR or management approaches to these dilemmas can be more prescriptive or formulaic: (1) analyze the presenting problem; (2) determine performance or conduct slippage; (3) identify any ethical breach; (4) make recommendations; and (5) take action such as discipline, a performance improvement plan or termination of employment. These approaches do not take the time to ask: "If we are at our best, what will be happening?" Or, "What is the ideal outcome for all in this situation?" "How can we support each other through this challenge?" "What can we learn from this?" The values added in practicing and scripting are tangible leadership competencies: (1) the ability to dissect a dilemma and see opportunities for resolution, (2) the competence of identifying enablers or champions to support working through challenges and (3) the skill of analyzing the risk of not taking action. Intangible added values include increased confidence – the feeling that "I can do this!" Comments such as, "I know **what** to do, I have prepared a script – the **how** steps of the conversation, I have **analyzed the risks,** and I have mastered my rationalizations."

At the heart of GVV is the belief that individuals can decide the right thing to do. It is in the "how to do it" where they get stuck. Most of the leaders I have worked with get mired in the "what if's" at this juncture. "What if I lose my job?" "What if I become isolated and marginalized?" "What if things get worse?"

My role in supporting these leaders was to create a safe place for exploration. During my coaching conversations, the leaders presented a leadership challenge. Scripts were created, often with multiple iterations. At times the leaders expressed fear and doubt. There were occasions when feelings of anger, resentment, and guilt needed to be voiced as we worked on the scripts. The process takes time and patience. We worked on taking baby steps initially versus tackling complex values conversations. I asked this type of question: who do you want to be in this conversation? What is the ideal outcome of the conversation? What do you want for others in the conversation? When you are at your very best, what is happening? What is the worst outcome that could occur? Once the scripts are fine-tuned, verbal practice is critical to gain confidence and increase the capacity to voice values. Actually, practicing out loud greatly enhances this capacity.

As time progressed, the leaders became clear that the cost to them of not voicing their values was important enough even though it might not be successful. To get to a place of clarity, leaders gave deep thought to their own purpose in life. In each example, we talked through the risks associated in voicing their values. We talked about letting go of perfection and focusing on possibilities.

Over time and with practice, leaders found that by voicing their values, they implicitly gave permission to others to do the same. This was a process of practice with some experiencing early successes and others less positive outcomes. With perseverance and practice in writing the scripts and saying the scripts out loud, successes increased.[4] In each situation I asked the client what they learned in the experience, how they would change the conversation and how they felt. Many expressed feeling anxious and fearful as they entered the conversation. With each success (as defined by the client), confidence deepened. Clients stated they were acutely aware of the presence of their values such as integrity, honesty, empathy, and compassion. Each leader observed that during the first five minutes of their conversations they felt anxiety. As the conversation continued, anxiety diminished.

Integrating GVV into leadership coaching

Over the years, I have worked with astronauts at NASA; physicians at the Texas Medical Center in Houston; lawyers in prestigious law firms in New York City, San Francisco, and Seattle; engineers in high tech companies; and academics in higher education. The commonality across these different professions is extremely intelligent individuals who are doing important work in our world. In each environment there were opportunities to provide support to leaders who might be perceived as abrasive or who might be struggling with ethics concerns, thus, impacting their relationships and results. In addition, the near constant pressure to deliver results occasionally created shortcuts in honoring ethics and values.

What follows is a description of how I have applied Mary's work in key leadership challenges. All names have been changed to maintain confidentiality of the clients.

Coaching abrasive leaders

Leaders perceived as abrasive are generally blind to how their words and actions impact others. Typical conduct may include public humiliation, shaming, threatening, condescending words, etc. Coupled with this may be slippage in ethical conduct and in honoring personal values. In the medical and legal world this conduct is described as *disruptive*.

At the heart of coaching a leader perceived as abrasive is a focus on discovering their values. Abrasive leaders are defined as rubbing their coworkers the wrong way. Their words and actions create interpersonal friction that grates on coworkers, eroding employee motivation and organizational productivity. Abrasive behaviors range on a continuum from mildly wounding to severely disruptive. Another term for abrasive behavior is unacceptable conduct.

As I coached leaders perceived as abrasive I wanted to know: what is important to them? How does integrity show up in their lives? What internal wisdom can support them in returning to and giving voice to their values in a non-abrasive manner? Where specifically have their ethics slipped?

Let's look at some case studies

A well-known law firm referred a partner (Larry) to me. Over the previous couple of years, Larry's conduct had devolved into a pattern of publicly humiliating chastisements – particularly towards young associates and support employees. Shaming, threatening, and instilling fear in others were dominant patterns in his conduct. Turnover in his department had reached an intolerable level. The law firm wanted significant changes in Larry's conduct or his departure would be imminent.

Using the principles Mary describes in GVV, Larry and I worked to define his personal and professional purpose and values – specifically around the impact he most wanted in his profession and his personal life. The principles included gathering data and information before acting; preparing versus blurting out a response or position on a matter; the importance of questions versus answers when engaging in dialog with others; understanding the needs, fears, and motivations of the audience; framing and setting the context when entering a dialog; and thinking through what he wanted as an outcome for these important conversations.

Larry quickly gained insight into the destructive path he was on. He became aware that drifting from his values was creating serious internal conflicts. His method of coping with the internal conflict was to attack others. He recognized his drive to control and manipulate his associates was to create fear in them. Larry realized he needed to resolve the conflicts in his work life. We worked on scripts to support him in preparing for upcoming pivotal conversations. Larry labored in preparing the scripts – particularly in recognizing his pattern of rationalizations. His main rationalization was, "All the partners treat the associates like this." My coaching centered on barriers Larry was creating by hanging on to his rationalizations. I asked him what he saw as consequences if he refused to change how he was approaching the challenges in his work life. Larry quickly recognized he needed to let go of his rationalizations. Larry was able to articulate that a consequence for hanging on to his rationalizations was to be released from the partnership. Further, he feared loss of client relationships, his community activities, and personal esteem. Larry needed support in how to identify rationalizations and the steps to navigate through them. Once this awareness dawned with Larry, he was able to catch himself before stating a rationalization.

Larry and I worked through the conversations he needed to have with his associates. In preparing for the meeting with them, Larry expressed to me his embarrassment and contrition for his past bullying conduct. We discussed what he wanted to accomplish in the meeting. He stated he wanted to ask for forgiveness for his past conduct and he wanted to give his associates permission to confront him if he slipped.

Over a two-week period Larry worked on his script and practiced with me. Larry was clear about the actions he wanted to take in meeting with the associates. He expressed concern that they might resist his apology and disbelieve his sincerity based on his history with them. He recognized he would need to gain their trust over time by his actions versus simply the words of his script. Larry recognized this was a long-term process versus a short-term, one time conversation. Larry asked me to attend this meeting as an observer. Larry began the meeting by thanking those present. In a voice choked with emotion, he said:

> Over the past several weeks, I have been working with a coach to gain insight into my bullying conduct. At first, I was very angry that I was being asked to work on my conduct. I have come to know that my words and actions caused you and others great pain. I am sorry and ask your forgiveness.

The room was completely silent. There were tears. One by one each associate gave Larry a hug and expressed forgiveness. After the meeting Larry shared, "I have never felt more authentic and true to myself as I do in this moment." Larry recognized that while forgiveness was stated in the meeting with the associates, he would need to be mindful of his actions and words with the associates going forward.

How did we go from an angry, bullying person to one who felt great attrition and desired a different path forward? The process started with empathy and non-judgment from me, the coach. I also provided relevant data as to how Larry was being perceived. Initial conversations involved navigating Larry's initial defensiveness, discomfort, and embarrassment. I used language that invited Larry to identify his values, and inquired how he might use them in taking action. I asked: "If you were to act on your values – what would you say or do?"

At the eight-week mark in the coaching, Larry was demonstrating markedly improved conduct in his interactions with others. He reported relationships at work with his associates and partners was progressing positively. Larry was most proud of the shift in his relationship with his teenage children. When I asked him what led to the shifts, he replied, "I am consciously living my values." He added that he makes it a point to ask others about their values and how he might be of support to them.

Working with university athletes and athletic departments

Being accepted into an Ivy League top 10 school with a full scholarship was the dream of a lifetime for Casey. Her growing up years found her in numerous softball leagues. Her skills on the pitching mound garnered the attention of many college recruiters. As she arrived on the Ivy League campus her freshman year, she was full of excitement for the athletic program as well as the rigorous academic regimen.

Early on, she noticed some of her teammates were incurring injuries as a result of certain training protocols demanded by the Head Coach. Further, once injured, the players were badgered into playing by the Head Coach against the advice of the team physician. Casey began to notice a pattern of the Head Coach and Assistant Coaches using abusive language on and off the field with the team. This resulted in a demoralized and fearful team. Playing statistics went down – mental health issues increased.

And then, it happened to Casey. She incurred a stress fracture in her tibia. The team physician prescribed an orthopedic boot to alleviate the pain and allow for better healing. In spite of the injury, Casey played game after game.

In the spring of her junior year, Casey determined she would speak directly with the Head Coach one-to-one to voice her concerns about the team culture. Casey had invited her teammates to go with her for the initial conversation with the Head Coach. All of them declined stating they were too afraid – adding their belief that nothing would change with the team culture. Casey reached out to me for advice as to how to open the conversation with the Head Coach. Her intention was to state her concerns and work collaboratively with the Head Coach towards a better team environment. We talked about various reactions the Head Coach might have when confronted – even in a respectful manner. I asked Casey, "What is the worst outcome you can foresee in this conversation?" Casey said, "The coach may blame me and punish me in some way." In spite of the risks, Casey was firm in her resolve to have the conversation. She was clear that not having the conversation would diminish her sense of who she truly is.

Over the following two weeks we worked on the script Casey would use. We discussed as well the reasons and rationalizations Casey confronted in anticipating the meeting with the Head Coach. For example, Casey questioned herself as to whether she was searching for individual solace or was she desiring a change in her softball community. Further, she gave serious thought to her wish that someone else would handle the conversation – perhaps one of the trainers or one of the Assistant Coaches. Casey was firm in her resolve to honor her values. I asked Casey to tell me more about her values. She replied, "I value respect for all, kindness, transparency, honesty, fairness, and compassion." Casey was clear about how she wanted to be in the conversation with her coach. She wanted to be calm, respectful, and candid.

Casey began her script by saying,

I want to talk with you about some concerns and observations I have. May I continue? I noticed when I injured my leg, the language towards me became hostile, demeaning, and accusatory. I'd like to better understand how we can work together to have a respectful and collaborative coach/player relationship.

Casey reported the coach was tense and defensive at the beginning of the conversation. Casey and I had worked together to develop some questions to support the script if there were moments of defensiveness. Some of the questions were: "What motivation strategies do you feel are most effective with our team? "How can the team measure success other than winning games?" "What can I do to support positive changes on the team?"

The Head Coach agreed to hold a subsequent team meeting. At the team meeting, teammates voiced concerns about the hostile language and treatment they were experiencing from the Head Coach. The team stated they felt fearful, unmotivated, and disempowered. They expressed concern there would be retaliation following the meeting. The Head Coach became angry and defensive. Casey intervened and suggested that each player and the Head Coach take some time to consider how they could each honor personal values. The team discussed what that would look like on the team. The team agreed to include an agenda item on values at each team meeting.

Two days following the team meeting, the Head Coach asked Casey to meet with her. During the meeting the Head Coach stated, "It's clear that the softball team here and the coaches cannot meet your expectations. I'm kicking you off the team." Casey was devastated. She believed in her heart that she had honored her values in her conversation with the Head Coach. She loved playing softball and thoroughly enjoyed her teammates. In spite of her disillusionment, Casey said she was proud of herself in that she used courage to speak with the Head Coach and honored her values.

Within hours the team surrounded Casey to give support. Feeling anger and frustration toward the Head Coach, the team decided to escalate their concerns to the university Athletic Director and the Vice President of Student Affairs. The student newspaper wrote scathing articles about the softball culture and the Head Coach's history with the softball team.

A month passed. The university sent a notice to the players and coach that an investigation with an outside lawyer would ensue over the summer. During this time two Assistant Coaches and the trainer resigned and accepted positions at other universities. Freshman athletes who had signed to join the team backed out of their commitments.

The results of the investigation revealed a toxic environment led by the abrasive Head Coach. In spite of the investigation facts, the university agreed to retain the Head Coach. She was placed on a performance plan that would be closely monitored by senior administration. She was asked to work with a consultant who specializes in working with leaders perceived as hostile, disruptive, or abrasive.

The university Athletic Director followed up with each team member. Casey considered returning to the team when invited by the Athletic Director. She chose to not return. She is deeply aware of the courage she demonstrated in facing her fears and honoring her values in the conversations with the Head Coach. Her teammates have all expressed how much they respect and admire her. Casey lost something she highly cherished – being a pitcher for an Ivy League team. Despite her initial sadness and deep disappointment, Casey gained a profound conviction that she took the honorable path of giving voice to her values. She is an honors student and graduated in May 2020. The Head Coach continues leadership development coaching.

This case profoundly demonstrates the power of giving voice to values, the courage to enter a conversation with a respectful script, the challenge of managing a myriad of emotions and the recognition that one cannot always control the outcome of a situation.

GVV played an important role in this case through supporting the process of creating a script for Casey in meeting with her coach. Casey had already made the decision that she needed to surface the dysfunctional team dynamics with the Head Coach. She and her teammates had discussed the reasons and rationalizations – it won't make any difference, our hands are tied, the Head Coach will get angry and retaliate, the university will not believe or support our concerns. Casey needed support in countering these rationalizations and moving to understand how to take action. Fortunately, there were a number of enablers for Casey, including the support of her parents, her grandmother, her university advisor, the team physician, and the team trainer.

The university sees the situation as coaches have a lot of pressure and need better team communication strategies. The team sees the situation as the university won't take actions leading to better sports team environments and are fearful of legal actions. They openly express belief the university will take care of and cover for their own versus foster accountability and a transparent approach to improve team conditions.

Casey's teammates frequently tell her they admire the courage and conviction she had in taking action. She is viewed as a role model by her teammates. Casey views the outcome as an initial loss, disillusionment, and disappointment. As time has gone by, she fervently believes she learned and modeled the GVV approach with awareness, analysis, decision-making and scripting leading to increased confidence. As Casey's coach, I see this as an ultimate win for her. Her confidence is grounded in her values and her deep belief that no matter the circumstances she will face in life, she will do so with dignity, grace, and deep conviction to give voice to her values – even when the outcome is less than positive.

I asked Casey if she would take these actions again knowing what she knows about the outcome. Her response, "Without a doubt. It was the right thing to do." I was Casey's coach as she navigated this dilemma.

Facilitating leadership development programs

Fred was a newly selected leader for a student services department in a large community college with multiple campuses. Fred had a stellar academic career as a faculty member, Dean, and Vice President. As he moved upward in his career, he began to wrestle with leadership skills he had not acquired. Complaints increased from his direct reports. They were being asked by Fred to cut corners through the purchasing process impacting the quality of construction projects centered on safety.

Fred was invited to participate in a leadership development class sponsored by the college. Early on in the class, Fred stated that he felt pressure to deliver results on time and within budget constraints. He was deeply concerned that the pressure was creating ethical breaches. Fred was acutely aware his employees were demoralized with the situation and were voicing complaints to the Office of Dispute Resolution. Fred was experiencing anxiety and internal conflicts.

Class discussion centered on questions to Fred to surface his personal values. He quickly was able to articulate them – honesty, transparency, and respect. Fred worked on scripting how he would frame a conversation with his boss. Fred practiced with the support of his classmates. He admitted feeling anxious and fearful that the conversation would break down into angry chaos. Class conversations centered on the skills of emotional self-management when in a challenging conversation with heated rhetoric. Fred practiced his script with various classmates (peer coaches) to gain confidence. Fred recognized the enablers to support the conversation and increase his confidence for the conversation were: (1) preparation – gathering information and data, (2) preparing a script, (3) practicing the script with his classmates,[5] and (4) thinking through possible emotions that could surface during the conversation. Fred felt confident that given the opportunity, his boss would choose to amend the current practice for the greater good in the college.

Following his script, Fred began the meeting with his boss by saying,

> Thanks for meeting with me. I've made some notes about a few things I'm concerned about. As you know, we've been cutting corners over the past few months in an effort to increase efficiency and productivity. This has impacted employee morale. I've been informed that employees are so concerned they are going to the Office of Dispute Resolution to file grievances. I want to work with you to find a better way for us to increase productivity without cutting corners.

Fred reported that he managed his emotions throughout the conversation. He stated that practicing with his peer coaches made all the difference in his confidence in entering the conversation with the boss.

Fred returned to class a few days later. He stated the conversation with his boss had occurred. He added the boss initially was very angry in the conversation. Fred told the class he remained calm and focused on his values and what he wanted to see through the purchasing process to gain realignment with his cherished values of honesty, transparency, and fairness in interactions with others.

Over the subsequent month, Fred reported that the boss did not change the production processes. Fred was relieved when the boss requested a second meeting. This time, the boss was calm and prepared to discuss what he and Fred needed to do to get back on track in the production department. The two worked together to prepare a project plan with a concrete timeline for the improved production changes.

Fred's situation and how he prepared, practiced, and delivered his script encouraged others in the leadership class to identify, plan, and prepare for their own values-based conversations. Other classmates identified situations they had been avoiding by using excuses such as it won't make any difference or that's the way it is here. Classmates recognized that it was relatively easy to make a decision about what to do when they needed to voice their values. The challenging part was in planning how to do it. Scripting was the critical component that follows the surfacing and articulation of values. Fred was a role model to the class in modeling the way with the GVV process.

Of particular value to this class was thinking through ways to voice and act on their values while side-stepping arguments and rationalizations. For example, we considered together and practiced how to say "no" respectively. The class was asked to confront the questions, "if my hands weren't tied, what would I do or say?"

These leaders shared that when they write out what they want to say and are able to practice the script in a safe environment, they gain confidence and competence prior to a pivotal conversation. These conversations may involve a measure of risk and feelings of fear and anxiety. Through participating in this class, Fred and the other leaders in the class gained confidence in knowing what to say, to whom, and especially how to say what needs to be voiced.

Guiding change management initiatives

In the spring of 2018, I was asked to support a large organization in a major reorganization project coupled with a significant downsizing. Entering the project, I quickly observed there had been no change management fundamental groundwork such as establishing a project team, developing a communication plan and conducting employee meetings to explain the rationale for the significant changes evolving. There was extreme stress and anxiety across the organization. Fear was rampant. Further, none of the senior leadership team had any experience in organization-wide change initiatives or downsizing fundamentals. The challenging dilemmas in this massive change initiative were not Black and White. There were many shades of gray. The organization was known for procrastination and avoidance. This initiative was perfect to introduce GVV. Individuals in the organization would readily articulate the actions they believed necessary to move the organization forward. Collectively, they experienced inertia when in group meetings. They would revert to individual wants and needs versus considering what was best for the organization. Their focus was frequently short-term versus a longer term view to move the organization forward. As I introduced the overview of GVV, the leadership team quickly grasped the actions they needed to take. They articulated their values. They voiced their concerns that the needed changes would impact their relationships with employees; they stated they felt they would not be liked and that the risks were high that friends would reject them. They did not know HOW to move forward constructively. Robust brainstorming meetings followed with a focus on HOW to step into values-based conversations and how to identify rationalizations as well as enablers.

John, the CEO, knew action and communication needed to get underway quickly. Working together, we identified the core transition team. This led to a project team charter that included the values that would guide the difficult work of the project. The Director of Marketing agreed to create a communication plan, and the Chief Human Resources Officer created talking points for John to use in his employee meetings. I worked with John to incorporate the personal values he wanted to articulate in his meetings across the organization. A project timeline was created to guide each part of the project.

GVV was used in the weekly core transition team meeting. Typical agenda items included: (1) articulating the purpose of the reorganization; (2) identifying all stakeholders in the reorganization; (3) surfacing legal and ethical possibilities in the work; (4) considering risk management concerns; and (5) understanding rationalizations, e.g., "This won't work," "Everyone will be angry at us," "I've never done this before." As we talked about and worked through these rationalizations, I introduced the topic of enablers. Among the most important enablers for this change management process were (1) a 100% commitment to honor the values of integrity, honesty, openness, and fairness; (2) a champion in John who was willing to provide needed resources such as money and consultants as needed; (3) creation of a core transition team and detailed project plan; and (4) specific dates with accountabilities assigned.

The departmental reorganizations occurred first in the project timeline. The layoffs followed. Preceding the layoff conversations, training was held for managers tasked with notifying employees who were losing their positions.

Scripts for the notification meetings were prepared by me. This responsibility became mine since I had experience in scripting departure conversations in other companies. I consulted with managers to provide support to them, get their input, and provide education regarding best practices in separation conversations. The scripts in an employee separation meeting are generally quite brief. This was the managers' script in meeting with the affected employee:

> Thank you for meeting with me. As you know, the institution has been encountering significant reduction in student enrollment which impacts the bottom line. As a result of this circumstance, your position has been eliminated. I want you to know, you're work here has been valued. The institution has created a separation package for you. Human Resources will be meeting with you next to review the package. I want to thank you again and wish you well.

It is important to note that preparing managers ahead of the notification meeting is critical. Managers must be able to handle strong emotions such as anger or tears. They must know how to manage defensiveness – their own and the impacted employees. They need to know how to answer questions such as "Why me?" Managers conducted many practice sessions with me and their fellow managers, who served as peer coaches. During the training and practice sessions, we focused on giving voice to our values – identified as transparency, respect, honesty, and empathy. We talked about typical responses employees have when informed they are losing their jobs. The Human Resources Department prepared off-boarding packets that included additional compensation, transition support including resume review, and interviewing tips.

A particular concern for me was providing emotional support for the managers tasked with delivering the termination conversations. Many rationalizations surfaced during the preparation of scripts and the delivery to impacted employees. Rationalizations included: "I think Rachel should handle these conversations. She has far more experience than I do," "I feel like I am betraying people I have known for many years." "Can't we just wait a little longer?" "What if we just send an email to these employees?" Time was spent in conversation and training about how leaders need to manage very challenging situations at times as fiduciaries of the institution.

We discussed the discomfort of going through this type of conversation. With time, peer coaching practice, and scripts, confidence and competence increased with the managers. These conversations are an extremely difficult task to accomplish even when well-prepared and experienced.

Following the separation conversations, we reconvened as a team to discuss what went well and what could be improved. Prepared scripts were noted as extremely valuable. Preparing and practicing the scripts lessened doubts and fear when managers entered the layoff conversations. The managers felt more competent in handling the conversation with empathy and candor. The team discussed the emotions they felt entering the conversations such as anxiety and doubt and the feelings they had after the conversations. Those feelings included relief, residues of sadness and a measure of confidence. The cadre of managers who worked together to navigate the challenging changes in this organization became a team of peer coaches. They continue to encourage and support each other in problem-solving and peer coaching.

In my work as a human resources executive, I have encountered situations where senior level executives have committed transgressions that could have resulted in immediate termination of employment. Transgressions included fudging expense accounts, inflating earnings reports, having an affair with a coworker or diverting company materials for personal use.

Bringing GVV to these situations has resulted in Boards of Directors pausing the immediate reaction to fire the executive to take the time (1) to reflect on the organization's values – what do we stand for; (2) to question, if we act on our stated values, what could we do or say; (3) to ask the tough questions – what is the right thing to do versus the legal or quick decision, or, when we look back at this situation in five years, how do we want the actions taken now to reflect our stated values? I have witnessed leaders confront their transgressions, make restoration, and maintain their positions. I have seen Boards of Directors choose the more challenging path of supporting these troubled leaders by walking beside the leader on the journey to restoration. The outcome is preserved reputations for the leader and for the companies they serve.

Conclusion

As I conclude this chapter, I am humbled to have been a part of the journeys in these case studies. The examples of honoring personal values and the experiences of voicing those values through preparation and scripting are noteworthy. Each person found courage to step into the unknown – the how of the conversations. They analyzed the risks in their dilemmas and concluded that to say or do nothing was not acceptable.

I believe that as a leadership coach, human resource leader. or CEO, learning about and using Mary C. Gentile's GVV work will greatly enhance your professional competencies. You will learn the skills of working through challenging situations in incremental steps, changing the frame of a problem to an opportunity, finding win-win solutions, appealing to a shared purpose, starting with questions versus answers or assumptions, and learning how to script conversations to guide the discussion. You will also gain a deep understanding of your own values.

I have grown both personally and professionally by reading Mary's book and integrating her teachings into my coaching practice. I know for sure I have gained deep confidence in my willingness to navigate values-based conversations for myself and in supporting others. Earlier in my life I framed these conversations as requiring tremendous courage. I experienced near paralyzing fear and anxiety. In spite of this, I was frequently asked by CEO's and others to support them in resolving these dilemmas. I came to understand that, perhaps, I had some talent in navigating these challenging workplace dilemmas. I wanted to gain a deeper understanding of contemporary research and best practices in giving voice to my values when faced with a conflict or ethical challenge. I needed a guide to support my personal development. Mary's GVV was spot on. I listened to Mary's recordings, completed the GVV coursework on Coursera and practiced with every opportunity that came my way.

Today, my executive coaching practice continues. My foundation for this work is grounded in Mary C. Gentile's GVV and research. They are my anchor in every coaching engagement where I serve.

Notes

1 Gentile, M. C. (2010). Preface see *how to act*. In *Giving voice to values* (p. 12). Retrieved from www.GivingVoiceToValues.org
2 Gentile, M. C. (2010). Preface. In *Giving voice to values* (p. 13). Retrieved from www.GivingVoiceToValues.org
3 Gentile, M. C. (2010). Reasons and rationalizations. In *Giving voice to values* (pp. 170–175). Retrieved from www.GivingVoiceToValues.org

4 Gentile, M. C. et al. (2010). Practice and roleplaying. In *Giving voice to values* (pp. 5–8, 160–161, 192–193). Retrieved from www.GivingVoiceToValues.org
5 Gentile, M. C. et al. (2010). Peer coaching. In *Giving voice to values* (p. 221). Retrieved from www.GivingVoiceToValues.org

References

Gentile, M. C. (2010). How to act. In *Giving voice to values* (p. 12). Retrieved from www.GivingVoiceToValues.org

Gentile, M. C. (2010). Peer coaching. In *Giving Voice to Values* (p. 221). Retrieved from www.GivingVoiceToValues.org

Gentile, M. C. (2010). Practice and roleplaying. In *Giving voice to values* (pp. 5–8, 160–161, 192–193). Retrieved from www.GivingVoiceToValues.org

Gentile, M. C. (2010). Preface. In *Giving voice to values* (p. 13). Retrieved from www.GivingVoiceToValues.org

Gentile, M. C. (2010). Reasons and rationalizations. In *Giving voice to values* (pp. 170–175). Retrieved from www.GivingVoiceToValues.org

12

INTRODUCING GIVING VOICE TO VALUES TO NEW AUDIENCES

Jane Cote and Claire Kamm Latham

Giving Voice to Values (GVV) began with the realization that new MBA graduates, well prepared for the technical demands of their new careers, were stymied by the continuous challenges to their values. Often superiors' requests fell into grey areas, many of which violated values new graduates held and had assumed would be respected in the workplace. The GVV framework has provided countless professionals the structure to address workplace concerns. As the reputation of GVV has risen, many scholars and trainers have recognized the need for GVV to evolve into new domains. This chapter will share our experiences and the approaches we have used to expand the GVV framework to professional accounting practitioners and two affinity groups with unique integrity boundary challenges:[1] women and social service professionals. For example, many individuals are in social work to assist others in improvement of their circumstances. In this role of helping others, the social worker may be challenged in maintaining clear boundaries, preserving confidentiality, and exercising appropriate rapport building.

Several factors motivated extending GVV to these audiences. First, as our accounting students graduated, they reached out to us to share experiences they were having in the workplace. They had participated in GVV exercises in the classroom but as they confronted integrity boundaries in their workplace, they sought further guidance. Workplace concerns were wide ranging. New professionals expressed challenges such as confronting superiors when decisions were made to manipulate employee assignments solely to avoid paying benefits; a colleague who was having a personal relationship with a superior was seen leaving work early and coming in late; and management's insistence on ignoring a new employee's prior illegal behavior within the same industry that could negatively impact the firm when it appeared the employee was repeating the same types of activities (i.e., submitting for reimbursement and requesting advances without appropriate documentation). These experiences and others created a growing need to expand GVV training beyond the university classroom. Moving beyond the university offered opportunities to learn more about the contexts in which GVV can be a productive framework for resolving workplace challenges.

The initial opportunity arose when conversations with CPAs highlighted concerns about the efficacy of biannual mandated ethics education. Most available courses were focused on regulatory compliance and not addressing those issues falling outside the code but potentially putting the professional and the firm at risk. Alumni who had participated in GVV workshops, created and conducted by the authors, advocated for GVV to be incorporated into the mandated ethics education. As faculty we saw this as an added opportunity to raise funds to support our accounting students and programs. With these events as backdrop, we created a workshop that met the requirements for mandated ethics education and in lieu of compensation for us as presenters, CPA firms made generous contributions to support our students and programs.

As events unfolded nationally, conversations surrounding women's challenges and capacity for voice in the workplace emerged. High profile cases were motivating more women to question the experiences they face and seek approaches to improve their workplace environment. As we discussed our GVV forums with CPA firms among various community members, we were encouraged to develop a GVV workshop targeted to women. Concurrently, one social service agency developing a series of workshops asked for a GVV workshop for their staff and constituents. Through the development of GVV workshops for three differing groups we have uncovered new insights into the depth and breadth of challenges in the workplace and how GVV can aid a broad set of audiences.

Those seeking to present GVV in new settings can be comforted by the strength of the framework. Our workshops all have followed a similar pattern and employed the same or similar GVV resources. The first step involves a series of exercises geared toward understanding yourself. Where have you navigated challenges to your values successfully in past settings? What approaches are most comfortable for you to address your concerns? Second, the workshop moves to recognizing the need to also understand others. What might be their motivations for observed behavior? Whereas you can clearly see the need for behavior or action change, others may not. Where are the spaces where values do align that you can begin to open the conversation for change? Finally, preparing to respond can take on many forms and each individual and each circumstance require one to devise an approach tailored to their strengths as well as the resources available to them.

The GVV framework provides structure but as we have experienced with students, the approach needs to be tailored to the audience for the message to resonate. As GVV workshops were developed for specific professional and community-based audiences, careful planning to understand the integrity boundaries experienced and the context of their environment was necessary for the energy and power of GVV to transfer to participants. In the next section, we provide details on the basic workshop framework and focus on the unique aspects in the public accounting profession. We then describe our experience in the other two arenas focusing on how we have tailored the basic workshop to each setting. This is followed by an evaluation of workshop efficacy and thoughts on new dimensions and directions.

GVV in public accounting profession

Most State Boards of Accountancy require ethics instruction as part of the required continuing professional education for continued licensure. Overwhelmingly, CPAs complain about the bland, ineffective ethics training they must endure biannually. Addressing these pervasive concerns, an ethics CPE workshop that included an introduction to GVV was developed and successfully implemented. In Oregon, the requirement is four hours of ethics training with at least one hour that covers ethics regulatory update. There is broad latitude for the remaining content, but workshops must be approved by the Board of Accountancy to count as continuing education in ethics.

The foundations of GVV emphasize that repeated practice is necessary to develop moral muscle memory. Moral muscle memory is the result of layers of activities participants can transfer to post-workshop experiences. With repeated practice using a variety of settings and methods, an individual develops a set of practiced schemas that can be elicited when circumstances arise. Recognizing that each circumstance is likely unique, the development of moral muscle memory offers individuals opportunities to recognize patterns and tailor solution schemas to the circumstances, organizations, and individuals. GVV is a thoughtful and nuanced tool to guide the development of action strategies. The workshop is highly interactive with several opportunities for participants to build their moral muscle memory as they engage with each other, participate in active tasks, and take time for reflective exercise. As described earlier, the workshop falls into the three sections: 1) Understanding Yourself, 2) Understanding Others, and 3) Preparing to Respond.

Understanding Yourself

Taking the time to understand one's own personal and professional integrity boundaries sets the stage. Many participants express angst about finding voice in the moment when their values are challenged. Research conducted with the accounting profession found that the most consistent and profound values challenges faced by CPAs occur with client interactions (Neesham & Azim, 2018). Our workshops with the accounting profession have reinforced these findings. For instance, conflict of interest was identified as a primary issue faced by firms. With more complicated, multi-firm engagements it is difficult to assess where the organizational boundaries lie. When circumstances become contentious, conflict of interest accusations can arise as well as concerns over client confidentiality. Prior workshop participants have expressed that GVV tools have provided the framework to develop a strategy that resolved the situations and preserved the relationships.

Client retention is another example where accounting professionals must balance the expectations from the firm with the needs to uphold the principles of accounting. Clients will ask for accommodations on their financial or tax statements that violate the code of professional conduct and/or generally accepted accounting principles. Navigating the need for client retention with the need to uphold the standards of the profession can create intolerable levels of stress for CPAs.

Along these lines, when work product from one firm is shared and that work product is substandard, professionals find it difficult to know how to address this with colleagues from another firm. Often, they rely on these relationships as a productive income stream and actions taken may impact the relationship. In one workshop, a participant struggled with whether he should inform the State Board of Accountancy of his concerns that a predecessor firm had not followed accounting standards. These and other instances highlight a recurring theme in the accounting profession where the actions of others that conflict with the boundaries of the professional code of conduct create heightened job stress, whether it be clients, internal/external colleagues or management pressures for client retention leading to accounting choices that are in the darker grey areas.

We explored situations like these and the role of GVV through an initial exercise. The Tale of Two Stories starts by asking participants to identify one situation where they have successfully addressed a value/principle-based challenge. They list the circumstances that motivated them to act, the set of actions, and resulting outcomes. Participants pair up and share their motivations and actions/outcomes with another. Due to requirements for client confidentiality, they are not asked to share the specific circumstance. Debriefing the exercise, the motivations and actions are elicited and once the audience recognizes both the commonality in their successes and the alternatives others have employed that they had not considered, the stage is set where participants are receptive to the GVV framework. Motivations to act center on a) maintaining firm reputation, b) their own professional identity, and c) the AICPA Code of Conduct.

Understanding Others

In an emotionally charged setting, it can be difficult to perceive the perspectives others will bring when concerns are expressed. Developing moral muscle memory includes assessing the perspectives of others, preparing for objections and rationalizations, and finding that common ground upon which productive voice can find traction.

Individuals, especially early in their careers, will often see others in a good versus evil dichotomy, that those who commit unethical acts are inescapably evil. As professional experience increases, individuals have more contextual understanding that attenuates the good/evil labeling. Professionals are typically working in teams where the need to balance strengths and personalities to accomplish the task is a priority. However, it is still important to emphasize that decisions are made in a context and that many who do step over the ethical line have not considered the impact of their actions or believe they are acting unethically. The activities in this section increase understanding of others' perspectives starting with a key exercise which helps participants see that there are values widely shared by all. As described in Shawver and Miller (2018, p. 33), "(k)nowing this allows an individual an opening to begin the conversation in a non-threatening atmosphere" and "(t)his interconnectedness serves to create a critical community of understanding and reinforce the concept that *one is not alone* in facing values challenges."

An interactive exercise serves to highlight our commonalities. To begin to discuss the GVV strategies we can develop to address integrity boundaries, we start by demonstrating where we have more in common that we might think. In a stressful situation, often we portray the actors in a binary, good versus evil framework. Our goal is to highlight that as individuals we hold common values that are important to us. Understanding what those common values are helps us to frame the situation more contextually. After a short presentation on the nature of values, participants identify the values that most strongly define themselves. Each value is written on a single sticky note and there is no limit to the number but participants complete the task in a few minutes, attempting to elicit their most closely held values. Each participant then places the notes on the wall and, as they do so, we begin to see commonalities. Similar to the word cloud concept, what emerges is a set of values that are shared by many. Typically, the five most universally shared values emerge: honesty, respect, responsibility, fairness and compassion (Gentile, 2010, p. 30). Debriefing the exercise, participants come to realize where they are more alike than different. As integrity boundaries are crossed, knowledge that others likely share their own values creates a starting point to open dialogue around critical concerns.

Depending on the participant profile and organizational culture of the firm other dominant clusters also emerge. For instance, in some organizations this exercise highlights the hierarchy or lack of hierarchy in the firm. In one firm, the teamwork value was evident among the participants. In a session with senior leaders and new professionals, it was clear that teamwork was an organizational value. The senior leaders openly discussed where they had experienced integrity boundaries and actively sought the input from new professionals. In contrast, when this exercise was conducted within another firm, teamwork was not a dominant cluster. During workshop discussions, new professionals were quieter and often waited for senior leaders to comment before they offered their own input. Senior leaders did not seek new professionals' input. The unique cultural dynamic between the two firms was striking. It reinforced the impact that organizational factors can have when employees seek to resolve concerns.

Understanding others also requires an assessment of the situation from the perspective of others. Seeking additional information from peers or authoritative sources, of particular importance in public accounting, can provide the context and environmental circumstances underlying the motivations of the observed actions of others. These actions help to frame the action plan and provide a knowledge foundation upon which one can find the appropriate level of authoritative strength underlying the concern. Equipped with such evidence, confidence matures and the individual is better prepared for productive dialogue. In responding to an integrity boundary concern, GVV advocates finding what works for the individual – a "comfort zone" for many in the public accounting arena is accepted accounting principles and the code of conduct. Often those confronted with a request for changed behavior or decisions will seek to defend their position. Recognizing in advance the underlying motivations will prepare the individual to counter rationalizations and to advance a position. One salient example where accounting professionals tend to ground their approach to integrity boundary breaches with authoritative sources is in the area of valuation. One example we present in the workshops is a scenario where the client insists on reporting a charitable contribution at a level that appears to be in excess of its market valuation. Tension arises when a major client for the firm attempts to pressure the CPA to accept the seemingly inflated valuation. Recognizing the risks to the firm and to the client if this valuation is challenged by the IRS, the CPA consults authoritative sources on the asset valuation and the degree to which the IRS will accept a range of valuations.

Building on what participants have learned about themselves and others, *Preparing to Respond* comprises the final workshop component. Continuing the example from the prior paragraph, once the CPA determines the client is asking for an inflated valuation, the CPA then develops an action strategy. Working with the partner who understands the client, they develop talking points that help the client see the risks entailed with inflated valuations. Knowing the client will insist and draw upon their importance to the firm several scenarios are developed in advance to address the potential pushback from the client.

A case activity is then used to explore the context in which actors are motivated to make decisions lacking in integrity. The case offers participants an opportunity to practice GVV concepts in a setting similar to their own. However, we have found that a third-party setting generates more conversation than using examples from the profession or their organization. The primary GVV case we employ is "Violation of Privacy (available at http://store.darden.virginia.edu/giving-voice-to-values)," incorporating peer coaching and scripting in this activity. "Violation of Privacy" is set in the technology industry where data on devices are not removed and when resold as reconditioned, may contain data from prior owners. The cost of fixing the problem is significant and comes at a time of budget constraints. Some case actors wonder if it would be better to ignore the problem so that they are not blamed for the additional cost to fix the problem. This concept of data privacy is analogous to client confidentiality in the public accounting profession. Moving it into another industry context allows participants to focus on the approach to resolving the dilemma the lead actor faces without complicating it with their own experiences in the accounting industry. We specifically make the link to the profession by having participants reflect, at the end of the activity, on the challenges they face with client confidentiality issues.

With this case activity in *Preparing to Respond*, each participant first crafts an individualized approach based on their preferred communication mode and setting. We then provide the guidance on peer coaching shown in Appendix A and have participants form pairs, alternating the roles of presenting and listening. The peer coaching exercise provides the opportunity for each individual to present their strategy and scripts to a colleague who also serves as a peer coach in the exercise. The peer coach can provide insights that may have been overlooked as well as give the individual added confidence for action. In the workshops, we have found both techniques are best practiced in a GVV case setting as a case creates a hypothetical situation where the emotional intensity of the setting is dampened. At workshops, time for both scripting and coaching has proven to be valuable experiences for participants. We debrief this activity including specifically prompting participants to share what they learned from their peer coach. Action plans have included (1) doing one's homework first and ensuring one has all of the facts, including the potential impact of disclosure of the flaw to the public (loss of trust, company reputation) and (2) enlisting allies from the various departments in the organization and ensuring that individuals are aware of the consequences of nonaction. Participants appeared to vary most in regards to how they would inform management with some advocating for individual sessions with different upper management and others supporting a presentation to an upper management group.

Nearing the end of the workshop, we use this opportunity to review key takeaways of the GVV framework. The final exercise in *Preparing to Respond* is for individual participants to reflect on a time where they did not respond to a values challenge but wished they had been able to. Using what they have learned, participants script a response to the previous values challenge. We have limited time at this point and do not formally debrief participants on their script however we have found that individuals often want to stay after and share the tools they have learned in anticipation of using them in future circumstances. Appendix B presents an agenda for the typical workshop format.

GVV and women in the workplace

As noted earlier, the basic workshop format is used in the other settings, that is, *Understanding Yourself*, *Understanding Others*, and *Preparing to Respond* comprise the three components. This forum brought together a broad cross section of women. We modeled the forum similarly to other women leadership forums in our community. We recruited sponsors, promoted it widely, and created an environment that included networking breaks and significant active learning exercises and discussion points. Many participants were senior executives, but many were early career stage too. More so than any other setting, women wanted time to talk about the matters of concern and time to support others when scripting and peer coaching. As such, some of the time devoted to the regulatory portion in the public accounting setting was used to expand the discussion in Tale of Two Stories, the values exercise, and *Preparing to Respond*.

A natural affinity emerges quickly among women. Hence, we built on this by creating a comfortable setting with built-in time to network. Concerns around being heard and taken seriously by colleagues, as well as having opportunities in the workplace that advance their careers are common conversation points. We augmented our workshop with presentations on research focused on issues women face as they advance in the workplace. For instance, women can experience a confidence gap (cf. Martin & Phillips, 2017; Sheppard & Aquino, 2017). It manifests in subtle and not so subtle ways. Women are less likely to speak up in work settings and are more likely than men to be interrupted when they do speak up. Women are less likely than men to take credit for their accomplishments and men tend to physically spread out more than women at the table, which signals to them and others more power and importance. However, women value relationships as the primary emphasis in building a healthy workplace. In the workshop, we emphasize that GVV asks us to recognize our own style to accentuate our talents and develop strategies to turn our challenges to our advantage.

Several unique outcomes organically arose with a women-only audience. First, the women perceived they had a safe forum to voice common workplace concerns they struggled to resolve. For instance, the lack of voice in a business setting among more assertive and more commonly male colleagues creates a challenge for women to surmount. Commonality around how women would make a comment or suggestion and be ignored, only to have the similar suggestion repeated by a male colleague and praised. Knowing that this was frequently experienced by women was an eye-opener for some. Developing simple voice empowering strategies, such as having another woman say that she just heard her female colleague make the same suggestion would alert the male colleagues that they should have realized they had ignored the female colleague voice. Second, in the limited time we had to present the foundations of GVV, women were able to recognize the need for an action strategy and build some initial ideas about how they could do this. For instance, at one table a senior professional was seated with several professional women at the early career stage. As the concerns about not being taken seriously in the workplace emerged, the senior professional provided her contact information and insisted they call her when this happens. Her experience succeeding in a male-dominated industry was one she was willing to share so that the next generation of women professionals was better prepared than she had been. The realization that common integrity boundaries are faced by professional women, and that a solution strategy using GVV tools created an opportunity to address it together was insightful for many.

Research on the ways in which women respond to each other in the workplace as well as how third parties tend to interpret the interaction to be problematic also sparked insights from participants (Sheppard & Aquino, 2017). Sheppard and Aquino (2017, p. 19) theorize that "the problematization of female same-sex conflict/relationships could actually cause or exacerbate conflict among women," that is, "third parties' interpretations of female same-sex conflict could spill over into the first parties' understandings about their own interactions." This was again eye-opening to many and had them considering the potential responses of a broader circle (i.e., understanding others). Presenting these and other research findings creates a shared community which opens conversations among participants.

Because of this dynamic and the fact that the manager in the case is female, we have found "Violation of Privacy" to be a successful case in *Preparing to Respond* for this setting also. In the women's workshop, the conversation changed. It becomes less about data privacy, which was the primary focus of discussions and actions strategies identified earlier in the CPA workshops where participants were both male and female, and more about women's voice in a male dominated environment. As this case was set in the technology industry, women spoke about the pervasive culture that makes it more difficult for women to develop the respect of their colleagues. With few women colleagues to rely upon for support, the participants mostly spoke of the barriers they might encounter in this setting yet found strength in the knowledge that they could reach out to each other, and as described earlier, to a later career individual external to the organization who expressed willingness to be a mentor.

GVV in social service agencies

We again used the same basic framework in a social service setting with expanded discussion time similar to the women's workshop. One of the co-authors has had extensive experience in the non-profit industry and provided context of areas which would be at the forefront of participants' concerns, helping to guide the debriefs and encourage discussion. Hence, though the three components are the same, participants' focus was on care for others and the challenges they face when advocating for the rights of others. They work in a high stress environment with high levels of unpredictability. Frequently, economically fragile individuals and the organizations which support them (who are also often economically fragile) struggle with the many assaults on their values and finding appropriate strategies to act. They are careful to advocate for their clients while not antagonizing the stakeholders they rely upon for funding and other mechanisms of support.

The "Violation of Privacy" case also resonated with participants in this setting, with particular emphasis on the peer coaching component. The case presents a relevant context for social service providers where client records need to be kept confidential. Any technology breaches that impact clients are serious. Participants reflect on current events where organizations did not respond to a data breach in a timely fashion and the dire consequences that followed. Peer coaching helps them to practice in the context of the case with small stakes values challenges, to build moral muscle memory that will aid them as they seek to tackle the bigger challenges they face in their mission-based work.

Participant discussions in the social services setting also solidified the potential of new dimensions of GVV for us.[2] With this community of social service professionals, diversity and equity topics were of the greatest concern expressed during discussions of potential integrity boundary challenges. For instance, a transgender participant sought approaches to communicate with their colleagues their needs and expectations to be treated appropriately. As a powerful example of impact, one participant reported back to us that she never lets a racially inappropriate comment go unacknowledged. Even if she needs to let days or weeks pass from the incident, she will find the time and space to address a colleague appropriately. When she first committed herself to this approach, it was hard, but over time she reports that it has become easier to open these conversations with her colleagues. Using GVV methods for finding shared values, anticipating pushback with the creation of respectful responses, and acknowledging during the conversation that she respects her colleagues and is attempting to build, not break their relationship, she finds that her conversations generally resolve professionally.

Thus, from a GVV perspective, the emphasis is not only on rehearsal but finding ways to have these conversations effectively, for example, buying time and finding the right way to lower the tone of the conversation. These are highly sensitive and personal concerns that can backfire if not considering just one's own concern but also how the other person might be receiving the conversation. In addition, during the shared values exercise a high level of cohesiveness emerged from the participants. They exhibited high correlation among their shared values, due to the environment they work within and the relationships they had developed among each other. Working within a mission driven organization where the mission is social and racial justice created a new shared value centered on this mission. It appeared that they had arrived at a point where they already had a foundation of common beliefs that supported them in the hard decisions they are faced with in their work. As such, appealing to shared values arose as a common action strategy for participants moving forward.

In sum, in each setting, we have used a similar structure and have been able to listen to participants so that we can provide examples and context that are relevant to them. In contrast with the CPA industry where in addition to the five common shared values others emerged such as teamwork, in the social service setting their justice mission saw an added difference in the common values identified. Keeping the three-segment framework intact, we tailor and integrate comments from the participants. That is, we take the time to understand the participant profile, build on comments that arise organically and present research findings relevant to the audience.

Workshop effectiveness

GVV is a versatile framework. There is an intuitive appeal to first-time participants. The active learning approach builds energy in the sessions and motivates participants to take an engaged role. Those who do participate report more value and a sense of investment in the process to address the workplace issues prevalent in every organization. Representative feedback from one participant emphasized "thinking of my decisions as impacting not only myself but others at the firm" and from another, "I liked the idea of constructive coaching versus role playing" and "gaining tools to process and address client issues."

For academic readers, we have found these workshops to be excellent venues to develop new academic research topics and, in some instances, collect data and provide feedback on workshop efficacy. For example, in the public accounting contexts, we conducted a research study which compared the impact of the GVV ethics training approach to one that has been the traditional focus of accounting ethics CPE (Cote & Latham, 2019). In the traditional workshops, conducted by CPE providers unfamiliar with GVV, the ethical decision-making portion introduced a decision-making framework and employed it during case and ethics violations discussions. In the GVV workshops, the ethical decision-making focus centered on the action-oriented GVV curriculum described earlier, including peer interaction in exercises such as reflection, identification of values, identification of reasons and rationalizations, and scripting responses.

At the conclusion of the workshops, the instructors provided participants with an ethical challenge scenario involving a tax partner and client pressure to accept a questionable value on a charitable donation. Participants answered a series of questions concerning how they would act in the setting (i.e., how likely is it that they would concede to the client), as well as the steps they might take to address the challenge (i.e., action plan alternatives). Results supported the efficacy of the GVV approach. The GVV training participants were significantly less likely to concede to the client than those who participated in the traditional training and were more likely to recognize the viability of multiple action plans. We suggest these study results are promising, that is, an ethics training approach which possesses active learning and an action-oriented framework enhanced the ethical capabilities of accountants in this professional context. The study also laid the groundwork for future research exploring different domains as well as longitudinal studies. We now request a six-month follow-up with participants to explore the longer-term effects of the GVV framework.

In the public accounting setting, we are required to have a course evaluation to provide to the State Board of Accountancy. We highlight a few comments which speak to the success of tailoring the course to the specific environment:

"The instructors made the course relatable to our profession and gave good examples to discuss."

"Good examples"; "Really liked the real-life examples."

"Multiple instances of audience participation were helpful and engaging. Real-life case examples also helped to cement concepts."

"Practical approaches to dealing w/ethical issues, not just telling stories. Thanks for introducing us to GVV."

Finally, one post-workshop trial represents an unfulfilled opportunity to date. Enthusiasm was so great in the women's workshop that participants suggested a closed Facebook group be created so that individuals could continue to share and seek feedback on approaches. The group was created, and participants were sent an invitation, with approximately one-third of the group joining. However, neither of the authors are experienced in social media and, as such, didn't post or encourage participation so that there was very limited activity. Managing this venue is a consideration for individuals considering developing a future workshop with other community groups.

New audiences and new dimensions

One of our biggest takeaways from these experiences is that, whereas the GVV framework is robust for presentation to many different audiences, successful workshops need to carefully consider the unique attributes of each setting. For instance, the number of participants matters. Even where we have conducted GVV workshops multiple times in the same industry (e.g., CPA profession), each circumstance is unique. The number of participants can impact the workshop approach and effectiveness. We have conducted workshops with CPA firms where the number of participants ranged from eight to over 100. Smaller settings are more intimate but can inhibit participants from frank conversation, depending on the dynamics between colleagues. When the workshop size is at 100 or more participants, the advantages of the activities and dialogue is diminished as the logistics become complicated and participation can be inhibited for some and other may seek to dominate discussions. The optimal size is 30–40 participants. At this size there is an opportunity for engagement with each individual and people can choose their level of participation or anonymity. Our willingness to be nimble and adaptive resulted in highly engaged participants.

Other variables that influence the dynamics include the culture of the organization and the demographics of the participants. Where GVV workshops are presented to a single organization the culture has a clear effect on the tone and content of the engagement. Firms with a flatter organizational hierarchy find participants at all levels actively engaged. Where there is a top-down hierarchy, lower-level employees typically turn to senior leaders for initial input into discussions. In the various activities in the workshops, we actively create pairs and groups reflecting several levels within the organization and specifically call on leaders to share and encourage discussion. Well-defined cultural values clearly surface in GVV workshops. In organizations where those values have not been articulated, more individualistic values surface. As noted earlier, one organization included clients in the workshops and this inhibits discussion of the client pressures, the top values conflict experienced by CPA professionals. Understanding audience demographics is critical to structuring active participation.

The popularity of our GVV workshops has led to repeated invitations to return to the same public accounting firms which we have decided will be our primary focus given the degree with which it significantly supports the accounting students at our university. Going forward we recognize this opens up new ways to further GVV. We are now building a series of intermediate and advanced workshops that both add to the knowledge and deepen the practice of GVV. For instance, we envision expanded practice with scripting and peer coaching, again tailored to the industry and experience of our participants. We are also developing a module that guides participants in the development of their professional profile. This includes introspective and reflective activities that develop the individual's personal boundaries, values, and brand.

In closing, to get to a high level of acceptance and satisfaction requires knowledge of the demographics of the audience, the values challenges most are facing, and the motivations for their presence at the workshops. We have provided detail in three settings and encourage others to consider expanding the approach in other industries and/or professions. The more the framework is tailored to the participants the more likely the power of GVV will be unlocked for them to adopt and use consistently.

Notes

1 While the GVV framework speaks to values challenges, we found that the term *values* was not well understood in the forums where we were presenting. When we use the term *integrity boundaries*, it's clear to participants that it is where a line has been crossed. For our participants, integrity also encompasses a range of acts including ethical, personal, and professional norms.

2 By *new dimensions*, we are referring to experiences beyond what we had previously come in contact with in workshops or classrooms or with the conversations with colleagues who also are actively involved with GVV. The potential of employing the GVV framework to address diversity and equity concerns was a new direction for us.

References

Cote, J., & Latham, C. K. (2019). Ethics training approaches in accountants' continuing professional education. *Journal of Accounting, Ethics and Public Policy, 20*(4), 533–576.

Gentile, M. C. (2010). *Giving voice to values: How to speak your mind when you know what's right.* New Haven, CT and London: Yale University Press.

Martin, A. E., & Phillips, K. W. (2017). What "blindness" to gender differences helps women see and do: Implications for confidence, agency, and action in male-dominated environments. *Organizational Behavior and Human Decision Processes, 142,* 28–44. https://doi.org/10.1016/j.obhdp.2017.07.004

Neesham, C., & Azim, M. I. (2018). Building ethical capability for accounting professionals: A needs analysis study. *Swinburne University of Technology.* https://doi.org/10.4225/50/5ab311664e7d4

Shawver, T. J., & Miller, W. F. (2018). *Giving voice to values in accounting.* London and New York: Routledge A Greenleaf Publishing Book. ISBN-13: 978-0815364184

Sheppard, L., & Aquino, K. (2017). Sisters at arms: A theory of female same-sex conflict at work and its problematization in organizations. *Journal of Management, 43*(3), 691–715. https://doi.org/10.1177%2F0149206314539348

The Giving Voice to Values Curriculum. (2018). Retrieved January 15, 2018, from http://store.darden.virginia.edu/giving-voice-to-values

A

APPENDIX

Peer coaching guidelines: prompts for session

Coach: Structure your coaching session using the following prompts:

What is at stake for the key people involved?

Will you do this solo? If with allies, then with whom?

Brainstorm the types of support you might need to be successful (peers, supervisors, documents, family)

Have you planned for their response to expressing your concerns?

What constitutes a successful outcome?

What is the optimal timing to present your concerns?

Do you have all the information you need?

Have you considered the motivations for the actions that concern you? What might be their rationale?

What is the biggest challenge you expect to face?

If not successful, what would be your next steps?

B

APPENDIX

Structure for introductory Giving Voice to Values workshop

Below is the structure for a three-hour GVV focus within a four-hour workshop. This structure can be adapted to a range of settings. For example, in the public accounting and/or legal setting, an hour is devoted to a regulatory and professional code update required for continuing professional education. We complete the regulatory update in the first hour. In the nonprofit and other general community settings, we found more time was needed during components 2–5 for participant discussions.

Components	Description	Key points	Approximate time
1	Introduction to GVV and what research has shown	• Tailor research to audience • GVV history and findings to date • Post-decision-making framework • Does not prescribe right from wrong • Practice builds moral muscle memory • End goal is a toolkit to help you tackle workplace challenges	20 minutes

Components	Description	Key points	Approximate time
2	Understanding Yourself	• Building on past success (Tale of Two Stories A): Pair and share • Debrief factors leading to success • Reflections on roadblocks to action and factors that inhibit success	50 minutes
3	Understanding Others	• Values exercise leading to five commonly shared values • Reasons and rationalizations: Pushback	40 minutes
4	Preparing to Respond	• Introduce GVV case (tailored to context) and main GVV questions • Provide guidance on peer coaching • Individual script • Peer coaching exercise • Debrief responses and summarize the preparation to respond	50 minutes
5	Conclusion	• Final exercise – Rescripting the past • Present key takeaways from workshop	20 minutes
Total			180 minutes

13

GIVING VOICE TO VALUES AND THE DIGITAL WORLD

Responding to today's and tomorrow's challenges and opportunities

Debra Newcomer

Introduction

When Mary and Jerry first asked me to contribute my perspective on how Giving Voice to Values (GVV) can better leverage digital tools (and why it is so important) to the newest GVV book, I was honored. It was early 2019, and I believed (and still do!) that there was tremendous untapped potential in how the GVV approach might intersect with the growing digital landscape and many digital transformations happening across our global organizations.

I had already seen firsthand how GVV can be learned, practiced, and applied through digital tools in my work at Nomadic Learning. I was also seeing how more and more of our workplace practices were becoming digital and mobile-first. So, I knew there was a growing need for GVV to be accessible through digital tools and that we would be more and more inspired to apply GVV through the many digital tools we were using. But I had no idea just how relevant the GVV digital discussion would quickly become.

Enter 2020

The intersection of the global pandemic and the renewed energy around the Black Lives Matter movement and other similar movements for social justice has shifted the way we live and work in unprecedented ways. It is inspiring organizations and individuals globally to reexamine our values, our purpose, and our actions. And, it has accelerated "digital transformation" efforts at nearly every global organization in ways we could never have predicted. Things that were slated to take years literally happened overnight.

Regardless of what happens next, the way we live and work has changed forever. We will never return to a pre-COVID-19 era where digital tools were a "nice to have," a complement to the work that we do in the office, or a set of tools leveraged by only a portion of the global workforce. They have become an integral part of the way so many of us get our work done, interact with each other, communicate, and collaborate inside and outside of our organizations.

How we respond to this crisis and this new world of remote work will be largely dependent on how well we collectively leverage the tools and technologies that have now become so integrated into our daily lives. And, in my opinion, it also hinges on how effectively we are able to voice our values across them.

In this chapter, I'll explore how the GVV approach can play a pivotal role in helping us to navigate the unique challenges of today and tomorrow – and how we can both learn and apply the GVV approach through digital channels.

GVV and today's crisis

The act of speaking up about values is very different today than in decades (and maybe even months) past. What we can do to voice our concerns and how that "voice" (in whatever medium it is delivered) can travel has been radically transformed by social media and a growing tide of digital activism that has real-world effects.

Where they might have been hushed up in years past, values discussions and concerns now have a space in the public conversation. When someone speaks up loudly and strategically – pulling the levers of PR and social media to bring attention to their cause – people actually listen. Movements are born. Movie stars fall. CEOs get fired. Governments respond. Companies change their cultures.

This sea change in what happens when we voice our values means that how we act on our values matters. While we may feel trapped by our conflict or completely alone, there may, in fact, be many thousands of others who feel the way we do – within our organizations and outside of them.

This moment – and the movements it is inspiring – is uncovering systemic, organizational, and individual challenges at a scale that most of us have never experienced in our lifetimes. We are living through a global crisis with little certainty of when or how we will come out of it or what work and life will look like on the other side.

Our values (and resilience and sanity) are being tested at every turn. The global public health system and economy are facing a crisis without precedent in modern times. Our teams and organizations are having to radically reimagine the way we work overnight. Even the lives of our families and communities have been disrupted beyond recognition.

But, it's not all doom and gloom. This crisis, like many before it, is also inspiring us. We are finding a shared sense of purpose that allows us to cut through the noise of the everyday. We are uncovering a sense of clarity about what our real priorities are. We are uncovering ways to leverage our strengths in new ways. We are giving ourselves permission to finally overcome, or even ignore, the barriers that have blocked us in the past.

And it's not only happening for us as individuals. It's happening for organizations, as well. In the face of shared adversity, the divisions, disagreements, and politics of business as usual are giving way to unity, true agility, and courage in service of the common good. Preserving hierarchy and the status quo are becoming secondary to surfacing and finding the best ideas. Collaborative innovation and creativity become the norm. We are learning how to trust and empower everyone, no matter their place in the organization.

Our task is not just to survive this moment, but to use it as a catalyst for lasting change. Can we adjust our priorities, our processes, and our ways of thinking to meet the challenges of a changed world? Can we adjust to those new priorities while staying true to our values? Can we voice those values to our team members, our global colleagues, and our leadership? And can we do so in a way that allows them to truly listen?

Crises can present us with an enormous opportunity. They open the door to big changes and realignments that might have been impossible before the crisis hit. But those changes will not happen on their own. They require us to voice our values, and to do so effectively, empathetically, strategically, and in ways that inspire others to join us.

The GVV approach is made for times like these – not because it offers us a magic formula for responding to values conflicts or navigating moments of uncertainty; it's more like a set of guidelines to help organize our thinking and planning around values issues. It is a way to help us feel less overwhelmed and more empowered when we face values conflicts. And as I discuss next, it is an approach that has great potential when applied through the digital channels and technologies that we are using in today's new world of work.

The evolution of the digital delivery of GVV

In order to understand how GVV can continue to grow across the digital landscape it is helpful to explore how it has evolved to date and consider some promising new directions for GVV that make use of digital channels and technologies.

GVV 1.0 – spreading GVV through traditional channels

The GVV approach has evolved a great deal since its creation in 2008. It has evolved far beyond its original intended business school audience – and is now being used across nearly every academic discipline (from business to nursing to accounting and liberal arts). The GVV approach has also evolved to include corporate and organizational use with the tools, case studies, and activities being used at hundreds of organizations globally across a wide range of industries and types of organizations: healthcare, finance, consulting, manufacturing, consumer goods, legal, accounting, military, defense. GVV has also expanded the way that students, professionals, and organizations access (and interact with) its principles and methodology. The GVV approach has been (and continues to be) shared through a number of non-digital avenues including:

- Formally in classrooms and seminars
- Informally in "lunch bunches" or book club style meetings
- Through videos created by Mary C. Gentile
- Through videos created by individual organizations, universities, and professors globally that adapt the GVV principles and approach to a wide range of situations
- Through the *Giving Voice to Values* book and the extensive curriculum – with various pieces available in Russian, English, Spanish, Chinese, Arabic, French, German, and Korean
- Through formal and informal case study discussions of the hundreds of GVV style cases and readings and exercises
- Via train-the-trainer style sessions with Mary C. Gentile and GVV's growing network of professors and facilitators

GVV 2.0 – scaling GVV through digital channels

The more traditional and in-person methods allow for a variety of people globally to be introduced to the GVV methodology, its history, and application. They allow for personal reflection, small group interaction, and often a deep understanding of the GVV approach. But, as with any in-person or individual approach, there are limits to the number of people GVV can reach based on resource availability.

Thinking at scale means figuring out how to leverage technology. And while it's getting better, digital training or e-learning had (and has) a fair number of problems that make it challenging for potential learners. Add a topic like values and the doubt and hesitations really begin to set in. There are a number of knee-jerk reactions people can have when you start to explore adding a digital component to a values-based training:

- "People don't want to talk about their values."
- "People won't talk about their values online."
- "We've tried digital tools in the past and no one liked them."
- "This may work in some countries but neither the technology nor the content will work with this audience."

- "It may work with leadership of an organization but not with our factory workers or administrative staff."
- "Legal would never approve of this."

But digital tools can be a tremendously successful avenue for discussing values broadly and learning the GVV approach specifically. Over the last decade, GVV has extended its reach through a variety of digital tools – each of them allowing for a different experience with GVV and each reaching new and broader audiences. A few of these digital tools/approaches include:

GVV's online resources center

Since 2008 GVV has made its hundreds of free pages of readings, action-oriented cases, exercises, teaching notes, and more available to educators, students, and professionals looking to learn about and implement the GVV methodology. Materials available for download at www. GivingVoiceToValues.org and http://store.darden.virginia.edu/giving-voice-to-values include:

- Annotated table of contents
- Foundational readings and exercises about the background of GVV
- Thought leadership about ethics in the workplace and values-driven leadership
- Individual GVV-style cases and modules spanning various industries, regions, and types of values conflicts
- Self-knowledge and self-assessment tools
- Sample scripts
- Skills modules and teaching plans for handling a wide range of ethical conflicts in the workplace
- Action-oriented frameworks to put GVV into practice no matter your level or position and much more

As of the date of publication, there have been more than 25,000 unique downloads of the materials between 2017 and 2020.

The site also shares information about the University of Texas-Austin McCombs School of Business "Ethics Unwrapped" Giving Voice to Values

Video Series – a series of short videos, including student comments and animation often used to introduce the GVV Seven Pillars to undergraduate students or other GVV beginners.

Additionally, teaching notes and B cases are available to verified, logged-in faculty members.

GVV webinars and digital workshops

Professor Mary C. Gentile has given many webinars over the years that offer an introduction to GVV and discuss how this innovative approach can address the five organizational obstacles to creating effective values-driven leadership development initiatives. She has shared illustrations of how corporations and other organizations have used GVV to address issues such as sexual harassment and organizational mistrust. Participants have used these webinars to learn about the methodology, explore how they might pilot GVV in their organizations, as well as plan for how they can apply GVV to their own personal workplace experience.

Organizations, Employee Resource Groups, student clubs, and membership societies globally have also used webinars as a way to bring like-minded colleagues together to explore and apply GVV. These webinars can stand on their own, serve as kickoffs to broader GVV in-person or other synchronous learning initiatives, or serve the function that informal check-ins do for colleagues unable to meet in person.

Coursera's Ethical Leadership through Giving Voice to Values MOOC

Since September 2017, the Darden School of Business, in partnership with Coursera, has offered a monthly four-week online course, *Ethical Leadership through Giving Voice to Values*. This course offers an introduction to the GVV approach to values-driven leadership development as well as the opportunity to engage in self-assessment, to rehearse GVV scripting and action-planning exercises, and to create a personalized implementation plan.

The course includes short videos introducing key GVV topics and approaches, as well as video presentations by GVV users from business, the military, and academia.

Audiences for this course include: business practitioners, corporate trainers and leadership/ethics professionals, faculty who wish to find ways to integrate values-related topics into their core curriculum, as well as students and individual learners. Faculty may wish to assign the entire course and/or selected videos and assignments to students in their own classes, as a way to introduce them to the GVV approach before asking them to apply the methodology to cases and topics in their existing syllabi.

Nomadic Learning's Giving Voice to Values Field Manual Program

The GVV team collaborated with Nomadic Learning to create a ground-breaking digital extension of the GVV curriculum. Learners go through the program as part of a group – typically 25–100 people. Through a series of highly engaging, meticulously designed social learning Field Manuals (what Nomadic calls their online modules), learners have a chance to explore the nature of values conflicts, to understand their own ethical priorities, and to strengthen their voice through intensive practice. Over three to six weeks, learners navigate a series of practical case studies, original animations, Hollywood film clips, and social polls and debates while working together to determine how to voice values with more confidence and increased effectiveness. Learners can jump on and off of the platform at their own pace, favorite or like elements that are most valuable or relevant, engage with other learners both publicly and privately, and post their own reflections and revelations through the Field Manual design and accompanying Resource Library. At the time of publication, more than 10,000 individuals have gone through Nomadic's GVV Field Manual Program.

The program enhances existing management, leadership, and communications curricula. It engages learners and supports instructors with innovative multimedia materials and effective analytics. Nomadic's GVV Program is delivered through a cutting-edge digital learning platform. It is mobile first, designed for the digital learner, and built for collaboration. The social learning elements are integrated within the content itself allowing for learners to collaborate on the real issues they are facing as they go through the learning. In addition to the Field Manuals, learners have access to a growing library of micro-learning resources that highlight key pieces of the GVV approach and highlight GVV in action.

Audiences for this experience currently include organizations globally that want to introduce their employees to the GVV approach or offer a way for them to uncover and work to solve some of the values issues they are experiencing. Additionally, the CFA Institute offers an instance of the program tailored for investment professionals and students globally. The Josh Bersin Academy launched a version of the GVV Field Manuals tailored to HR professionals globally that helps them think through how to integrate GVV into their learning offerings, employee experience, and culture initiatives, as well as think through their role in creating a culture of voice. Similarly, the Darden School of Business's Executive Education has offered an instance of this collaborative experience for leaders seeking to develop a culture of integrity and moral competence and individuals who want to defend their values with confidence.

GVV 3.0 – Integrating GVV into our daily routines/ further leveraging existing technologies and tools

Digital tools like webinars, the Coursera MOOC, and Nomadic's Field Manual Program are already greatly increasing the reach of GVV, but they are still mostly seen as part of formal learning programs or traditional ways to access content. There are a number of technologies and tools currently available that offer new ways to deliver GVV content, continue to increase awareness of GVV, and offer more access points and ways to interact with it. Four key avenues include podcasts, social media, communities of practice, and collaboration tools. Many of these are already being leveraged to share and interact with GVV, but there is still untapped potential that I see as a key next step for scaling GVV.

Podcasts

The podcast as an avenue for education and entertainment has become mainstream in the United States, and interest and access continue to increase globally. According to Podcast Insights, www.podcastinsights.com/podcast-statistics/, as of August 2020, there are reported to be more than 1 million podcasts in existence with more than 30 million podcast episodes as of April 2020. Past reports from The Infinite Dial showed a creeping increase in podcasts from year to year. That changed in 2019, when there was a dramatic jump. Compared with 2018 figures, the number of people who have listened to at least one podcast in their lives increased by 20 million, and an additional 14 million people described themselves as weekly listeners. *The New York Times* reports that the number of podcast listeners increased sharply in 2019, "more than half the people in the United States have listened to one, and nearly one out of three people listen to at least one podcast every month. [In 2018], it was more like one in four."

Podcasts are also gaining appeal across all age groups and demographics. "Forty percent of people between the ages of 12 and 24 listened to a podcast [in February 2019] – a 10 percent jump from 2018."

The University of Texas-Austin McCombs School of Business created a short podcast series that highlights each of the GVV pillars based on the videos mentioned earlier. Mary C. Gentile has been a guest on a number of podcasts including *Compliance Weekly*'s podcast, Australian National Radio's podcast, the Henessey Report's podcast series, and the College of William & Mary's podcast, to name just a few.

As the network of people who use GVV continues to increase there is a growing body of experts and supporters who are available to share their stories, best practices, and lessons learned through a podcast dedicated to GVV specifically and/or by being guests on the growing number of podcast shows and channels that exist within relevant academic, organizational, and organizational culture-based podcasts.

Part of what is so powerful about the GVV approach is the way it can be tailored to individuals and their own strengths – so hearing stories of people in a podcast format and the many ways they were able to act on their values successfully will continue to lower the barrier to entry for others doing so, as well. It will also help to normalize the act of voicing values when it becomes something we feel comfortable discussing more broadly with our communities and colleagues – and podcasts are a natural way in which to do this at a larger scale.

Social media

According to *Statista*,

Social media usage is one of the most popular online activities. In 2020, an estimated 3.6 billion people were using social media worldwide, a number projected to increase to almost 4.41 billion in 2025. Social network penetration is constantly increasing worldwide and as of January 2020 stood at 49 percent.

This figure is anticipated to grow as lesser developed digital markets catch up with other regions when it comes to infrastructure development and the availability of cheap mobile devices.

Social media is being used in ways that shape politics, business, world culture, education, careers, innovation, and more. And we are becoming more and more inspired to share about our personal lives, fears, motivations, and concerns. We are seeing more and more movements leverage social media to voice their collective values as they organize, educate, and engage supporters. GVV could play an interesting role in how we expand our use of social media to voice our individual values. It could also help movements to be more effective and strategic as they bring stakeholders together around common values conflicts.

For example, the Black Lives Matters movement in the United States as well as many grassroots elections and Get Out the Vote campaigns globally can use the GVV approach to help individual organizers and members streamline their messages, anticipate pushback, and create shareable scripts to help counter those responses. But rather than thinking about some of the more traditional methods for voicing values, social media would allow values to be voiced in relevant memes, powerful images, video clips, or short but powerful captions. Additionally, when organizers and supporters think at the scale that social media provides it can help in the search for allies; substantially decrease the isolation that many can feel when thinking they are the only ones voicing their values; and provide a highly scalable and low-risk way for more people to voice the values of the movement (and their own).

It is also worth noting that there will be a new book on GVV for building racial justice coming out in 2021 by Shannon Prince in the GVV Book Collection from Routledge Publishing/Greenleaf Imprint.

Additionally, perhaps one of the most prominent ways that the GVV approach could help to enhance the way people and groups are sharing is by helping to create a social media culture where we rehearse and anticipate reactions in a more comprehensive manner rather than being quick to post, quick to judge, and quick to "cancel."

Although "cancel culture" trends toward celebrities or public figures, ordinary individuals and brands are not immune. If more of us use the GVV framework for thinking through our own social media behavior and approach voicing our values and opinions through the GVV lens we will be more thoughtful about what we post, when, how, and to whom. We may also be more empathetic when we see something taken out of context or dug up from years past, and we can help create a culture where we can have more authentic discussion and encourage growth rather than instant "cancellation" or ostracization.

Social media could also create additional ways for us to share GVV stories, peer coach, and rehearse through its private or semi-private groups. Similarly, internal social networking sites within organizations could provide a way to practice the GVV approach with colleagues globally, connect with allies as a part of the GVV approach, or even raise issues together to the larger organization or leadership.

Digital communities of practice

Another trend that is increasing with the proliferation of digital tools and digital work is the digital community of practice. Wenger and Trayner explain that the term

> community of practice is of relatively recent coinage, even though the phenomenon it refers to is age-old. The concept has turned out to provide a useful perspective on knowing and learning. A growing number of people and organizations in various sectors are now focusing on communities of practice as a key to improving their performance.

They continue:

> Communities of practice are formed by people who engage in a process of collective learning in a shared domain of human endeavor: a band of artists seeking new forms of expression, a group of engineers working on similar problems, a clique of pupils defining their identity in the school, a network of surgeons exploring novel techniques, a gathering of first-time managers helping each other cope. In

a nutshell: Communities of practice are groups of people who share a concern or a passion for something they do and learn how to do it better as they interact regularly.

Social media platforms and digital learning companies that focus on social learning are helping to create the space and interest for these communities of practice to take shape online. Involving and connecting the vast network of GVV professors, practitioners, and users globally creates opportunities for informal learning, community building, and networking. These digital communities of practice also allow for the sharing of formal resources like the many GVV cases and exercises, but also the equally important personalized elements of sharing advice – on and off the record. These communities allow for synchronous and asynchronous sharing of information, peer coaching, reflecting, and learning together through message boards, video chatting, posting, and connecting directly with other like-minded colleagues globally. It could also be a place where the GVV team could post specific challenges industries or employees are having and crowd source insights, offer the many GVV activities for reflection and personal growth, or direct members to tools and specific cases – which could be enhanced through machine learning and AI technology as they become more sophisticated.

And given the importance of allies to the GVV approach, all of these help to foster the global GVV community and dramatically increase the networks of which we are a part and offer connections to new and different forms of allies as well as new connections for peer coaching across industries, companies, and geographies.

"In the flow of work" with collaboration tools

As we have introduced more tools to the overall employee experience, there has been a strong trend toward the adoption of tools that keep employees "in the flow of work" rather than seeing digital tools or employee experience platforms as things that require people to stop working in order to use them. The simplest examples of these are collaborative tools like Microsoft Teams and Slack that allow employees to instantly interact with their colleagues, clients, and counterparts through threaded conversations, channels, and direct messages. They also allow employees to have meetings, share files, and have video or non-video calls without having to close their computers or stop work. They are accessible from all devices and already integrate with thousands of apps and digital platforms, making them core to the way an increasing number of organizations operate globally. These tools will likely continue to adapt as more of them come on the market and we spend more and more of our days working remotely.

Linking GVV content, elements, and discussions to existing collaboration and "flow of work" tools across our increasingly networked organizations provides an interesting opportunity for us to further normalize both values conflicts and the GVV approach. There could be channels within these collaboration tools dedicated to values discussions or voicing concerns; peer coaches and allies could use these tools to connect with employees; and these tools could be used to surface learning materials related to GVV. There could even be quick polls within the tools for employees to check their thinking, see if their experience aligns with others, or gather data about the broader values landscape or specific issues within their teams. There could be GVV moments that automatically surface quick information, reminders, exercises, or stories within these platforms that individuals could work on alone or in small groups. They could do this work entirely through these collaboration tools or use the prompts for further discussion through video conferencing, book club style gatherings, or in person.

GVV 4.0 – continuing to leverage new technologies

As we all know, technology is constantly being developed, iterated on, and replaced as it becomes more and more advanced. No matter how it changes, it will continue to help evolve the way we deliver and interact with the GVV approach. The following are a handful of technologies that are evolving currently that provide interesting opportunities for GVV. In order for these to really take off, I think we need to build a coalition of GVV ambassadors and supporters across a wide range of domains to help GVV take the next step into the digital age. Many leaders, managers, trainers, and educators are already exploring ways to elevate the ways they train employees – some specifically with

GVV – but if we were to bring thought leaders, executives, investors, developers, coders, design thinkers, educators, artists, innovators, and students together to explore and develop the GVV offerings there would be endless possibilities!

Virtual reality training

Immersive learning is revolutionizing the way many companies and organizations train their employees across a variety of skill sets. Through virtual reality (VR), employees are able to learn by doing, but have the safety of an altered reality. This allows them to be more engaged, be better prepared, and develop new skills faster with data-driven insights for themselves and their employers.

The fast-growing field of VR is an increasingly common part of training, from retailers to hospitals to oil rigs and athletic fields. Employers are using it to help recruit, train, and retain employees with VR simulations. Energy and mining companies are using it to increase safety training; fast food chains are using it to help line workers learn cooking procedures; delivery companies are using it for road safety and logistics; and retailers are using it for safety, security, and supply-chain training. Some companies and leadership institutes are also looking at VR as a way to help employees at all levels practice their interpersonal and soft skills – such as practicing for high impact career conversations like hiring, firing, and mergers.

GVV is already exploring the use of avatars as part of trainings which help to make simulations feel more life-like. The development of an avatar can also be a key step in helping some individuals feel more confident in the rehearsal stage – plus it's fun and creative to build out your GVV avatar, which doesn't hurt!

In these simulations – with or without avatars – individuals can practice difficult conversations through rehearsal – which is key to the GVV methodology. These simulations feel extremely real and can allow users to interact with a variety of nuanced reactions (their own and others within the simulation) to help anticipate reactions, identify risks of those involved, and get comfortable with their own scripts. It can tap into the user's specific state muscle memory as well as help them to feel empowered when they face these difficult conversations in real life.

AI and machine learning

There are a number of potential adaptations of machine learning, AI, and other augmented software related to the use of the technologies explored earlier. They can help to recommend specific cases in existing learning management systems or through collaboration tools, helping individuals gain faster access to the most relevant GVV content.

There may be opportunities around an integration with or a GVV extension of Microsoft's Workplace Analytics technology. One of the adaptations of this software is a tool that "pings" and "nudges" the user, serving up gentle suggestions to pause, rethink, or perhaps not take an action.

For example, if you are getting ready to send an email to a colleague at 11 PM, a little notification pops up to ask you if you really want to send the email at this time. It also has settings for scheduling meetings, and reminders pop up to tell you when you might be scheduling too many meetings in a row, or if an employee is sending you messages outside of their working hours on a regular basis. There is huge potential for similar reminders that could be GVV focused, helping to increase the pause between when you encounter something and when you act. This can be critical to effectively voicing our values and creating cultures of true voice.

There may also be ways that we can integrate the GVV mindset more formally through integrations or "pop up" reminders similar to what we are seeing with the advent of AI and machine learning tools and apps that may prompt us to "look at this post through a GVV lens" or "be sure" prior to posting something publicly.

AI-based software applications and data collection could also help to identify patterns within specific organizations and workplace environments that could help to increase relevant content or tools (case studies based on those patterns and themes). The most effective GVV case studies are based on what people experience most frequently, so if we leverage the technology and analytics to better understand which values conflicts are happening most often, we'd be better prepared to educate, rehearse, and coach around these areas at all levels across the organization.

GVV "checkers"

AI has enhanced the technology behind the "spell check" functionality. Now, language processing and recognition software powered by AI can screen our writing for spelling, grammar, tone, potential bias, and more.

Some interesting applications include:

- *Our Family Wizard* is an online co-parenting communication platform that helps ease the discomfort of co-parenting. Its "tone-o-meter" scans emails divorced co-parents send to each other and flags words and phrases that could be perceived as antagonistic. It also offers suggestions for where rephrasing might be helpful.
- *The design firm Doberman designed an app* that charts gender bias through voice recognition. The GenderEQ app monitors and evaluates meetings based on voice recognition, then analyzes the data to show the percentage of time taken up by male and female speakers. The app works on a phone or tablet, the idea being that the device can be set down on a table in the middle of a meeting and chart, in real time, who is speaking and for how long. The app doesn't record the conversation or analyze the content of a person's speech – it won't infringe on the user's privacy. It just recognizes the frequency of voices and labels them as male or female. While the designers at Doberman know merely charting and displaying data on who talks the most in meetings won't solve gender inequality, they are hoping to spark a conversation about it. Users can share the data with their team, and chart how meetings evolve over time.
- *The Just Not Sorry* internet browser extension helps users (often women) stop using demeaning language by underlining those phrases similar to a spelling or grammar checker. It highlights phrases like "I'm no expert" and qualifying words like "actually" and when you hover over the text, you'll see explanatory quotes from thought-leading women like "'Just' demeans what you have to say. 'Just' shrinks your power." The creator, Tami Reiss, got the idea for the app after a conversation with fellow female entrepreneurs, many of whom shared her habit. "Sometimes the environment needs to change in order to enable better behavior," Reiss says. "We thought: What if we changed the environment? What if we pinged someone to say, 'Hey, you're doing this thing that you probably don't want to do.' The response is going to be unconscious to someone else, but it's going to have a really big impact."

Having a similar GVV technology that helps us as we script our responses or draft emails, offering reminders or pings, flagging non-GVV language, or simply getting us to pause could go a long way to infusing GVV into the culture of our organizations.

GVV app and gamification

One of the best ways we can prepare for standing up for our values is to practice. A lot. Rehearsing what we're going to say or do, anticipating how our audience will respond, and preparing to handle objections and tough responses can build our confidence and reduce any fears we have about voicing our values. Including a friend or close colleague can also help, so we're not in it alone.

A GVV app – for use on your smartphone or computer – could offer quick and easy access to tips and tools and offer daily reminders and exercises to practice the GVV methodology. It could also allow you to take notes or favorite or like helpful content so it could be more accessible throughout the day when needed. Additionally, it could offer gamification similar to the gamification applied in other habit-changing apps – like meditation – that also require frequent use and offer progress tracking, small incentives, and rewards. This would help users to build their moral muscle memory, normalize the act of thinking about our values, and make it something we look forward to doing in small ways daily or weekly.

Virtual GVV coaching

Even before the global pandemic of 2020, there was a steady increase in telehealth and teletherapy globally. People were becoming more and more comfortable and providers were seeing the benefits to partial or fully remote options for certain patients. A parallel trend was also growing in the organizational coaching and wellbeing spaces with more providers coming on the scene like BetterUp – which aims to democratize coaching so that it can scale to anyone within an organization, not only the C-suite.

As more managers and employees are working remotely, this trend is continuing to rise for formal coaching programs sponsored by the organization and informal use of video-based conference technologies and chat features that allow managers to quickly coach and offer feedback in the flow of work.

BetterUp uses evidence-based assessments and machine learning to help match employees with world-class coaches and personalized development strategies. Employees complete profiles and answer a series of questions about personal and professional purpose, communication style, and needs to help match them with the right coaches. Their platform manages the end-to-end coaching experience, from coaching operations and scheduling to engagement, making it easy for organizations to scale expert coaching with the highest levels of data privacy and security. Coaches connect with employees through digital channels like teleconference, chat tools, and video calls.

There could be a similar application for the peer coaching element of the GVV approach where employees are matched with professional GVV coaches or volunteer peer coaches within their own organizations. Or there could be formal partnerships with organizations already offering other forms of coaching to train them in the GVV methodology.

Conclusion

As digital tools get smarter and GVV becomes more digitally integrated with emerging technologies like machine learning, AI, and virtual reality, there is the potential for the impact and scale of the GVV approach inside of organizations and within our global communities to grow exponentially. There are five primary reasons why I am optimistic about the future growth and evolution of GVV. First, in many ways we live and work through our digital tools – even before the 2020 shift to increased remote work, we were largely a society that lived and worked with the digital tools by our side. We interacted with friends and larger communities through social media. More and more of our actual work was shifting to digital platforms – both individually and in how we collaborate. And now, many of us are working through our computers and wifi for at least part (if not all) of our days. Today's community organizing, activism, and advocacy have reached a new threshold through (and because of) digital channels globally.

Second, values issues are not separate from the other issues we face in the workplace and beyond. Not only does it make practical sense to shift our learning to the digital tools we spend our time on – it also makes the more symbolic point that values issues shouldn't be separate from the rest of our day-to-day work. One of the keys to GVV is the act of normalizing values conflicts – both for ourselves and for our organizations. Digital is the new normal, but it also provides a place for us to keep track of our thoughts, favorite or like the elements that we find particularly useful for easy access, and it literally helps us practice talking about values in the channels we use each day.

Third, there's room for everyone in the digital world. The digital revolution has created the ability for global connections and communities that were previously unimaginable. It has opened up the ability for us to seamlessly and cost-effectively interact with people from every corner of our organizations and all areas of the world. Going through a values-based training with that kind of connectivity allows for more (and varied) perspectives; an instant community to learn with; and a network of people with whom to work through your conflicts, test ideas, and build solutions. And, perhaps most importantly, if the content is engaging and it's accessible via mobile, with the right mix of incentives, people across all levels – from factory floor to C-suite – not only have the time, but make the time to join the discussions.

Fourth, we can feel more comfortable in this digital world interacting with each other around values-based issues. The digital native often feels more comfortable sharing their opinions through digital tools because it has been so compulsory in schooling and professional life. But others may also find more comfort voicing values or raising sensitive issues because there is an element of safety in being able to take more time to compose arguments and edit thoughts prior to putting them out into the world. It can also feel less intimidating to post, email, or text something privately rather than having to share through in-person or live communication channels.

Fifth and lastly, digital allows for more customization. Digital learning tools (when created with these goals in mind) can be more effective ways of meeting each individual where they are; allowing everyone the time and space to reflect on the concepts before requiring a response; providing equally powerful experiences for introverts and extroverts; and creating a sense of shared understanding and language with which to talk about any issue. And, this is particularly valuable for learning the skills needed to voice our values effectively.

As GVV expands its reach through these digital tools and technologies, touching more and more people throughout the world, I believe we will see its impact not only professionally, but in all areas of our lives.

Additional references

https://blog.hootsuite.com/facebook-secret-groups/

https://podcasts.apple.com/mn/podcast/giving-voice-to-values/id776119893?mt=2

https://publicpolicy.stanford.edu/publications/impact-social-media-social-unrest-arab-spring

https://slate.com/human-interest/2015/12/new-chrome-app-helps-women-stop-saying-just-and-sorry-in-emails.html

www.compt.io/hr-articles/hr-podcasts

www.facebook.com/notes/mark-zuckerberg/building-global-community/10154544292806634/

www.geeksforgeeks.org/difference-between-machine-learning-and-artificial-intelligence/

www.givingvoicetovaluesthebook.com/media-room/

www.myhrfuture.com/blog/2019/3/22/how-to-create-a-people-analytics-function-for-good

www.nytimes.com/2019/03/06/business/media/podcast-growth.html

www.swoopanalytics.com/building-online-communities-of-practice/

www.viar360.com/companies-using-virtual-reality-employee-training/

www.nomadiclearning.com

CONCLUSION

Looking back and looking ahead: Giving Voice to Values

Mary C. Gentile

Beginnings

When I talk about Giving Voice to Values (GVV) with different audiences around the world – educators, students, corporate managers, investment professionals, healthcare professionals, lawyers, the military, NGOs, professional associations, and so on – I typically start my remarks by saying that several decades ago I suffered what I call a "crisis of faith." I was working with leading schools and educators to integrate ethics into the graduate business curriculum and I felt that the work we were doing was at best, futile and at worst, hypocritical.

I go on to talk about the origins of these doubts. It was easy to point to the long list of corporate scandals and misconduct, but I would always conclude that the most powerful doubts grew out of my experiences in conversation with students and practitioners. It seemed that we would typically pose ethical challenges as "dilemmas" where there seemed to be no good options: either we speak out, often with little positive impact and to the detriment of our own careers; or we remain quiet, put our heads down, and just do as we're told. And if we chose the latter option, it seemed that the ethics course simply meant that we were more aware of our own moral failing in doing so.

Perhaps even worse, because these values conflicts were presented as "dilemmas," the discussion would be framed as an analysis to determine whether a course of action was ethical or which choice was less unethical. This conversation, of course, was an invitation to rationalize and it positioned the problem as a purely cognitive challenge. It would seem that the students or practitioners in the discussion who wanted to behave ethically would be left with the choice to either find a way to defend what they sensed was wrong; to act with the conviction that they were doomed to fail and pay a price; or to accept that ethics were a luxury they could not afford: that is, rationalization, martyrdom, or surrender to cynicism.

Not only was this an unattractive and not particularly constructive set of options for the students or practitioners, it was an unappealing conversation for the faculty or organizational trainers to lead. They found themselves in a position of lecturing to the learners, while inwardly believing that the actions they proposed were often unlikely to succeed. I call this the "preach and pretend" pedagogy. No wonder business faculty in the functional disciplines – finance, marketing, operations, etc. – were frequently not that excited about integrating ethics into their courses.

For all these reasons, and because one of my primary roles while at Harvard Business School was to work with the "non-ethics" faculty – those who taught courses other than ethics – to find ways to build values into their syllabi, I was frustrated with the way we tended to approach the teaching of business ethics.

The preceding "story" is true and is the way I often introduce my motivation to find a different way to teach business ethics. I usually go on to explain how a variety of experiences as well as insights from research in psychology, cognitive neuroscience, as well as organizational studies led me to generate the action-focused approach of GVV. That is, instead of focusing primarily and exclusively on answering the question of "what is the right thing to do?" in any particular business situation, GVV focuses on the question "once I know what I believe is right, how can I get it done, effectively?" This pedagogical sleight of hand skips over the problematic "ethical dilemma" framing to bring the learner to what I call the "GVV Thought Experiment." We don't ask learners what they would do, as that tends to trigger the automatic rationalizing and unconscious decision-making biases that can limit our sense of possibility. Instead, we ask first, WHAT IF they wanted to act on the values-based position proposed in our scenarios? How could they do so successfully? The conceptual foundations beneath this accessible but powerful re-framing are described in the original book and many subsequent articles, and it has been referenced throughout this volume.

But in this chapter, I want to talk about the fact that the usual introduction to GVV I just described is not the whole story. I want to get a bit more personal as I believe that doing so will help myself and hopefully the readers here to see why and how they can take the ideas behind GVV further than I originally imagined – further than even the contributors to this volume have imagined although many of them have already taken it beyond my vision – and hopefully begin to set a course for the future of this work.

So, I just said that my frustration with business ethics education was not the whole story of GVV's origins. For that whole story, I think we need to go further back and I ask the reader for a bit of indulgence on the personal nature of the next few paragraphs. I share it because I think that often getting in touch with who we have always been, at core, is what allows us to tap into the deep wells of energy and commitment needed to enact our highest and most significant aspirations. And of course, that is what GVV is all about at heart.

So, as I often tell people, I have always been an earnest sort of person. When I was a kid, my aspiration was to write a book that would teach people how to be happy, and not only that, it had to be less than 100 pages, preferably with pictures of animals. I thought that this accessibility was what would make it connect with people. So perhaps you can see a reflection of this early aspiration in GVV which, at its core, is a simple idea – that is, ask a new question ("how to do the right thing" rather than simply "what is the right thing") and then give folks the opportunity to pre-script and rehearse their implementation plans. And it is this simplicity that gives GVV much of its power. But the other, less obvious part of GVV that this childhood story foreshadows is the assumption that many of us *want* to act in alignment with our values; it makes us happier.

Later when I was in college and then in my early career, I would spend endless fraught hours trying to figure out what I should do with my life.

I would make lists of my strengths and weaknesses, my likes and dislikes, the needs I saw in the world around me, and so on. I somehow wanted to find that intersection in the Venn diagram of my life and world that would tell me where I belonged, how I could make a positive difference, and what would make me most happy. There was a good bit of ego in this as I wanted to feel that I had made a positive impact, but I told myself that this was okay because my goal reflected the convergence of the public and the private good.

However, despite the energy and reflection I dedicated to this task, I failed. I could not seem to figure out "how to be happy." It seemed that all the things that seemed worth doing were either things that seemed beyond my reach or capability, or things that I just did not feel motivated, personally, to do. This latter led to a good bit of self-recrimination as I felt I should be able to force myself to do what is good for the world. But there was this also strong drive to be personally happy that prevented me from a self-sacrificing pursuit of professions or roles that my rational analysis suggested would be optimal for others but for which I did not feel an appetite. I was still looking for that "convergence."

With a sense of failure, I settled on my "good enough for now" life plan: I would just *try to be helpful* wherever I was planted. Even if the role or task was not the grand convergence I longed for, at least I would be helping those who seemed to have found their own positive goals. And it is this plan that led me to a variety of roles, including my work at Harvard Business School on the development of their ethics and leadership curriculum and eventually my work as an advisor to The Aspen Institute Business & Society Program. It is there where the support of BSP's founder and Executive Director, Judy Samuelson; the early investments of Dean Joel Podolny at Yale School of Management to whom Judy reached out; and the insights gained from a consulting engagement at Columbia Business School, also arranged through Aspen BSP, provided the fertile ground for me to develop the first iterations of GVV. Perhaps you can see here another reflection of one of GVV's guiding principles: that is, that we try to act where and how we can, knowing that perfection may not be possible but that the effort is still important and that it can be part of staying on a journey of continuous improvement.

Another formative influence on GVV was my own academic background; before joining HBS, I had completed a doctorate in the humanities and had written a book on feminist film theory. I believe that had I not been trained in the study and structure of narrative, I probably would not have generated an idea like GVV. That is, my first experience at Harvard Business School was auditing a course there and I noticed that the focus of case study discussions seemed to be to gather a large amount of information and data and to bring it all down to a single pointed solution or plan of action. This was utterly contrary to my experience as a student of literature and film where often the point was rather to take a single line of text or a particular sequence of images and to open them up to as many multiple interpretations and meanings as conceivable. And I think it is this training that allowed me to see that GVV is all about looking at the same set of facts and influences as another but seeing more options, more choices of how one might respond and act. And this background also helped me recognize and build upon the power of stories – stories we tell others to influence and persuade them and stories we tell ourselves in order to help us feel that a values-driven course of action can be possible (or not).

Yet another significant contributor to the development of GVV was the work I did while at HBS to develop their first course on managing diversity in the mid-'90s. It was in developing this course that I began to craft some of the early pedagogical tools that grew into GVV. I invited students to examine how the ways that they framed a position contributed to and could determine their sense of what was possible. I remember teaching a class on Affirmative Action. I knew that this would be a "hot" topic with my group of second year MBA students, mostly White (although this was a course on diversity, the student body at the time was not very diverse), who were largely invested in their sense that business was a meritocracy and that anyone who has the talent and drive can succeed. So, I decided to raise the topic more indirectly, using "potholders" to help students handle the heat: that is, I used a case study that discussed the Federal Communication Commission's efforts to diversify access to the Spectrum rights by means of a lottery. The hope was to allow smaller as well as minority-owned businesses a better chance of gaining a share of the radio waves than if the distribution was a traditional bidding process. Although this process was not directly analogous to Affirmative Action, I hoped it would be a way into a discussion of different approaches to fairness in the distribution of access and goods.

But I was wrong. The students were immediately on to me, and they were unwilling to jump into the discussion. They must have felt it was a sort of trap, too dangerous, and in an educational environment where class participation is often one of the largest contributors to one's grade, my students were silent. So, I had to change course. I told them that I could see they were not going to fall for my effort to ease them into the conversation so we would take another tack. I drew a vertical line down the center of the blackboard and I asked them to "pretend" for a moment that they were all vehement opponents of Affirmative Action: what values would they base their opposition upon? Because they were freed from having to "own" the position, it became easier for them to suggest a list of values and I wrote them down on one side of the line: fairness, meritocracy, justice, etc. Then I asked them to all "pretend" that they were dedicated supporters of Affirmative Action: what values would they base their support upon? And I wrote that list on the other side of the line . . . and of course, as you have likely guessed, the list was the same.

At that point I turned to the class and said: "Okay. Having generated these lists does not make this conversation easy. But it does illustrate that we are now engaged in a discussion of IMPLEMENTATION, rather than one based on the moral deficiency of one group of you or the other. By finding this short list of high level but shared values, we can at least begin to talk about what would work." Now we all know that the emotions, fears, resentments, and historical realities that underlie our nation's history of racial injustices are not ONLY an implementation problem. But the point here is that we found a way for the students to engage in a conversation and a collaborative problem-solving process that didn't exclude some of them at the outset due to judgment by others in the room.

Although not exactly GVV, I think I learned from this experience about the power of re-framing a conversation; the power of finding common ground, even if it is limited and very high level; and the usefulness of moving to an action-focused conversation about what might be possible: all components of the GVV pedagogical approach.

I think this early experience with developing a diversity course at HBS provided another input to the eventual development of GVV. I recall that on the last day of this MBA course I reflected on my objectives and the reality of my experience building, lobbying for, and teaching the course. One of the reasons I wanted to do that work was – selfishly – because

I have always seen myself as an introvert, somewhat risk averse, and not someone who enjoys arguments or confrontation. However, I was also someone who tended to notice injustices around me and it was painful to see this sort of thing but to feel unable or unwilling to intervene. I was aware that I enjoyed certain privileges due to my race, my education, my middle-class family, and so on. I thought that perhaps by developing this course, I could learn how to be a better ally myself, even as I taught my students. So, after a two-year process of developing the curriculum and then finally teaching it, and despite the fact that the students rated the course very highly, I felt that I had failed at one of my core goals. I believed that despite all this effort, I was still the same introverted, risk averse person I had always been and so I was probably doomed to continue to fail to intervene (effectively or at all) when confronted with injustices in my own life.

I will not go into the stories now but to my surprise, in the subsequent months after the course ended, I encountered a number of experiences when I witnessed discriminatory behaviors or prejudicial judgments on the part of clients or my manager, and almost automatically I found myself intervening. I did not intervene in the ways that an extrovert or a dedicated risk-taker might have, but I intervened in ways that felt natural to me: by asking questions; by making observations, sometimes with gentle humor; by proposing alternative framings or viewpoints. And I found that I was effective. Those of you who are familiar with GVV will recognize this as an illustration of the fifth pillar: Self-Knowledge and Alignment. The idea here is that there are many ways to enact our values and if I urge the risk-taker to be more conservative, they may say "that's fine, but it's just not natural to me." And if I urge the introverted, risk averse folks to be bolder and to have "moral courage, they may say "that's nice, but I'm just not that sort of person." Instead, we explore the many ways that we can learn from the times we have been effective in the past and then frame our values conflicts in ways that allow us to play to our strengths – just as I found myself doing, naturally, after spending a time preparing and teaching a course that allowed me to pre-script and rehearse these approaches. So rather than preaching "moral courage" – a wonderful goal but one that may feel out of reach, unrealistic, or too daunting for many – GVV tries to build "moral competence" where we practice the many ways we might voice and enact our values and work to build the habit and "moral muscle memory" that makes these approaches come more naturally, accompanied by less stridency and emotion.

Growing pains and choices

Once I "found" the core ideas behind GVV – asking a new question (that is, rather than "what is the right thing to do?", asking "how do we get the right thing done?") and building a "moral muscle memory" (that is, a habit through pre-scripting, action planning, rehearsal, and peer coaching) – I faced a number of decision points and challenges regarding how to develop, launch, and grow the ideas behind the methodology. My initial goal, although it may sound grandiose, was to transform the way we talk about ethics and values in business education, particularly MBA education. As the years have gone by, this objective has morphed and grown larger into a desire to try to transform the wider conversation about values and ethics to embrace more choice and enable more positive voice and action across educational arenas and within organizational practice across professions and contexts. Much of this expansion has been driven by the wonderful creativity and energy of the many faculty and professionals who see this potential and run with it, as evidenced in the preceding chapters of this volume.

Probably due to my own academic background, I believed that one of the most powerful paths toward my goal – or perhaps the most powerful pathway that played to my particular strengths and preferences – was through identifying and communicating an idea. I was not drawn to institution building in the traditional sense; I did not see myself as a manager, and I did not enjoy the process of administration and organizational management. However, I believed in the power of ideas and GVV seemed a good one. So it seemed I had stumbled upon that convergence of the private and public good, after all. Similarly, my own introversion and self-doubts limited my sense that I had the "answers" to conflicts across professions and contexts, but GVV was about asking enabling questions and providing tools to help those who did possess the necessary expertise and insights to believe in their own ability and freedom to create and implement those answers.

What's more, I believed that no one "owned" ideas; their impact grew from their accessibility to all. Thus, it became important to design GVV in such a way that it was not dependent upon one person or upon outside funding or even upon the curricular materials I and others created. All of those things were hugely helpful of course, and even necessary in the early years, but I wanted GVV to find its audience and have its impact without continued dependency on those things. I was fortunate because the research from a variety of fields such as behavioral ethics, social psychology, and design thinking that influenced the development of GVV was also influencing many others in education, business, and elsewhere around the same time as this work was starting. GVV is not alone in its focus upon action and rehearsal, and that has only served to reinforce its growth. For example, many organizations today try to promote what they call a "speak up culture." Although this approach is often more of an exhortation (sort of like "If you see something, say something") as opposed to the GVV methodology of pre-scripting, rehearsal, and peer coaching; and although it often tends to focus on "reporting" (through hot-lines and compliance officers and such) as opposed to the GVV focus on raising issues early, before reporting is required, to change the conversation and decision-making process within one's immediate team of colleagues, nevertheless this "speak up" focus certainly reinforces the GVV message and has served to extend its growth.

The conviction that GVV was an idea and that ideas are free and open to all certainly helped in the spread of GVV, but it also created some challenges. There were those who warned me that users would not value or appreciate what they did not have to pay dearly for. And there were those who argued that my approach would not be sustainable and would prevent GVV's survival. I recall working with an executive from a major multinational company who confided to me that what he loved about GVV was that it was not one of these huge, complex, pre-packaged, inflexible, and hugely expensive programs that consultants swoop in to deliver from on high; rather it was flexible, inexpensive, engaged ownership from within the firm, and seemed more about the organization than about the consultants. On the other hand, he admitted that those were the same things that made it challenging for him as he had to find individuals from within the firm to take ownership and work with us to bring GVV to their teams. In other words, they complained about high fees but on the other hand, it allowed them to "out-source" the work, even when that might not serve their ultimate objectives of culture change.

Additionally, locating sources of funding for GVV has also been challenging but I have tried to design it in such a way that it can nevertheless survive. Although most of the curricular materials are free and institutions like The Aspen Institute, Yale School of Management, Babson College, and now the University of Virginia Darden School of Business, which serves as GVV's home base, have been hugely supportive in making that possible, these institutions have also seen the extensive, global attention that they have received by providing a home for this work. And there have been partners – publishers like Yale University Press and Routledge Publishing/Greenleaf Imprint with its GVV Book Collection and Business Expert Press; Nomadic.fm with its sophisticated online educational programs; Coursera with its MOOCs; Mursion with its avatar-based simulations – who have helped to extend this work . . . and of course, they do charge for their products. My objective and hope is that all of these mechanisms serve to reinforce each other and to spread the ideas behind GVV. And of course, I continue to share GVV on an almost weekly basis with educational institutions, companies, organizations, and so on across the United States and around the world. Increasingly it is other users of GVV who are doing such presentations, lectures, workshops, and so on. I have tried to design GVV so that once you understand the concepts behind it – the ideas – it does not matter if I disappear or even if the curricular materials disappear because the idea itself is so easily applied and customized for different contexts. At least that is the hope – and time will tell!

The future

So, as I conclude this chapter, I find myself at the beginning again. I look back at the choices I made consciously, as well as the ones that I made without recognizing I was doing so. I wonder if there are ways I might have approached this work that would have been more impactful. For example, while I have always seemed to find institutions who valued and supported this work enough to house it, support it, and/or support me – The Aspen Institute Business & Society Program, Yale School of Management, Babson College, and now the University of Virginia Darden School of Business – I have not been able to secure funding to more deeply institutionalize GVV. I sometimes am frustrated when I recognize work and progress that we could do if there were more support, but then I remember that I did not want to "OWN" GVV; that GVV is an idea and that ideas belong to everyone and that, in fact, that was how we started this whole journey. I believed that ideas are the way to make change. It was, after all, one of those convergences of the private and public good because I really didn't want to spend my time running and managing an organization. I wanted GVV to be in the world and hopefully inspiring others to design their own educational and training efforts, and their own personal choices, as informed by it.

I hope and believe that this strategy has been effective. I believe that this book is just a small reflection of the impacts others are having, when informed by GVV. There are many other stories we could tell: the organizations that are using GVV in their online training of practitioners (the Chartered Financial Institute, the Australian Institute of Health and Safety, the Government Financial Officers Association); the many faculty around the world who have come across GVV online or in conversation with a colleague or by attending a lecture and who now are integrating it into their teaching; the network of ethics and compliance professionals globally who are influenced by the way other companies have used the approach, whether they call it GVV or not; the many books written by contributors to the GVV book series from Routledge Publishing/Greenleaf Imprint who write about values in different contexts with an orientation toward action and positive solutions rather than simply exhortations to do better; the scholars who have begun to craft research to explore the impact of an action orientation in values education; and so on.

As I consider my hopes for the future of GVV, some of the things that emerge are:

- I hope that ethics education would *always* include the opportunity not only to raise awareness and hone our ethical analysis skills, but to actually examine and rehearse scripts and strategies for enacting our values effectively, successfully. I hope that this emphasis – and the "GVV Thought Experiment" – would become an expected and necessary part of any ethics discussions, whether they are in business, in healthcare, in law, in liberal arts courses, in elementary and secondary education, or in corporate and other organizational settings.

- I hope that the ability to have this sort of GVV conversation becomes part of the training for public sector professionals – in law school, schools of government and public policy, and in on-boarding for elected officials.
- I hope that more scholars research what is effective when voicing and enacting values, rather than focusing only or primarily on why we don't voice and act at all (or successfully).
- I hope that more books in the GVV Book Series from Routledge/ Greenleaf – and from other publishers – share and analyze successful efforts at values-driven change. For example, we have books forthcoming on effective values-driven voice and action for racial justice, for sustainability, for young adult development, for career planning, and so on.
- I am excited at experiments with new modalities such as avatar training and more interactive, online social cohort-based learning.
- I hope that corporate efforts to integrate GVV will go beyond formal ethics training – although that is important – and that the "GVV Thought Experiment" will become part of the regular daily conversations led by business leaders and part of the framing of every business team discussion.
- I hope that students will not only learn the GVV methodology and apply it to their own experiences, but that they will participate in training and facilitating this approach with their peers, as accounting seniors did for accounting sophomores at Washington State University.
- I hope to see more translations of the GVV materials into many more languages.
- And on and on.

  - Most of all, I hope that this emphasis upon training and rehearsal for values-driven action becomes a taken-for-granted part of every conversation, every training program, every class, in every profession – whether it is named Giving Voice to Values or not. As I mentioned at the start of this chapter, I hope that GVV can help to "change the conversation" about ethics. And I hope that all these "users" of GVV feel that they OWN the approach and want to extend it, enhance it, and practice it.

As I look ahead, my profound hope is that the cadre of GVV ambassadors around the world will continue to grow; to take inspiration and heart from the basic re-frame at the heart of GVV; and that they will take this work much further than I could ever imagine or attempt. To these ambassadors I offer this chapter as, hopefully, a source of encouragement and hope. I encourage them to look for those convergences of private and public good, and to focus on the goal even when the path seems counter-intuitive. And to everyone who has used GVV, who has contributed to GVV, who has offered me insights and constructive feedback and support, thank you!

INDEX

Note: numbers in **bold** indicate a table on the corresponding page

reframing as Giving Voice to Values
(GVV) strategy 29, **34**, 111–112,
124, 132, 134, 140; of medical
ethics teaching 94; of reasons and
rationalizations 102
Reiss, T. 236
responsibility, locus of 130
Rogers, C. 46
Rogers, L. 41–42, 46, 49–51
Roi, R. 145, 147, 150–151, 156, 158
Rorty, R. 36, 32
Routledge Publishing/Greenleaf
Imprint 230, 250–252
Rubino, K. 143n15

Samuelson, J. 244
self-awareness and self-knowledge
160, 224, 247
Shawver, T. J. 204
Sheppard, L. 209
Sierra Leone 117–118
social media 229–231
Specia, M. 142n9
stakes in Giving Voice to Values
(GVV) 28–29; Johnson & Johnson
(case study) 59–60; normalizing
62; scripting 46; "table stakes" 36
Stevens, D. 68

"Tale of Two Stories" exercise 22,
24, 203; among Ashesi University
alumni 109–111, 115, 117; in
business school 75, 77, 81; and
understanding yourself **219**; and
women in the workplace 208
Tam, T. 145, 147–149, 151–152, 159
tanning, ethical concerns regarding
59–60
Tan, Y. 142n8
Thomasma, D. 17
"toolkit": for ethical action 115;
legal 123; managerial 150; of
strategies 76

Tsinghua University 177–178
Tylenol scare of 1982 58–59, 61

understanding yourself/others and
preparing to respond 202–210,
219
unethical behavior 107; by authority
figures (China) 170; complicity
in 104; consequences of 124; in
decision-making (business) 126,
134; as being evil 204; in legal
settings 125; managerial 57;
rationalizations of 111–112; and
value conflicts 242
University of Notre Dame 73, 75–76,
79–83, 85
University of Notre Dame Australia
91, 94–99
University of Texas-Austin McCombs
Schools 225–226, 229
University of Virginia 38, 250
Utilitarianism 10, 62

value conflicts 25–27, 31–33, 223,
227; and "apology" role-play 97;
in China 170, 177; in coaching
185, 191, 197; commonly
experienced 230, 235; in CPA
work 214; communicating to
resolve 88–90, 100; as "dilemmas"
242; in Ghanian workplace 106,
110; manager training in 52; as
natural 96; normalizing 233,
239; "playing to one's strengths"
160, 247; "rehearsing" 102; tasks
and training 109–113, 117; in
workplace 141, 146, 152, 155–158,
182
values, listening for *see* listening
virtual coaching 237–238
virtual reality (VR) 234
virtue ethics 7–21; Confucian
166–168; and ethical decisions

Made in United States
North Haven, CT
04 August 2022

22286649R00153